Unleashing AI

Unleashing AI

Harnessing Artificial Intelligence for Business Success

Milan Frankl

Unleashing AI: Harnessing Artificial Intelligence for Business Success

Cover design by Charlene Kronstedt

Interior design by Exeter Premedia Services Private Ltd., Chennai, India

First published in 2025 by
Business Expert Press, LLC
222 East 46th Street, New York, NY 10017
www.businessexpertpress.com

ISBN-13: 978-1-63742-800-9 (paperback)
ISBN-13: 978-1-63742-801-6 (e-book)

Business Expert Press Big Data, Business Analytics, and Smart Technology Collection

First edition: 2025

10 9 8 7 6 5 4 3 2 1

EU SAFETY REPRESENTATIVE

Mare Nostrum Group B.V.
Mauritskade 21D
1091 GC Amsterdam
The Netherlands
gpsr@mare-nostrum.co.uk

Description

***Unleashing AI: Harnessing Artificial Intelligence for Business Success* is a comprehensive guide for business leaders, professionals, and entrepreneurs looking to understand and leverage the transformative potential of AI technologies.**

Unleashing AI is an actionable resource that equips the readers with the knowledge and strategies to harness the power of AI for competitive advantage. This book goes beyond the hype and technical jargon, offering a clear and accessible exploration of AI's applications, implementation challenges, and ethical considerations. It reviews the fundamental concepts of AI, its applications across various business functions, and the ethical considerations associated with its deployment. Through detailed chapters and practical insights, readers will gain a deep understanding of how to integrate AI into their business strategies to drive innovation, efficiency, and competitive advantage.

By combining expert insights, and practical frameworks, *Unleashing AI* empowers readers to navigate the AI landscape, identify opportunities, and develop effective AI strategies aligned with their business goals.

Contents

Acknowledgments

I would like to express my heartfelt gratitude to those who have supported me throughout the journey of writing this book. My sincere thanks to Brian Harper (mPhD), whose expertise and insights into artificial intelligence have profoundly shaped my understanding of the field. I am equally grateful to Victor Barwin (CPA) for his invaluable guidance and encouragement, which have been instrumental in refining my ideas on financial and management matters. A special acknowledgment goes to Dr. Bill Wadge (PhD), whose innovative perspectives on AI applications in business inspired many of the concepts discussed herein. Finally, I extend my deepest appreciation to my wife, whose unwavering support, patience, and love have been my greatest motivation. This work would not have been possible without each of you.

Acknowledgments

Introduction

We are living in the age of artificial intelligence (AI), where machines are learning to think, act, and interact with humans like never before. AI has come a long way since its inception, and its applications are vast and varied. From virtual assistants such as Siri and Alexa to self-driving cars and personalized product recommendations, AI is transforming the way we live and work.

The business case for AI is strong. According to a recent report by the World Economic Forum and McKinsey, AI has the potential to add up to $16 trillion to the global economy by 2030 thanks to AI.[*,†] AI can help businesses reduce costs, increase revenue, and improve customer satisfaction. It can also help businesses make better decisions, faster and more accurately.

In the fast-paced and competitive world of business, organizations are constantly seeking innovative ways to stay ahead of the curve. AI has the potential to revolutionize the way businesses operate, making them more efficient, productive, and profitable.

The AI Revolution in Business

In the annals of business history, little technological advancement has promised as much transformative potential as AI. As one stands on the cusp of 2025, AI is no longer a futuristic concept confined to science fiction or academic research labs. It has emerged as a powerful, versatile, and increasingly accessible tool that is reshaping the very foundations of how businesses operate, compete, and create value.

---

[*] **The global economy** will be $16 trillion bigger by 2030 thanks to AI. www.weforum.org/agenda/2017/06/the-global-economy-will-be-14-bigger-in-2030-because-of-ai/.

[†] **The economic potential of generative AI: The next productivity frontier.** June 14, 2023 | Repor www.mckinsey.com/capabilities/mckinsey-digital/our-insights/the-economic-potential-of-generative-ai-the-next-productivity-frontier.

The integration of AI into business processes marks the beginning of a new era in commerce and industry. Much like the steam engine ignited the Industrial Revolution or the internet ushered in the Digital Age, AI is catalyzing a profound shift in how to approach problem-solving, decision making, and innovation in the business world.

This book aims to be your guide through this AI-driven transformation, offering insights, strategies, and practical applications to help you harness the power of AI in your organization.

AI: More Than Just Automation

AI is revolutionizing the business landscape in several key ways. It enhances decision making by processing vast amounts of data and identifying patterns that humans might miss, leading to more informed choices at all levels of an organization. AI also enables unprecedented personalization at scale, allowing companies to tailor their offerings to individual customers. The technology's predictive analytics capabilities help businesses anticipate market trends and potential issues, giving them a competitive edge. Furthermore, AI is accelerating innovation by opening up new possibilities for products, services, and business models. Finally, it's proving to be a valuable tool in risk management, helping companies identify and mitigate potential problems before they escalate. Together, these advancements are transforming how businesses operate and compete in the modern marketplace.

The Democratization of AI

One of the most exciting developments in recent years has been the increasing accessibility of AI technologies. Once the domain of tech giants and specialized research institutions, AI is now within reach of businesses of all sizes. Cloud-based AI services, open-source tools, and user-friendly platforms are democratizing access to AI capabilities, leveling the playing field, and spurring innovation across industries.

Navigating the AI Landscape

As with any transformative technology, the integration of AI into business operations comes with its own set of challenges and considerations. From ethical concerns and data privacy issues to the need for reskilling workforces and redesigning organizational structures, businesses must navigate a complex landscape as they embrace AI.

This book addresses these challenges head-on, providing frameworks for ethical AI adoption, strategies for managing change, and insights into the skills and organizational structures needed to thrive in an AI-driven business environment.

Looking Ahead

The chapters that follow explore specific AI applications across various business functions, from marketing and customer service to supply chain management and product development. Case studies of successful AI implementations, discussions of emerging trends, and practical guidance for developing and executing an AI strategy are covered.

The AI revolution in business is not a distant future—it is happening now. Whether you are a CEO charting your company's course, a manager looking to optimize your department's operations, or an entrepreneur seeking to disrupt your industry, understanding and leveraging AI will be crucial to your success in the years to come.

Investigating the role of AI in automation, data analysis, customer service, and decision making and how it can help businesses gain a competitive edge in the market are also addressed. Different types of AI, its applications in various industries, and its benefits and challenges as well as the ethical implications of AI and its impact on society are studied.

This book explores the transformative power of AI as a business tool by examining the various applications of AI in different industries, its benefits, and its challenges.

Join us on this journey through the exciting world of AI and its potential to transform businesses to discover how AI can help businesses innovate, disrupt, and thrive in a rapidly changing world, and harness its transformative power to drive growth, innovation, and competitive advantage in the business realm.

What Is Artificial Intelligence

What Is Human Intelligence?

By and large, human intelligence consists of one's capability to comprehend the objective world and apply knowledge to solve problems. The intelligence of an individual consists of wide-ranging abilities, such as the aptitude to:

- Perceive and understand objective things, the objective world, and oneself;
- Gain experience and acquire knowledge through learning;
- Comprehend the knowledge and apply knowledge and experience for problem analysis and problem-solving;
- Perform linguistic abstraction and generalization;
- Appropriate, promptly, and reasonably cope with the complex environments;
- Predict insights into the development and changes of things;
- Associate, reasoning, judgment, and decision making; and
- Discover, invent, create, and innovate.

Intelligence Relevant to Business Applications

In the dynamic world of business, various forms of intelligence play crucial roles in driving success and innovation. Understanding and leveraging different types of intelligence can provide a competitive edge and foster a more adaptive and resilient organization.

This section explores several key forms of intelligence that are particularly relevant to business applications:

Logical Intelligence: This involves the ability to reason, think critically, and solve problems systematically. Logical intelligence is essential for strategic planning, decision making, and troubleshooting complex issues.

Mathematical Intelligence: Closely related to logical intelligence, mathematical intelligence encompasses skills in numerical analysis, data interpretation, and quantitative reasoning. It is vital for financial management, market analysis, and operational efficiency.

Interpersonal Intelligence: This type of intelligence refers to the ability to understand and interact effectively with others. It includes skills in communication, empathy, and conflict resolution, which are crucial for leadership, teamwork, and customer relations.

Intrapersonal Intelligence: Intrapersonal intelligence involves self-awareness and the ability to manage one's own emotions and motivations. It is important for personal development, stress management, and maintaining a balanced work–life dynamic.

Spatial Intelligence: This form of intelligence relates to the ability to visualize and manipulate objects and spaces. Spatial intelligence is valuable in fields such as design, architecture, and logistics, where spatial reasoning and visualization are key.

By harnessing these diverse forms of intelligence, businesses can enhance their strategic capabilities, foster innovation, and create a more cohesive and effective organizational culture. Each type of intelligence offers unique strengths that, when combined, can drive comprehensive growth and success.

Moreover, these intelligences intersect and complement each other. Businesses benefit from a diverse mix of these skills to thrive in today's data-centric markets. Business intelligence tools such as dashboards, visualizations, reporting, and predictive analytics empower organizations to extract valuable insights from data, optimize operations, and make informed decisions. AI applications, such as machine learning (ML) and natural language processing (NLP), are highly relevant in business contexts.

The Distinction Between Data, Information, Knowledge, and Wisdom

In the digital age, the terms Data, Information, Knowledge, and Wisdom (**DIKW**) are often used interchangeably, yet they represent distinct concepts that build upon one another in a hierarchy. Understanding these distinctions is crucial for effectively managing and utilizing the vast amounts of data generated in today's world.[‡]

Data is the raw, unprocessed facts and figures without context. It is the foundation upon which information is built. For example, a list of numbers or a collection of dates are data points.

Information emerges when data is processed, organized, or structured in a way that adds meaning. It answers questions such as "who," "what," "where," and "when." For instance, a report summarizing sales figures over a quarter transforms raw sales data into information.

Knowledge is derived from information by applying rules, context, and experience. It answers "how" questions and provides insights that can guide decisions. For example, understanding that sales increase during certain months based on historical data is knowledge.

Wisdom is the pinnacle of this hierarchy. It involves applying knowledge in a practical, judicious manner to make sound decisions. Wisdom answers "why" questions and reflects deep understanding and foresight. For instance, using knowledge of sales trends to develop a strategic plan for future growth demonstrates wisdom.

This section delves into each of these concepts, exploring their characteristics, interrelationships, and the ways they contribute to effective decision making in business and beyond.

DIKW: Definitions, Characteristics, Examples, and Role in AI

Data is a fundamental concept in the digital age, encompassing anything represented in digital form, including nonexecuting knowledge stored digitally. It is characterized by its passive and inert nature, consisting of raw symbols or signals that lack inherent meaning. Data only becomes meaningful when interpreted

‡ www.ontotext.com/knowledgehub/fundamentals/dikw-pyramid/.

or transformed through various processes. Examples of data are diverse and ubiquitous in our digital world. They include database rows, spreadsheets, images, and emails, among many other forms. These examples illustrate a wide range of information that can be captured and stored digitally.

Information is a dynamic concept that emerges from the interpretation of data. It can be defined as the momentary extraction of structure from data, which modifies the perspective of the interpreter, leading to new data or insights. This process highlights the transformative nature of information. The characteristics of information are distinct from those of raw data. Information exists during the active interpretation of data, revealing context and highlighting discontinuities between existing knowledge and new insights. It is ephemeral and transformational, constantly evolving as new interpretations and analyses occur. Examples of information include infographics, summaries, and structured reports. These formats present data in a way that is more easily digestible and meaningful to the interpreter, often revealing patterns or trends that may not be immediately apparent in the raw data. In the context of AI, information plays a crucial role. AI systems excel at transforming vast amounts of raw data into meaningful information by extracting patterns, creating summaries, and providing insights. This ability to process and interpret data at scale is one of the key strengths of AI, enabling it to uncover valuable information that might otherwise remain hidden in large datasets.

Knowledge represents a higher level of understanding and capability in the hierarchy of data and information. It can be defined as the rules, algorithms, interpreters (such as pattern recognizers), or other mechanisms that transform data into information. This definition emphasizes the active and transformative nature of knowledge. The characteristics of knowledge are multifaceted. Importantly, knowledge is not static; it may change through interaction with information, allowing for learning and adaptation. This dynamic nature applies to both human and machine-based knowledge systems. Knowledge is what enables understanding and problem-solving, serving as the foundation for interpreting data and deriving meaningful insights. Examples of knowledge include expertise in a particular field, procedural knowledge (knowing how to perform specific tasks), and algorithms that can process and analyze data. These forms of knowledge represent the ability to not just possess information but to also apply it effectively to solve problems or generate new insights. In the realm of AI, knowledge plays a crucial role. AI systems acquire knowledge through various means, including training on large datasets, learning from examples, and adapting to new situations. This acquired knowledge is what enables AI to perform complex tasks, solve problems, and make decisions. As AI systems continue to evolve, their ability to acquire, refine, and apply knowledge becomes increasingly sophisticated, allowing them to tackle more complex challenges and provide more valuable insights.

Wisdom represents the pinnacle of the data–information–knowledge hierarchy, defined as specialized knowledge that filters and activates the most relevant information from data. This definition highlights the discerning and selective nature of wisdom, emphasizing its ability to identify and apply the most pertinent insights in any given situation. The characteristics of wisdom are distinct and powerful. It integrates experience and context, allowing for a more nuanced and comprehensive understanding of complex situations. Wisdom produces super-useful insights that go beyond mere knowledge, offering profound understanding and guidance. Importantly, wisdom is not static; it may evolve through positive or negative reinforcement, reflecting the learning process that comes from applying knowledge in real-world situations. Examples of wisdom include deep insights that cut to the heart of complex issues, practical judgment that guides effective decision making, and the ability to make sound choices in challenging circumstances. These examples illustrate how wisdom transcends mere knowledge, incorporating a deeper understanding of context and consequences. In the context of AI, the concept of wisdom presents an interesting challenge. While AI systems don't possess wisdom in the human sense, with their emotional and experiential components, they can provide valuable recommendations and optimize decisions based on learned knowledge. Advanced AI systems can analyze vast amounts of data and knowledge to generate insights that may appear wise, even if they lack the true depth of human wisdom. As AI continues to evolve, the line between machine-generated recommendations and humanlike wisdom may become increasingly blurred, raising fascinating questions about the nature of intelligence and decision making in both artificial and human contexts.

These concepts build upon each other, with wisdom representing the highest level of understanding and practical application. The relationship between Data, Information, Knowledge, Wisdom, and AI is summarized hereafter:

Data: *AI processes and enriches data.*	**Information:** *AI extracts insights and context from data.*	**Knowledge:** *AI learns and applies rules and algorithms.*	**Wisdom:** *AI optimizes decisions and provides valuable recommendations.*

Summary

In summary, AI relies on data, transforms it into information, acquires knowledge, and contributes to informed decision making. AI enhances our ability to extract valuable insights from data.

AI and Consciousness

Consciousness is a complex and multifaceted concept. At its core, it refers to the state of being aware of and able to think about one's existence, thoughts, and surroundings. It involves several aspects, including:

- **Awareness:** Being conscious of internal and external experiences.
- **Self-Awareness:** Recognizing oneself as an individual separate from the environment and others.
- **Subjective Experience:** Having personal experiences and feelings.

AI, as it currently stands, does not possess consciousness. AI systems, including advanced models like GPT-4, operate based on algorithms and data processing without any subjective experience or self-awareness.

Here are some key points on how AI deals with the concept of consciousness:

- **Simulation of Behavior:** AI can simulate behaviors that appear conscious, such as understanding and generating humanlike text, but this is based on pattern recognition and prediction rather than true awareness.
- **Philosophical and Ethical Debates:** The possibility of AI achieving consciousness is a topic of ongoing debate among philosophers, cognitive scientists, and AI researchers. Some argue that with advancements in technology, AI might oneday exhibit forms of consciousness, while others believe that true consciousness requires biological processes that AI cannot replicate.
- **Ethical Considerations:** If AI were to achieve consciousness, it would raise significant ethical questions about the rights and treatment of such entities. This is a largely speculative area, but it underscores the importance of careful consideration as AI technology advances.

In summary, while AI can mimic certain aspects of human behavior, it does not possess consciousness. The exploration of AI consciousness remains a fascinating and complex field, blending technology, philosophy, and ethics.

Ready for an AI Definition?

Based on the proposed definition of human intelligence as having the ability to understand and apply knowledge to solve problems, encompassing various capabilities such as perception, learning, problem-solving, reasoning, creativity, adaptation to complex environments, and predicting changes, some more common definitions of AI are presented hereafter:[§]

- **AI in Simple Terms:** AI is intelligence in computers or machines, especially when it mimics human intelligence. It covers various types of machine intelligence, including tools for creating art, and content and summarizing or transcribing information.
- **Artificial General Intelligence (AGI):** Most AIs developed so far have been "narrow" or "weak," excelling at specific tasks but lacking broader abilities. AGI, on the other hand, would possess the flexibility of thought similar to humans and potentially even consciousness. Companies such as OpenAI and DeepMind aim to create AGI, although concerns exist about superintelligences surpassing human capabilities.
- **Alignment:** While one focuses on individual differences, humanity shares common values that bind societies together. Alignment refers to ensuring that AI systems align with these shared values, preventing unintended consequences or harmful behavior.

IBM's Definition: AI enables computers and machines to simulate human intelligence and problem-solving capabilities. It can perform tasks that would otherwise require human intervention, often combined with other technologies such as sensors or robotics.

Summary

In summary, AI involves rapid data processing, ML, and automation to simulate intelligent behavior in machines and software, distinct from natural human intelligence.

[§] Artificial intelligence (July 17, 2024). In Wikipedia. https://en.wikipedia.org/wiki/Artificial_intelligence.

However, the definition of AI is vast and complex. What does it mean for machines to understand speech or write a sentence? What tasks could they perform and how much could they be "trusted?"

The term "AI" remains a topic of debate, with some suggesting that it can learn to behave like humans, while others argue that it is a slang term for "Mathy Math."[5]

The debate continues.

---

[5] **"Mathy Math"** is an informal term often used to describe advanced or abstract mathematical concepts. It is a playful way of referring to the more intricate and theoretical aspects of mathematics.

PART 1

AI Fundamentals for Business

Part I of this book lays the groundwork for comprehending AI technologies, the significance of data and algorithms, and the broader AI ecosystem.

By mastering these concepts, you will be well-prepared to leverage AI's potential to drive innovation and competitive advantage in your organization.

Chapter 1 Understanding AI Technologies

Chapter 1 introduces the core technologies that power AI.

- **Machine Learning:** Learn how algorithms can autonomously learn from data to make predictions and decisions.
- **Deep Learning:** Explore neural networks that mimic the human brain, enabling sophisticated pattern recognition and decision making.
- **Natural Language Processing:** Understand how AI interprets and generates human language, enhancing communication between humans and machines.
- **Computer Vision:** Discover how AI systems analyze and interpret visual information from the world around us.
- **Robotic Process Automation:** Learn about automating repetitive tasks to improve efficiency and accuracy in business processes.

Chapter 2 AI Data and Algorithms: The Building Blocks of Intelligent Systems

Chapter 2 covers the fundamental components that drive AI.

- **The Importance of Data for AI:** Understand why data is crucial for AI and how it fuels intelligent decision making.
- **Types of Data for AI Applications:** Explore the various types of data, including structured, unstructured, and semistructured data, and their relevance to AI.
- **AI Algorithms Explained:** Gain insights into the algorithms that power AI, from simple linear regression to complex neural networks.
- **Evaluating AI Model Performance:** Learn how to assess the effectiveness of AI models using metrics and validation techniques.

Chapter 3 The AI Ecosystem

Chapter 3 introduces the infrastructure and services that support AI development and deployment.

- **AI Hardware and Cloud Computing:** Discover the role of specialized hardware and cloud platforms in accelerating AI computations and scalability.
- **AI Software Platforms and Tools:** Explore the software solutions that facilitate AI development, from frameworks to integrated development environments.
- **AI Service Providers:** Learn about the companies and organizations that offer AI services, from consulting to managing the implementation of AI solutions.

CHAPTER 1

Understanding AI Technologies

While probing deeper into the world of Artificial Intelligence (AI), it is crucial to understand the key technologies that form its foundation.

This chapter explores five fundamental AI technologies that are driving innovation and transformation across industries.

It begins with **machine learning (ML)**, the backbone of many AI systems, enabling computers to learn from data without explicit programming.

Next, it examines **deep learning**, a subset of ML that uses neural networks to mimic human brain function, allowing for more complex pattern recognition and decision making.

Exploring **natural language processing (NLP)** follows the technology that allows computers to understand, interpret, and generate human language.

Computer vision, which enables machines to gain high-level understanding from digital images or videos, mimicking human visual perception ensues.

Finally, **robotic process automation (RPA)**, a technology that uses software robots or "bots" to automate repetitive, rule-based tasks traditionally performed by humans, is discussed.

Each of these technologies plays a crucial role in the AI ecosystem, often working in concert to create powerful, intelligent systems. By understanding these core technologies, identifying potential AI applications in business and making informed decisions about AI adoption and implementation becomes easier.

The journey into the fascinating world of AI technologies starts.

What Is Machine Learning

ML is a fascinating branch of AI that's changing the way computers work and how they help us. But what exactly is it? Let us break it down in simple terms.

The Basics of Machine Learning

At its core, ML is about teaching computers to learn from data, rather than explicitly programmed for every task. It is like teaching a child. Instead of giving the child step-by-step instructions for every situation, we teach them general principles and let them learn from experience.

In ML, one feeds computers large amounts of data and lets them find patterns and make decisions based on what they've "learned." This approach allows computers to improve their performance on a specific task over time, without a human constantly telling them what to do.

How Does Machine Learning Work

ML typically involves three main steps:

1. **Training:** The computer is given a large dataset to learn from.
2. **Learning:** The computer analyzes the data to find patterns and relationships.
3. **Testing and Application:** The computer uses what it has learned to make predictions or decisions about new data.

For example, if we want to teach a computer to recognize cats in pictures, we would start by showing it thousands of cat pictures. The computer would learn to identify features common to cats (such as whiskers and pointy ears). Then, when shown a new picture, it could use what it learned to decide if the image contains a cat.

Types of Machine Learning

There are three main types of ML:

1. **Supervised Learning:** The computer is given labeled data (e.g., pictures labeled "cat" or "not cat") and learns to classify new, unlabeled data.

2. **Unsupervised Learning:** The computer is given unlabeled data and must find patterns and relationships on its own.
3. **Reinforcement Learning:** The computer learns by interacting with an environment and receiving rewards or penalties for its actions.

Business Applications

- **Supply Chain Optimization:** AI agents can learn to manage inventory and logistics more efficiently.
- **Financial Trading:** Developing sophisticated trading strategies that adapt to market conditions.
- **Energy Management:** Optimizing energy consumption in smart buildings and grids.

Neuromorphic Computing

Neuromorphic computing aims to mimic the structure and function of the human brain in hardware, potentially leading to more efficient and powerful AI systems.

Key Advancements

- **Brain-Inspired Hardware:** Development of chips that simulate neural networks more efficiently than traditional processors.
- **Spiking Neural Networks:** AI models that more closely resemble biological neural networks, potentially leading to more energy-efficient AI.
- **In-Memory Computing:** Integrating memory and processing to reduce data movement and increase efficiency.

Business Applications

- **Edge Computing:** Enabling powerful AI processing on small, low-power devices for Internet of Things (IoT) applications.
- **Real-Time Decision Making:** Faster, more efficient AI for applications such as autonomous vehicles and robotics.
- **Predictive Maintenance:** More efficient processing of sensor data for equipment monitoring and maintenance prediction.

Quantum Machine Learning

While still in its early stages, quantum computing has the potential to revolutionize ML by solving complex problems exponentially faster than classical computers.

Key Advancements

- **Quantum Algorithms:** Development of quantum versions of ML algorithms that can handle larger datasets and more complex problems.
- **Quantum Classical Hybrid Systems:** Combining quantum and classical computing to leverage the strengths of both.
- **Quantum Feature Spaces:** Using quantum systems to represent data in ways that are difficult or impossible with classical computers.

Business Applications

- **Drug Discovery:** Accelerating the process of finding new medications by simulating molecular interactions.
- **Financial Modeling:** More accurate and complex financial simulations for risk assessment and portfolio optimization.
- **Optimization Problems:** Solving complex logistics and scheduling problems more efficiently.

Real-World Applications of Machine Learning

ML is already used in many areas of our daily lives. Some examples are as follows:

- Recommendation systems on streaming platforms and online stores.
- Voice assistants such as Siri or Alexa.
- Fraud detection in banking.
- Email spam filters.
- Self-driving cars.
- Medical diagnosis.

The Power and Limitations of Machine Learning

ML is powerful because it can:

- Process and analyze vast amounts of data quickly.
- Identify patterns that humans might miss.
- Continuously improve its performance over time.
- Make predictions and decisions in real time.

However, ML has its limitations.

- ML systems are only as good as the data they're trained on.
- ML systems can inherit biases present in the training data.
- ML systems may struggle with tasks requiring common sense or emotional intelligence.
- ML systems' decision-making processes can be difficult for humans to interpret.

The Future of Machine Learning

As technology advances, ML is becoming more sophisticated and widespread. Developments are occurring in areas such as:

- **Deep Learning:** A subset of ML that uses neural networks to mimic human brain function.
- **Transfer Learning:** Where knowledge gained in one task is applied to a different but related task.
- **Federated Learning:** This allows ML models to be trained across multiple devices.

These advancements are opening up new possibilities in fields such as health care, environmental protection, and scientific research. Some exciting ML trends that are likely to emerge in the near future include the following:

- **Customized Chatbots:** In 2024, tech companies are focusing on making generative AI more accessible. Google and OpenAI are developing user-friendly platforms that allow people to customize powerful language models and create their mini chatbots without coding skills. These chatbots can handle not only text but also images and videos, opening up new possibilities for applications. For example, AI-powered chatbots can handle customer inquiries, freeing up human agents to deal with more complex issues. In finance, AI systems can process transactions and detect fraud, reducing the need for manual oversight.

- **Automated Machine Learning (AutoML):** AutoML is gaining prominence. It automates the process of selecting and optimizing ML models, making it easier for nonexperts to build effective models.
- **Tiny Machine Learning (TinyML):** TinyML focuses on deploying ML models on resource-constrained devices, such as IoT sensors* and edge devices.† It enables efficient inference with minimal computational resources.
- **Generative AI:** State-of-the-art models such as GPT-4 and Gemini are multimodal, processing text, images, and videos. This capability could lead to innovative applications in various domains.
- **No-Code ML:** Simplified tools allow users to create ML models without extensive coding. This democratizes ML development and encourages broader adoption.

---

* **IoT (Internet of Things) sensors** are devices that collect and transmit data from their environment. These sensors are used in various applications to monitor and measure physical conditions such as temperature, humidity, light, motion, and pressure. The data gathered by IoT sensors is sent to a central system or cloud platform for processing and analysis, enabling real-time decision making and automation. Common types of IoT sensors include the following:

Temperature sensors: measure ambient temperature; Humidity sensors: track moisture levels; Motion sensors: detect movement; Light sensors: monitor light intensity; Pressure sensors: gauge atmospheric or fluid pressure.

These sensors are fundamental to smart home systems, industrial automation, health care monitoring, environmental monitoring, and many other fields.

† **Edge devices** are hardware components that operate at the edge of a network, meaning they process data close to the source of data generation rather than sending it to a centralized server or cloud. These devices are integral to edge computing, where processing, analysis, and storage occur near the data source to reduce latency and bandwidth usage. Examples include smart sensors, IoT devices, gateways, and edge servers. They are widely used in applications such as smart cities, industrial automation, and health care to enable real-time data processing and faster decision making.

- **Ethical and Explainable ML:** Researchers and practitioners are emphasizing fairness, transparency, and interpretability in ML models to address biases and build trust.
- **MLOps:** MLOps combines DevOps practices with ML workflows, streamlining model deployment, monitoring, and maintenance.[‡]

Keep an eye on these trends—they'll shape the future of ML!

Summary

ML is a powerful tool that is transforming how one interacts with technology and solves complex problems. By allowing computers to learn from data and improve over time, ML is enabling innovations that were once thought impossible.

As the development and refinement of ML technologies continue, one is likely to see even more exciting applications emerge. However, these developments must be approached thoughtfully, considering both the potential benefits and the ethical implications of increasingly intelligent machines.

Understanding ML is becoming increasingly important in our data-driven world. Whether you are a business leader, a policy maker, or simply a curious individual, having a grasp of what ML is and how it works can help you navigate and *shape* the future of technology.[§]

[‡] **MLOps or ML Ops** is a paradigm that aims to deploy and maintain machine learning models in production reliably and efficiently. The word is a compound of "machine learning" and the continuous delivery practice (CI/CD) of DevOps in the software field. Machine learning models are tested and developed in isolated experimental systems. When an algorithm is ready to be launched, MLOps is practiced between data scientists, DevOps, and machine learning engineers to transition the algorithm to production systems. Ref: https://en.wikipedia.org/wiki/MLOps.

[§] ***Machine Learning***

MIT Technology Review
What's next for AI in 2024 |www.technologyreview.com/2024/01/04/1086046/whats-next-for-ai-in-2024/.

Merehead
New Projects and Trends of Machine Learning 2024—https://merehead.com/blog/machine-learning-trends-2024/.

What Is Deep Learning

Deep learning is a cutting-edge subset of ML that is making waves in the world of AI. But what exactly is it, and why is it so important? Let us break it down in simple terms.

The Basics of Deep Learning

Deep learning is a more advanced form of ML that tries to mimic how the human brain works. It uses complex structures called neural networks, which are inspired by the networks of neurons in our brains. These artificial neural networks are capable of learning from vast amounts of data and can perform tasks that were once thought to be uniquely human, such as recognizing speech, identifying objects in images, or even creating art.[5]

How Does Deep Learning Work

Deep learning systems, often called deep neural networks, consist of multiple layers of interconnected nodes (like neurons in the brain). Each layer processes information and passes it on to the next layer. The "deep" in deep learning refers to the many layers in these networks.

Here's a simplified step-by-step process:

- **Input:** Data is fed into the network (e.g., an image).
- **Processing:** Each layer extracts features from the data, starting with simple features and progressing to more complex ones.
- **Output:** The final layer produces the result (e.g., "This image contains a cat").
- **Learning:** The network compares its output to the correct answer and adjusts its internal connections to improve accuracy.

This process is repeated millions of times with different data, allowing the network to become increasingly accurate.

[5] **A neural network** is a machine learning program, or model, that makes decisions in a manner similar to the human brain, by using processes that mimic the way biological neurons work together to identify phenomena, weigh options, and arrive at conclusions. Ref: www.ibm.com/topics/neural-networks.

What Makes Deep Learning Special

Deep learning has several advantages over traditional ML:

- **Feature Learning:** Deep learning can automatically learn important features from raw data, whereas traditional ML often requires human experts to define these features.
- **Handling Complex Data:** It excels at processing unstructured data such as images, video, and text.
- **Scalability:** Deep learning models often improve with more data and larger networks, making them well-suited for the big data era.
- **Versatility:** The same basic neural network architecture can be applied to many different types of problems.

Challenges and Limitations of Deep Learning

While powerful, deep learning is not without its challenges:

- **Data Hunger:** Deep learning typically requires vast amounts of data to train effectively.
- **Computational Intensity:** Training deep neural networks often requires significant computing power.
- **Black Box Problem:** The decision-making process in deep networks can be difficult to interpret or explain.
- **Potential for Bias:** If trained on biased data, deep learning systems can perpetuate or amplify these biases.

The Future of Deep Learning

As technology advances, we're seeing exciting developments in deep learning:

- **More Efficient Architectures:** Researchers are developing neural network designs that require less data and computing power.
- **Explainable AI:** There's a push to create deep learning systems that can explain their decision-making process.

- **Multimodal Learning:** Systems that can process and understand multiple types of data (text, images, and sound) simultaneously.
- **Few-Shot Learning:** Techniques that allow deep networks to learn from smaller amounts of data.

These advancements are expanding the potential applications of deep learning and addressing some of its current limitations.

Some Key Real-World Examples of Deep Learning in use Today

1. **Computer Vision and Image Recognition**
    - Facial recognition systems for security and authentication.
    - Object detection and classification in self-driving cars.
    - Medical image analysis for disease detection (e.g., identifying tumors in X-rays/Magnetic Resonance Imaging (MRI)).
2. **Natural Language Processing**
    - Voice assistants such as Siri, Alexa, and Google Assistant.
    - Machine translation services such as Google Translate.
    - Chatbots and conversational AI.
3. **Speech Recognition**
    - Voice-to-text transcription services.
    - Voice control systems in smart home devices and cars.
4. **Recommendation Systems**
    - Product recommendations on ecommerce sites such as Amazon.
    - Content recommendations on streaming platforms such as Netflix and Spotify.
5. **Financial Services**
    - Fraud detection in banking and credit card transactions.
    - Algorithmic trading and stock price prediction.
    - Credit scoring and loan approval systems.
6. **Health Care**
    - Drug discovery and development.
    - Personalized medicine and treatment recommendations.
    - Disease diagnosis from medical imaging.

7. **Robotics**
    - Motion planning and control in industrial robots.
    - Autonomous navigation in robots and drones.
8. **Gaming**
    - AI opponents in video games.
    - Procedural content generation in games.
9. **Autonomous Vehicles**
    - Object detection, path planning, and decision making in self-driving cars.
10. **Art and Creativity**
    - AI-generated art, music, and writing.
    - Style transfer in image and video editing.

These examples showcase how deep learning is applied across a wide range of industries and applications to solve complex problems and create new capabilities. The technology continues to advance rapidly, with new use cases emerging regularly.

Summary

Deep learning represents a significant leap forward in the quest to create intelligent machines. By mimicking the structure and function of the human brain, deep learning systems can tackle complex problems that were previously out of reach for computers.

From powering the voice assistants on phones to revolutionizing medical diagnosis, deep learning is already having a profound impact on people. As the technology continues to evolve, we can expect to see even more ground-breaking applications emerge.

However, approach deep learning with both excitement and caution. While its potential is enormous, one must also be mindful of its limitations and potential risks, particularly in areas such as privacy and algorithmic bias. Understanding deep learning is becoming increasingly important as it shapes the future of AI and, by extension, society.

Whether looking to leverage AI, a policy maker considering its implications, or simply a curious individual, having a grasp of deep learning can help businesses navigate and contribute to the ongoing AI revolution.[**]

** ***Some excellent resources about Deep Learning***

DataCamp's Guide on Deep Learning
DataCamp offers a comprehensive guide that covers topics from basics to neural networks. It explains deep learning concepts and their applications, including natural language processing, computer vision, and speech recognition. www.datacamp.com/blog/how-to-learn-deep-learning.

Free Resources for Learning Deep Learning With PyTorch
This Medium article provides a curated list of free resources specifically focused on deep learning using PyTorch. It includes online courses, tutorials, textbooks, blogs, and software tools. https://medium.com/analytics-vidhya/top-5-free-resources-to-learn-deep-learning-with-pytorch-a92fd1d718bd.

DeepLearning.AI's Resource Center
DeepLearning.AI offers a collection of eBooks, guides, course slides, AI notes, and more. It's a valuable resource for both beginners and experienced practitioners in the field of AI and machine learning. www.deeplearning.ai/resources/.

What Is Natural Language Processing

NLP is a fascinating field of AI that focuses on the interaction between computers and humans through natural language. In simpler terms, it is about teaching computers to understand, interpret, and respond to human language in a way that is both meaningful and useful. NLP has made significant strides in recent years, enabling machines to understand and generate human language with unprecedented accuracy. Advanced NLP technologies are set to revolutionize business communication and customer interactions.

The Basics of Natural Language Processing

Human language is incredibly complex and diverse. It includes not just words and sentences but also context, tone, and nuances that can change the meaning of what is said. NLP aims to bridge the gap between human communication and computer understanding.

NLP combines several disciplines, including linguistics, computer science, and ML, to enable computers to process and analyze large amounts of natural language data.

How Does Natural Language Processing Work

NLP involves several key steps to transform human language into a format that computers can understand and act upon:

- **Tokenization:** Breaking down text into smaller units, such as words or phrases.
- **Parsing:** Analyzing the grammatical structure of a sentence.
- **Stemming and Lemmatization:** Reducing words to their base or root form.
- **Part-of-Speech Tagging:** Identifying the grammatical role of each word in a sentence (e.g., noun, verb, adjective).
- **Named Entity Recognition:** Identifying and classifying key elements in text, such as names of people, organizations, dates, and locations.

- **Sentiment Analysis:** AI can now accurately detect emotions and sentiments in text, enabling businesses to gauge customer satisfaction and market trends more effectively by determining the sentiment or emotional tone behind a piece of text (e.g., positive, negative, and neutral).
- **Large Language Models:** Models such as GPT-3 and its successors can generate human-like text, answer questions, and even write code. These models are becoming more sophisticated, with an improved understanding of context and nuance.

Real-World Applications of Natural Language Processing

NLP is already used in many areas of our daily lives, often without us even realizing it. Here are some common applications:

- **Voice Assistants:** Siri, Alexa, and Google Assistant use NLP to understand and respond to voice commands.
- **Machine Translation:** Services such as Google Translate use NLP to translate text from one language to another.
- **Chatbots:** Many customer-service chatbots use NLP to understand and respond to customer inquiries.
- **Email Filters:** Spam filters use NLP to identify and filter out unwanted emails.
- **Sentiment Analysis:** Companies use NLP to analyze customer reviews and social media posts to gauge public opinion about their products or services.
- **Text Summarization:** NLP can automatically generate summaries of long documents, making it easier to digest large amounts of information quickly.
- **Autocorrect and Predictive Text:** NLP powers the autocorrect and predictive text features.

The Power and Limitations of Natural Language Processing

NLP has several advantages:

- **Efficiency:** It can process and analyze vast amounts of text data quickly.
- **Automation:** It automates tasks that would be time-consuming and tedious for humans.
- **Insight:** It can uncover patterns and insights in text data missed by human analysts.

However, NLP also has its limitations:

- **Ambiguity:** Human language is often ambiguous and context-dependent, making it challenging for computers to interpret accurately.
- **Complexity:** Understanding nuances, idioms, and cultural references can be difficult for NLP systems.
- **Bias:** NLP systems can inherit biases present in the data they are trained on, leading to biased or unfair outcomes.

The Future of Natural Language Processing

The field of NLP is rapidly evolving, with ongoing research and advancements pushing the boundaries of what is possible. Some exciting developments include the following:

- **Improved Language Models:** Advanced models such as GPT-4 and beyond are capable of generating human-like text and understanding context more effectively.
- **Multilingual NLP:** Efforts are made to improve NLP capabilities across multiple languages, making technology more accessible globally. Advanced systems can now process and translate multiple languages in real time, breaking down language barriers.
- **Explainable AI:** There is a growing focus on making NLP systems more transparent and explainable, so users can understand how decisions are made.

- **Human–AI Collaboration:** Future NLP systems will likely focus on enhancing collaboration between humans and AI, making interactions more seamless and intuitive.

Summary

NLP is a powerful technology that is transforming how one interacts with machines. By enabling computers to understand and respond to human language, NLP is making technology more accessible and useful in everyday life. From voice assistants and chatbots to translation services and sentiment analysis, NLP is already having a significant impact across various industries. As technology continues to advance, one can expect even more innovative applications to emerge, further enhancing our ability to communicate and interact with machines.

Understanding NLP is becoming increasingly important as it shapes the future of AI and human–computer interaction. Whether you are a business leader looking to leverage AI, a developer working on the next big thing, or simply a curious individual, having a grasp of NLP can help you navigate and contribute to the ongoing AI revolution.[††]

[††] ***Some sources that provide information on natural language processing (NLP)***

OpenSource
12 open source tools for natural language processing. https://opensource.com/article/19/3/natural-language-processing-tools.

DeepLearning.AI
Natural Language Processing (NLP)—A Complete Guide. www.deeplearning.ai/resources/natural-language-processing/.

IBM
What Is NLP (Natural Language Processing)? | IBM. www.ibm.com/topics/natural-language-processing.

What Is Computer Vision

Computer vision is a rapidly advancing field of AI that enables machines to interpret and understand the visual world. Simply put, it is about teaching computers to see and make sense of images and videos, much like humans do.

This technology is transforming various industries and becoming an integral part of daily life.

The Basics of Computer Vision

At its core, computer vision involves the automatic extraction, analysis, and understanding of useful information from a single image or a sequence of images. This process mimics the way humans use their eyes and brains to perceive and interpret the world around them.

Computer vision combines several disciplines, including computer science, mathematics, and engineering, to develop algorithms and models that can process visual data.

How Does Computer Vision Work

Computer vision systems typically follow a series of steps to analyze visual data:

- **Image Acquisition:** Capturing images or video using cameras or sensors.
- **Preprocessing:** Enhancing the quality of the images, such as adjusting brightness or removing noise.
- **Feature Extraction:** Identifying important features in the images, like edges, shapes, and textures.
- **Object Detection and Recognition:** Identifying and classifying objects within the images (e.g., recognizing a cat in a photo). AI can now identify and classify objects in images and videos with high accuracy, even in complex scenes.
- **Postprocessing:** Analyzing the results and making decisions based on the extracted information.

Real-World Applications of Computer Vision

Computer vision is already used in many areas of our daily lives and across various industries. Here are some common applications:

- **Facial Recognition:** Computer vision is used in security systems, smartphones, and social media platforms to identify individuals. Advanced systems can recognize faces and emotions, with applications in security and customer experience.
- **3D Vision:** AI can now interpret 3D environments, crucial for robotics and augmented reality (AR) applications.
- **Autonomous Vehicles:** Self-driving cars use computer vision to detect and interpret road signs, pedestrians, and other vehicles.
- **Medical Imaging:** Computer vision assists doctors in diagnosing diseases by analyzing medical images such as X-rays, MRIs, and CT scans.
- **Retail:** Computer vision enhances shopping experiences with features such as virtual try-ons and automated checkouts.
- **Manufacturing:** Quality control systems use computer vision to inspect products for defects.
- **Agriculture:** Computer vision is monitoring crop health and detecting pests using aerial images from drones.
- **Entertainment:** Computer vision is powering AR and virtual reality (VR) experiences.

The Power and Limitations of Computer Vision

Computer vision has several advantages:

- **Automation:** It can automate tasks that would be time-consuming and labor-intensive for humans.
- **Precision:** It can analyze visual data with high accuracy and consistency.
- **Scalability:** It can process large volumes of images and videos quickly.

However, computer vision also has its limitations:

- **Complexity:** Visual data is inherently complex and can be challenging to interpret accurately.
- **Variability:** Changes in lighting, angle, and occlusion can affect the performance of computer vision systems.
- **Bias:** Computer vision models can inherit biases present in the training data, leading to unfair outcomes.

The Future of Computer Vision

The field of computer vision is rapidly evolving, with ongoing research and advancements pushing the boundaries of what is possible. Some exciting developments include the following:

- **Improved Algorithms:** Developing more sophisticated algorithms that can handle complex visual tasks with greater accuracy.
- **Edge Computing:** Bringing computer vision capabilities to devices at the edge of the network, such as smartphones and IoT devices, for faster processing and real-time analysis.
- **Explainable AI:** Making computer vision systems more transparent and interpretable, so users can understand how decisions are made.[‡‡]
- **Integration with Other AI Technologies:** Combining computer vision with other AI technologies, such as NLP and ML, to create more powerful and versatile systems.

Summary

Computer vision is a powerful technology that is transforming how machines interact with the visual world. By enabling computers to "see and understand" images and videos, computer vision is making

---

[‡‡] The term *IoT*, **or Internet of Things,** refers to the collective network of connected devices and the technology that facilitates communication between devices and the cloud, as well as between the devices themselves.

technology more accessible and useful in everyday life. From facial recognition and autonomous vehicles to medical imaging and retail, computer vision is already having a significant impact across various industries. As technology continues to advance, one can expect even more innovative applications to emerge, further enhancing the human ability to interact with and interpret the visual world. Understanding computer vision is becoming increasingly important as it shapes the future of AI and human–computer interaction.[§§]

---

§§ ***Computer vision***

NVIDIA Technical Blog
The Future of Computer Vision | https://developer.nvidia.com/blog/the-future-of-computer-vision/.

Augmented Start-Up
The Future of Computer Vision: Trends, Applications, and Impacts in 2023. www.augmentedstartups.com/blog/the-future-of-computer-vision-trends-applications-and-impacts-in-2023.

viso.ai
Computer Vision Trends—The Ultimate 2024 Overview—https://viso.ai/computer-vision/computer-vision-trends/.

What Is Robotic Process Automation

Robotic process automation (RPA) is a powerful technology that is transforming the way businesses operate by automating repetitive and mundane tasks. RPA involves software robots, or "bots," that can perform digital tasks just like a human would.

Let us dive into what RPA is and how it is making a difference in the business world.

The Basics of Robotic Process Automation

At its core, RPA is about using software to create "robots" that can mimic human actions on a computer. These bots can interact with applications, enter data, process transactions, and even respond to emails. The goal is to free up human workers from tedious tasks so they can focus on more strategic and creative work.

RPA doesn't require complex programming. Instead, it uses simple, user-friendly tools that allow business users to create bots by recording their actions or by using a visual interface to design workflows.

How Does Robotic Process Automation Work

RPA bots can perform a wide range of tasks by following a set of rules and instructions. Here's a simplified step-by-step process of how RPA works:

- **Task Identification:** Identify repetitive tasks that can be automated, such as data entry, invoice processing, or customer support.
- **Bot Creation:** Use RPA software to create bots. This can be done by recording human actions or by designing workflows using a drag-and-drop interface.
- **Deployment:** Deploy the bots to perform the tasks. Bots can work 24/7 without breaks, ensuring efficiency and consistency.
- **Monitoring and Maintenance:** Monitor the performance of the bots and make adjustments as needed to ensure that they continue to operate effectively.

Real-World Applications of Robotic Process Automation

RPA is used across various industries to streamline operations and improve efficiency. Here are some common applications:

- **Finance and Accounting:** Automating tasks such as invoice processing, payroll, and financial reporting.
- **Customer Service:** AI-powered chatbots and virtual assistants can provide 24/7 support by responding to routine customer inquiries, processing orders, and updating customer records.
- **Human Resources:** Automating employee onboarding, offboarding, and benefits administration.
- **Health Care:** Managing patient records, scheduling appointments, and processing insurance claims.
- **Supply Chain Management:** Tracking shipments, managing inventory, and processing orders.
- **Retail:** Automating inventory management, order processing, and customer support.
- **Content Creation:** Automated content generation for marketing, reports, and documentation.
- **Market Research:** Analyzing social media and customer feedback to gain insights into consumer preferences and trends.

The Power and Limitations of Robotic Process Automation

RPA offers several advantages:

- **Efficiency:** Bots can perform tasks faster and more accurately than humans, reducing errors and increasing productivity.
- **Cost Savings:** Automating repetitive tasks can lead to significant cost savings by reducing the need for manual labor.
- **Scalability:** RPA can be easily scaled up or down to meet changing business needs.
- **Compliance:** Bots can ensure that tasks are performed consistently and in compliance with regulations.

However, RPA also has its limitations:

- **Limited Scope:** RPA is best suited for rule-based tasks and may struggle with more complex, judgment-based tasks.
- **Maintenance:** Bots need to be regularly monitored and updated to ensure that they continue to function correctly, especially when underlying systems change.
- **Initial Setup:** Implementing RPA requires an initial investment of time and resources to identify suitable tasks and create bots.

The Future of Robotic Process Automation

The field of RPA is rapidly evolving, with ongoing advancements making it even more powerful and versatile. Some exciting developments include the following:

- **Intelligent Automation:** Combining RPA with AI technologies such as ML and NLP to handle more complex tasks and make smarter decisions.
- **Integration with Other Systems:** Enhancing RPA capabilities by integrating with other business systems and applications, creating seamless workflows.
- **User-Friendly Tools:** Developing more intuitive and user-friendly RPA tools that allow even nontechnical users to create and manage bots.
- **Enhanced Security:** Improving the security of RPA systems to protect sensitive data and ensure compliance with regulations.

Summary

RPA is a transformative technology that is reshaping the way businesses operate. By automating repetitive and mundane tasks, RPA allows human workers to focus on more valuable and creative activities, leading to increased efficiency and productivity.

From finance and customer service to health care and retail, RPA is already having a significant impact across various industries. As the technology continues to advance, more innovative applications will emerge, further enhancing humans' ability to automate and streamline business processes.

Understanding RPA is becoming increasingly important as it shapes the future of work and business operations. Whether you are a business leader looking to leverage RPA, a developer working on the next big thing, or simply a curious individual, having a grasp of RPA can help you navigate and contribute to the ongoing automation revolution.[¶]

[¶] ***Robotic Process Automation***

IBM Blog

The Future of Robotic Process Automation (RPA)—www.ibm.com/blog/the-future-of-robotic-process-automation/.

Robots at Work

Robotics Process Automation and the Future of Employment. https://easychair.org/publications/preprint/46XL.

Capgemini

The Future of Robotic Process Automation (RPA)—www.capgemini.com/insights/expert-perspectives/the-future-of-robotic-process-automation-rpa-integrated-intelligent-automation-platforms/.

CHAPTER 2

AI Data and Algorithms

The Building Blocks of Intelligent Systems

In the realm of AI, **data** and **algorithms** are the fundamental components that breathe life into intelligent systems. This chapter delves into these crucial elements, exploring how they work together to create AI applications that can learn, reason, and make decisions.

This chapter begins by examining the critical role of data in AI. Just as humans learn from experience, AI systems learn from data. Why high-quality, diverse, and abundant data is essential for training effective AI models and how it impacts the performance and reliability of AI systems are examined.

Next, various types of data used in AI applications are explored. From structured data such as spreadsheets to unstructured data such as images and text, each type presents unique challenges and opportunities. How different data types are used across various AI applications and the considerations for collecting and preparing each are reviewed.

The heart of this chapter focuses on AI algorithms—the step-by-step procedures that enable machines to learn from data and make intelligent decisions by demystifying common AI algorithms, explaining their principles in straightforward terms, and illustrating how they are applied in real-world scenarios.

Finally, the crucial process of evaluating AI model performance is discussed. Understanding how well an AI system is performing is essential for improving its capabilities and ensuring its reliability. Various metrics and techniques are used to assess AI models, helping to understand how to measure and interpret AI performance effectively.

By the end of this chapter, you will have a solid grasp of the data and algorithmic foundations that power AI systems. This knowledge will equip you to better understand, implement, and evaluate AI solutions in your business context.

Let us embark on this exploration of the building blocks that make AI possible.

The Importance of Data for AI

Just as one gains knowledge and skills through interactions with the world, AI systems learn and improve through exposure to vast amounts of data. This section explores why data is so crucial for AI and how it affects the development and performance of intelligent systems.

Data: The Lifeblood of AI

At its core, AI is about creating systems that can learn, reason, and make decisions. But unlike humans, who can learn from a relatively small number of experiences, AI systems typically require enormous amounts of data to become proficient at their tasks. This data serves as the foundation on which AI models build their understanding of the world. Think of an AI system as a newborn child. A child learns to recognize objects, understand language, and navigate their environment through countless interactions and observations. Similarly, an AI system needs to be exposed to numerous examples to learn patterns, make connections, and develop the ability to generalize from what it has seen to new, unseen situations.

Quality Matters: The Need for High-Quality Data

While quantity is important, the quality of data is equally crucial. High-quality data for AI should be:

- **Accurate:** Free from errors and correctly representing the real-world scenario it is meant to capture.
- **Relevant:** Directly related to the problem the AI is trying to solve.

- **Consistent:** Following a uniform format and structure.
- **Timely:** Up-to-date and reflective of current conditions.

Poor quality data can lead to what's often called GIGO (garbage in, garbage out) in AI. If an AI system is trained on inaccurate or irrelevant data, it will make poor decisions or predictions, regardless of how sophisticated the underlying algorithms are.

Diversity: Representing the Real World

Diversity in data is crucial for creating AI systems that can perform well in varied, real-world conditions. A diverse dataset helps AI models to:

- **Avoid Bias:** If data is not diverse, AI systems can develop biases that lead to unfair or inaccurate results for certain groups.
- **Handle Variability:** The real world is complex and varied. Diverse data helps AI systems cope with this variability.
- **Generalize Better:** With exposure to a wide range of scenarios, AI systems can better apply their learning to new, unseen situations.

For example, a facial recognition system trained only on images of light-skinned individuals will perform poorly when trying to recognize people with darker skin tones. Diverse data helps prevent such limitations.

Abundance: More Data Equals Better Performance

In many cases, the performance of AI systems improves with more data. This is particularly true for complex tasks and advanced AI techniques such as deep learning. More data allows AI systems to:

- **Identify Subtle Patterns:** With larger datasets, AI can detect nuanced patterns that might be missed with smaller amounts of data.

- **Reduce Overfitting:** Overfitting occurs when an AI model learns the training data too well, including its noise and peculiarities, leading to poor performance on new data. More data helps prevent this.
- **Improve Accuracy:** Generally, more data leads to more accurate models, especially for complex tasks.

However, there can be diminishing returns. At some point, adding more data may not significantly improve performance, and the focus should shift to improving the quality and diversity of the data or enhancing the AI algorithms themselves.

Impact on AI System Performance and Reliability

The quality, diversity, and abundance of data directly impact the performance and reliability of AI systems:

- **Performance:** AI systems trained on high-quality, diverse, and abundant data generally perform better across a wide range of scenarios. They make more accurate predictions, classifications, or decisions.
- **Reliability:** With better data, AI systems become more reliable and consistent in their outputs. They're less likely to make unexpected errors or behave erratically when faced with new situations.
- **Robustness:** Diverse data helps create more robust AI systems that can handle variations and anomalies in input data without significant degradation in performance.
- **Fairness:** Properly diverse datasets help ensure that AI systems perform equitably across different demographic groups, reducing the risk of bias and discrimination.

Summary

In the world of AI, data is not just important—it is fundamental because it is fueling intelligent systems. High-quality, diverse, and abundant data forms the foundation upon which successful AI systems are built. It enables AI to learn, adapt, and make accurate decisions across a wide range of scenarios. While continuing to develop and deploy AI systems, the focus on data—its collection, preparation, and use—remains crucial. Organizations looking to leverage AI must prioritize not just the development of sophisticated algorithms, but also the cultivation of high-quality, diverse datasets.

In AI, the system is only as good as the data it learns from. By focusing on data quality, diversity, and abundance, one can create AI systems that are not only powerful and accurate but also fair, reliable, and truly beneficial to society.*

---

* ***Here are three sources that cover the topic of data as the foundation of AI success:***

Encora
Data Excellence as the Foundation for AI Success
www.encora.com/insights/data-excellence-as-the-foundation-for-ai-success.

Building a foundation for AI success
Technology and data strategy
www.microsoft.com/en-us/microsoft-cloud/blog/2024/01/29/building-a-foundation-for-ai-success-technology-and-data-strategy/.

Forbes
A Successful Data Strategy Is the Foundation for Your AI Strategy
www.forbes.com/sites/forbestechcouncil/2024/06/03/a-successful-data-strategy-is-the-foundation-for-your-ai- strategy/.

Types of Data for AI Applications

In the realm of AI, data is the cornerstone that enables machines to learn, adapt, and make decisions. Just as humans rely on diverse experiences to gain knowledge, AI systems require various types of data to function effectively.

This section explores the different types of data used in AI applications, highlighting their unique challenges and opportunities, and discussing how they are collected and prepared.

Structured Data

Structured data is highly organized and easily searchable. It is typically stored in tabular formats such as spreadsheets or databases, where each piece of information is contained within predefined fields.

Examples

- Customer databases with names, addresses, and purchase histories.
- Financial records with transactions, account balances, and dates.

Applications

- **Customer Relationship Management (CRM)**: AI analyzes customer data to predict purchasing behavior and improve customer service.
- **Financial Forecasting**: AI models predict market trends and financial risks using historical financial data.

Challenges

- **Data Consistency:** Ensuring that data is consistently formatted and free from errors.
- **Data Integration:** Combining data from different sources can be complex and time-consuming.

Preparation

- **Cleaning:** Removing duplicates and correcting errors.
- **Normalization:** Standardizing data formats to ensure consistency.

Unstructured Data

Unstructured data lacks a predefined format, making it more challenging to analyze. This type of data includes text, images, audio, and video.

Examples

- Social media posts, emails, and documents.
- Photos, videos, and audio recordings.

Applications

- **Natural Language Processing (NLP):** AI systems analyze text data to understand and generate human language, powering applications such as chatbots and language translation.
- **Computer Vision:** AI models interpret visual data to recognize objects, faces, and scenes used in applications such as facial recognition and autonomous vehicles.

Challenges

- **Data Complexity:** Unstructured data is more difficult to process and analyze due to its varied formats.
- **Volume:** The sheer amount of unstructured data can be overwhelming.

Preparation

- **Data Annotation:** Labeling data to provide context (e.g., tagging objects in images).
- **Preprocessing:** Converting data into a usable format, such as transcribing audio to text.

Semistructured Data

Semistructured data falls between structured and unstructured data. It does not reside in a traditional database but has some organizational properties, such as tags or markers.

Examples

- JSON or XML files
- HTML documents

Applications

- **Web Scraping:** Extracting data from websites to analyze trends and consumer behavior.
- **APIs:** Integrating data from different systems to create comprehensive datasets.

Challenges

- **Data Parsing:** Extracting and interpreting data from semistructured formats can be complex.
- **Standardization:** Ensuring that data from different sources follows a consistent structure.

Preparation

- **Parsing:** Extracting relevant information from semistructured formats.
- **Transformation:** Converting data into a structured format for easier analysis.

Time-Series Data

Time-series data consists of sequences of data points collected or recorded at specific time intervals.

Examples

- Stock prices are recorded every minute.
- Sensor readings from IoT devices.

Applications

- **Predictive Maintenance:** Analyzing sensor data to predict equipment failures and schedule maintenance.
- **Financial Analysis:** Using historical stock prices to forecast future market trends.

Challenges

- **Temporal Dependencies:** Accounting for the time-based relationships between data points.
- **Data Volume:** Managing large volumes of data collected over time.

Preparation

- **Resampling:** Adjusting the frequency of data points to a consistent interval.
- **Smoothing:** Reducing noise in the data to highlight trends.

Collecting and Preparing Data for AI

The process of collecting and preparing data is crucial for the success of AI applications. Here are some key considerations:

Data Collection

- **Relevance:** Ensure that the data collected is relevant to the specific AI application.
- **Sources:** Data can be sourced from public databases, web APIs, sensors, and user-generated content.

Data Cleaning

- **Accuracy:** Remove errors, duplicates, and inconsistencies.
- **Completeness:** Ensure that the dataset is complete and contains all necessary information.

Data Annotation

- **Data Labeling:** Annotate data to provide context, such as tagging objects in images or labeling text sentiment.
- **Data Quality Control:** Ensure that annotations are accurate and consistent.

Data Transformation

- **Data Normalization:** Standardize data formats and scales.
- **Data Feature Engineering:** Create new features from raw data to improve model performance.

Summary

Understanding the various types of data used in AI applications is essential for developing effective AI systems. From structured data in spreadsheets to unstructured data such as images and text, each type presents unique challenges and opportunities. Properly collecting, cleaning, annotating, and transforming data ensures that AI models are trained on high-quality, diverse, and abundant datasets, leading to better performance and reliability. By recognizing the importance of data and the specific considerations for each type, organizations can harness the full potential of AI to drive innovation and achieve their goals.[†]

[†] ***Here are some sources that cover the topic of types of data for AI applications:***

AI for all data types: structured, unstructured, and semi-structured
https://data.world/blog/ai-for-all-data-types/.

Types of Artificial Intelligence | IBM
www.ibm.com/think/topics/artificial-intelligence-types.

Google Cloud
Applications of artificial intelligence. https://cloud.google.com/discover/ai-applications.

AI Algorithms Explained

AI algorithms are the engines that power intelligent machines, enabling them to learn from data and make decisions. While they may seem complex, the basic principles behind many AI algorithms can be understood in simple terms. Let us explore some common AI algorithms, how they work, and their real-world applications.

AI Algorithms Explained: How Machines Learn and Make Decisions

Supervised Learning Algorithms

Supervised learning is like teaching with examples. The machine is given labeled data (input and correct output) and learns to predict outputs for new inputs.

How It Works

- The AI algorithm is given a dataset with correct answers (labels).
- It learns patterns from this data.
- When given new, unlabeled data, it uses these patterns to make predictions.

Common Supervised Learning Algorithms

a. **Linear Regression**
  - Used for predicting numerical values.
  - Finds the best-fitting straight line through a set of points.
    - **Real-World Application:** Predicting house prices based on features such as size and location.

b. **Logistic Regression**
  - Used for binary classification (yes/no decisions).
  - Calculates the probability of an input belonging to a particular category.
    - **Real-World Application:** Predicting whether an email is spam or not.

c. **Decision Trees**
- Makes decisions by following a treelike model of decisions.
- Splits data based on features to make predictions.
    - **Real-World Application:** Diagnosing diseases based on symptoms.

Unsupervised Learning Algorithms

Unsupervised learning is about finding patterns in data without labeled answers. It is like discovering groups or structures in data on your own.

How It Works

- The algorithm is given unlabeled data.
- It looks for patterns or similarities in the data.
- It groups or organizes the data based on these patterns.

Common Unsupervised Learning Algorithms

a. **K-Means Clustering**
- Groups similar data points together.
- Divide data into "k" number of clusters.
    - **Real-World Application:** Customer segmentation for targeted marketing.

b. **Principal Component Analysis (PCA)**
- Reduces the dimensionality of data while preserving important information.
- Finds the most important features in a dataset.
    - **Real-World Application:** Image compression, reducing noise in data.

Reinforcement Learning Algorithms

Reinforcement learning (RL) is an area of ML where AI agents learn to make decisions by interacting with an environment. This technology is particularly promising for optimizing complex systems and processes.

Reinforcement learning is like learning through trial and error. The algorithm learns to make decisions by receiving feedback from its environment.

How It Works

- The algorithm (agent) interacts with an environment.
- It receives rewards or penalties based on its actions.
- Over time, it learns which actions lead to the highest rewards.

Common Reinforcement Learning Algorithms

Q-Learning.

- Learned the value of actions in different states.
- Chooses actions that maximize long-term rewards.
    - **Real-World Application:** Game playing AI, autonomous vehicles.

Deep Learning Algorithms

Deep learning uses artificial neural networks inspired by the human brain. These networks can learn complex patterns from large amounts of data.

How It Works.

- Data is fed into a network of interconnected nodes (neurons).
- Each node processes the data and passes it to the next layer.
- The network adjusts its connections to improve its predictions.

Common Deep Learning Algorithms Architectures

a. **Convolutional Neural Networks (CNNs)**
- Specialized for processing grid-like data, such as images.
- Uses filters to detect features in data.
    - **Real-World Application:** Image recognition, facial recognition.

b. **Recurrent Neural Networks (RNNs)**
- Processes sequences of data, remembering previous inputs.
- Suitable for time-series data or text.
    - **Real-World Application:** Language translation, speech recognition.

Ensemble Methods

Ensemble methods combine multiple algorithms to create a more powerful model.

How It Works.

- Multiple models are trained on the same data.
- Their predictions are combined to make a final decision.
- This often leads to better performance than individual models.

Common Ensemble Methods

Random Forest.

- Combines multiple decision trees.
- Each tree votes on the final prediction.
    - **Real-World Application:** Recommendation systems predictions in stock market trends or fraud detection.

Many online platforms use a combination of these algorithms to create personalized recommendations:

Collaborative Filtering (Unsupervised Learning)

- Groups users with similar preferences.
- Recommends items liked by similar users.

Content-Based Filtering (Supervised Learning)

- Analyzes features of items a user has liked.
- Recommends similar items based on these features.

Deep Learning

- Uses neural networks to learn complex patterns in user behavior and item characteristics.

Reinforcement Learning

- Optimizes recommendations over time based on user interactions.

By combining these approaches, platforms such as Netflix, Amazon, and Spotify can provide highly personalized recommendations to their users.

Summary

While AI algorithms can be complex, their basic principles often follow intuitive patterns of learning and decision making. From supervised learning that learns from examples to unsupervised learning that discovers patterns to reinforcement learning that learns through trial and error, these algorithms power a wide range of AI applications. Understanding these fundamental concepts can help demystify AI and provide insight into how machines can perform tasks that once seemed uniquely human. As AI continues to advance, these algorithms will evolve and combine in new ways, opening up even more possibilities for intelligent systems.[‡]

---

‡ ***Here are some sources that cover the topic of AI algorithms:***

BBC
Google just updated its algorithm. The internet will never be the same. www.bbc.com/future/article/20240524-how-googles-new-algorithm-will-shape-your-internet.

ScienceDaily
Artificial Intelligence News
www.sciencedaily.com/news/computers_math/artificial_intelligence/.

MIT News
AI accelerates problem-solving in complex scenarios.
https://news.mit.edu/2023/ai-accelerates-problem-solving-complex-scenarios-1205.

Evaluating AI Model Performance

In the world of AI, building a model is just the beginning. To ensure that an AI system is effective, reliable, and capable of continuous improvement, it is crucial to evaluate its performance. This process involves using various metrics and techniques to measure how well the model is doing its job.

Let us explore why evaluating AI model performance is essential and how to do it effectively.

Why Evaluating AI Model Performance Is Important

- **Ensuring Accuracy:** The primary goal of any AI model is to make accurate predictions or decisions. Evaluating performance helps determine if the model is meeting this goal.
- **Improving Capabilities:** By understanding where a model excels and where it falls short, developers can make necessary adjustments to improve its performance.
- **Ensuring Reliability:** Regular evaluation ensures that the model performs consistently across different scenarios and datasets.
- **Avoiding Bias:** Evaluation helps identify and mitigate biases in the model, ensuring fair and equitable outcomes.
- **Building Trust:** Reliable and accurate models build trust among users and stakeholders, making it easier to adopt AI solutions.

Key Metrics for Evaluating AI Models

Different types of AI models require different evaluation metrics. Here are some common metrics used to assess AI model performance:

For Classification Models

- Accuracy: The percentage of correct predictions out of all predictions made.
  - **Formula:** (Number of Correct Predictions)/(Total Number of Predictions)

  - **Use Case:** Useful when the classes are balanced (e.g., predicting if an email is spam or not).
- Precision: The percentage of true positive predictions out of all positive predictions made.
  - **Formula:** (True Positives)/(True Positives + False Positives)
  - **Use Case:** Important when the cost of false positives is high (e.g., predicting a disease).
- Recall: The percentage of true positive predictions out of all actual positives.
  - **Formula:** (True Positives)/(True Positives + False Negatives)
  - **Use Case:** Important when the cost of false negatives is high (e.g., detecting fraud).
- F1 Score: The harmonic mean of precision and recall, providing a balance between the two.
  - **Formula:** 2 * (Precision * Recall)/(Precision + Recall)
  - **Use Case:** Useful when both precision and recall are important.

For Regression Models

- Mean Absolute Error (MAE): The average of absolute differences between predicted and actual values.
  - **Formula:** (Sum of |Predicted - Actual|)/(Number of Predictions)
  - **Use Case:** Easy to interpret and useful for understanding the average error.
- Mean Squared Error (MSE): The average of squared differences between predicted and actual values.
  - **Formula:** (Sum of (Predicted - Actual)^2)/(Number of Predictions)
  - **Use Case:** Penalizes larger errors more than MAE, useful for emphasizing larger mistakes.
- R-squared (R^2): The proportion of variance in the dependent variable that is predictable from the independent variables.
  - **Formula:** 1 - (Sum of Squared Residuals)/(Total Sum of Squares)
  - **Use Case:** Indicates how well the model explains the variability of the target variable.

Techniques for Evaluating AI Models

- **Train-Test Split:** Dividing the dataset into training and testing sets. The model is trained on the training set and evaluated on the testing set.
    - **Purpose:** Ensures that the model's performance is evaluated on unseen data, simulating real-world scenarios.
- **Cross-Validation:** Dividing the dataset into multiple subsets (folds) and training/testing the model on different combinations of these folds.
    - **Purpose:** Provides a more robust evaluation by using different parts of the data for training and testing.
- **Confusion Matrix:** A table used for evaluating the performance of a classification model. It shows the true positives, true negatives, false positives, and false negatives.
    - **Purpose:** Helps visualize the performance and understand the types of errors the model is making.
- **ROC Curve and AUC:** The receiver operating characteristic (ROC) curve plots the true positive rate against the false positive rate. The area under the curve (AUC) measures the overall performance.
    - **Purpose:** Useful for evaluating the performance of classification models, especially with imbalanced classes.
- **Residual Analysis:** Examining the differences between predicted and actual values (residuals) in regression models.
    - **Purpose:** Identify patterns in the residuals that indicate model errors or biases.

Interpreting AI Model Performance

Interpreting the results of these metrics and techniques is crucial for understanding the model's strengths and weaknesses:

- **Context Matters:** The importance of different metrics can vary depending on the application. For example, in medical diagnosis, recall might be more important than precision.

- **Balanced View:** No single metric tells the whole story. It is essential to consider multiple metrics to get a comprehensive view of the model's performance.
- **Continuous Monitoring:** AI models should be continuously monitored and reevaluated as new data becomes available. This ensures that they remain accurate and reliable over time.

Summary

Evaluating AI model performance is a critical step in developing effective and reliable AI systems. By using various metrics and techniques, one can measure how well a model is performing, identify areas for improvement, and ensure that the model is fair and unbiased. Understanding these evaluation methods helps build trust in AI systems and ensures that they deliver accurate and reliable results. As AI continues to evolve, ongoing evaluation and refinement will remain essential for harnessing the full potential of this transformative technology.[§]

[§] ***Here are some sources that cover the topic of evaluating AI model performance:***

MIT News
How to assess a general-purpose AI model's reliability. https://news.mit.edu/2024/how-assess-general-purpose-ai-models-reliability-its-deployed.

Proofnews
How we tested leading AI models performance on election queries. www.proofnews.org/how-we-tested-leading-ai-models-performance-on-election-queries/.

Science Daily
New open-source platform allows users to evaluate performance of AI. www.sciencedaily.com/releases/2024/06/240604132115.htm.

CHAPTER 3

The AI Ecosystem

As AI continues to revolutionize industries and reshape business operations, understanding the complex ecosystem that supports AI development and deployment becomes crucial. This chapter delves into the key components that make up the AI ecosystem, providing a comprehensive overview of the infrastructure, tools, and strategies necessary for successful AI implementation.

This section begins by exploring **AI Hardware** and **AI Cloud Computing**, the foundational elements that power AI applications. From specialized processors designed for ML to scalable cloud platforms that enable massive computational tasks, it will examine how these technologies are evolving to meet the growing demands of AI workloads.

Next, it will dive into **AI Software Platforms and Tools**, the engines that drive AI development. It will survey the landscape of frameworks, libraries, and development environments that enable data scientists and engineers to build, train, and deploy AI models efficiently.

The journey through the ecosystem continues with an exploration of **AI Service Providers** by examining the companies and organizations offering AIaaS, from tech giants to specialized start-ups, and discussing how these providers are making AI more accessible to businesses of all sizes.

By the end of this chapter, one will have a comprehensive understanding of the AI ecosystem and be better equipped to navigate its complexities. As a business leader looking to leverage AI or a technologist aiming to build AI solutions, this knowledge will be valuable in harnessing the power of AI.

Exploration of the AI ecosystem, uncovering the tools, technologies, and strategies that are shaping the future of AI begins.

AI Hardware and AI Cloud Computing Powering the Future of AI

AI has become a transformative force across industries, but its power relies heavily on two foundational elements: specialized hardware and cloud computing. These technologies work in tandem to enable the complex computations and massive data processing required for AI applications. Let us explore how AI hardware and cloud computing are evolving to meet the growing demands of AI workloads.

At the heart of AI's computational prowess lies specialized hardware designed to handle the unique requirements of ML and deep learning algorithms.

- **Graphics Processing Units (GPUs)**
  Originally designed for rendering graphics in video games, GPUs have found a new calling in AI. Their ability to perform many calculations simultaneously makes them ideal for the parallel processing needs of neural networks. NVIDIA, a leader in this field, has developed GPUs specifically optimized for AI workloads, enabling faster training and inference of complex models.
- **Tensor Processing Units (TPUs)**
  Google introduced TPUs as custom-designed chips for ML tasks. These specialized processors are optimized for tensor operations, which are fundamental to many AI algorithms. TPUs can significantly accelerate ML workloads, particularly those using Google's TensorFlow framework.*
- **Field-Programmable Gate Arrays (FPGAs)**
  FPGAs offer a flexible hardware solution that can be reconfigured for specific AI tasks. This adaptability makes them valuable for organizations that need to optimize their hardware for different AI workloads over time.

* **TensorFlow** is an open-source machine learning framework developed by Google. It provides a comprehensive ecosystem of tools, libraries, and community resources to build and deploy machine learning models.

- **AI-Specific Chips**
  As AI continues to grow, we're seeing the development of chips designed exclusively for AI tasks. Companies such as Intel and start-ups such as Graphcore are creating processors that aim to push the boundaries of AI performance and efficiency.
- **Cloud Computing: Scalability and Accessibility**
  While specialized hardware provides the raw computational power, cloud computing offers the scalability, flexibility, and accessibility needed to deploy AI solutions effectively.
- **Scalable Computing Resources**
  Cloud platforms such as Amazon Web Services (AWS), Microsoft Azure, and Google Cloud Platform offer virtually unlimited computing resources on demand. This scalability is crucial for AI workloads, which can require enormous computational power for training large models or processing vast amounts of data.
- **AI-as-a-Service (AIaaS)**
  Cloud providers are increasingly offering AI capabilities as services, making advanced AI technologies accessible to organizations without the need for significant upfront investment in hardware or expertise. These services range from pretrained models for common tasks such as image recognition or NLP to platforms for building and deploying custom AI models.
- **Distributed Computing**
  Cloud platforms enable distributed computing, allowing AI workloads to be spread across multiple machines or data centers. This capability is essential for training very large models or processing enormous datasets that exceed the capacity of a single machine.
- **Edge Computing Integration**
  As AI applications move closer to end-users and devices, cloud providers are integrating edge computing capabilities into their offerings. This allows for AI inference to occur closer to where data is generated, reducing latency and enabling real-time AI applications.

The Synergy of Hardware and Cloud

The true power of modern AI comes from the synergy between specialized hardware and cloud computing:

- **Accessibility:** Cloud platforms make specialized AI hardware accessible to organizations of all sizes, democratizing access to advanced AI capabilities.
- **Flexibility:** Users can choose the right hardware for their specific AI tasks without having to invest in and maintain physical infrastructure.
- **Cost-Efficiency:** Pay-as-you-go models allow organizations to use expensive AI hardware only when needed, optimizing costs.
- **Rapid Innovation**: Cloud providers continuously update their hardware offerings, allowing users to benefit from the latest advancements without capital investment.

Challenges and Future Directions

Despite the rapid advancements, several challenges remain:

- **Energy Consumption:** AI hardware, particularly when scaled in cloud data centers, consumes significant amounts of energy. Developing more energy-efficient AI hardware is a key focus area.
- **Specialization Versus Generalization:** As AI hardware becomes more specialized, finding the right balance between task-specific optimization and general-purpose flexibility is crucial.
- **Data Privacy and Security:** As more AI workloads move to the cloud, ensuring the privacy and security of sensitive data becomes increasingly important.
- **Quantum Computing:** Looking ahead, quantum computing holds the promise of solving certain AI problems exponentially faster than classical computers, potentially revolutionizing the field once again.

Summary

The combination of specialized AI hardware and cloud computing is driving the AI revolution, making powerful AI capabilities more accessible and scalable than ever before. As these technologies continue to evolve, one can expect to see even more innovative AI applications emerging across industries, transforming how one lives and works. The future of AI is bright, powered by the formidable duo of advanced hardware and cloud computing.[†]

[†] ***AI Hardware and Cloud Computing***

Forbes
"How Businesses Are Using Artificial Intelligence in 2024," www.forbes.com/sites/technology/article/ai-software/.

Predictive Analytics Today
"Top Artificial Intelligence Platforms for Predictive Analytics," www.predictiveanalyticstoday.com/artificial-intelligence-platforms/.

Red Hat
"AI Infrastructure Explained: Building the Foundation for AI/ML," www.redhat.com/en/topics/ai/ai-infrastructure-explained.

AI Software Platforms and Tools: The Engines of AI Development

AI has become a cornerstone of technological innovation, driving advancements in various fields from health care to finance. Central to this revolution are the AI software platforms and tools that empower data scientists and engineers to build, train, and deploy AI models efficiently. This section surveys the landscape of these frameworks, libraries, and development environments, highlighting their roles and evolution in the AI ecosystem.

Development Environments and Platforms

Development environments and platforms provide integrated tools for the entire AI model life cycle, from data preparation to deployment.

AI Frameworks and Libraries

AI frameworks and libraries are essential tools that provide the building blocks for developing AI models. They offer prebuilt functions and modules that simplify the complex tasks of data processing, model training, and deployment.

- **TensorFlow:** Developed by Google, TensorFlow is one of the most popular open-source AI frameworks.
- **PyTorch:** Developed by Facebook's AI Research lab is another leading open-source framework. It is praised for its dynamic computation graph, which makes it easier to debug and modify models on the fly. PyTorch has gained popularity in the research community because of its flexibility and ease of use, particularly for deep learning applications.

- **Scikit-Learn:** A widely used library for classical ML tasks. Built on top of NumPy,[‡] SciPy,[§] and Matplotlib,[¶] Scikit-learn provides simple and efficient tools for data mining and data analysis. It is particularly well-suited for tasks such as classification, regression, clustering, and dimensionality reduction.
- **Jupyter Notebooks:** An open-source web application that allows developers to create and share documents containing live code, equations, visualizations, and narrative text. They are widely used in data science for exploratory data analysis, visualization, and prototyping of ML models.
- **Google Colab:** A cloud-based Jupyter Notebook environment that provides free access to GPUs and TPUs, making it an excellent tool for developing and training deep learning models. It integrates seamlessly with Google Drive, allowing for easy collaboration and sharing of notebooks.
- **IBM Watson Studio:** Watson Studio provides a suite of tools for data scientists, application developers, and subject matter experts to collaboratively and easily work with data. It supports the entire AI life cycle, from data preparation to model building, training, and deployment. Watson Studio also offers automated machine learning capabilities, making it accessible to users with varying levels of expertise.

[‡] **NumPy** (Numerical Python) is a library for working with arrays and mathematical operations in Python. It is a fundamental library for scientific computing and data analysis, providing support for large, multi-dimensional arrays and matrices, and a wide range of high-performance mathematical functions to manipulate them.

[§] **SciPy** (Scientific Python) is a Python-based ecosystem of open-source software for mathematics, science, and engineering. It is built on top of NumPy and provides functions for scientific and engineering applications.

[¶] **Matplotlib** is a popular Python library for creating static, animated, and interactive visualizations in python. It provides a comprehensive set of tools for creating high-quality 2D and 3D plots, charts, and graphs.

Machine Learning Operations (MLOps) Platforms

MLOps platforms streamline the deployment and management of ML models, ensuring that they can be integrated into production environments efficiently and reliably.

- **Mlflow:** An open-source platform for managing the end-to-end ML life-cycle providing tools for experiment tracking, model packaging, and deployment, enabling reproducibility and collaboration among researchers.
- **Kubeflow:** A Kubernetes-native platform for deploying, scaling, and managing ML models in production. It leverages the power of Kubernetes to provide a scalable and portable environment for running AI workloads, making it easier to deploy ML pipelines on various cloud platforms.

The Evolution and Future of AI Software Platforms

The landscape of AI software platforms and tools is continuously evolving to meet the growing demands of AI workloads. Key trends shaping the future of AI development include the following:

- **Increased Accessibility:** AI platforms are becoming more user-friendly, with low-code and no-code solutions making AI development accessible to a broader audience.
- **Integration With Cloud Services:** The integration of AI tools with cloud platforms is enabling scalable and flexible AI development, allowing organizations to leverage powerful computational resources on demand.
- **Focus on MLOps:** The emphasis on MLOps is growing, with more tools developed to streamline the deployment and management of AI models in production environments.
- **Advancements in Open Source:** The open-source movement continues to drive innovation in AI, with frameworks such as TensorFlow and PyTorch leading the way in providing powerful, community-driven tools for AI development.

Summary

In summary, AI software platforms and tools are the engines that drive AI development, providing the necessary infrastructure for building, training, and deploying AI models efficiently.

As these technologies continue to evolve, they will play a crucial role in democratizing AI and enabling innovative applications across various industries.**

** ***AI Software Platforms and Tools***

VEED.IO
15 Best AI Tools in 2024 (The Only List You'll Need). www.veed.io/learn/best-ai-tools.

Founderjar
13 Best Artificial Intelligence Software, Tools, and Platforms of 2024. www.founderjar.com/best-artificial-intelligence-software/.

Best Artificial Intelligence Software and Platforms
https://project-management.com/artificial-intelligence-software/.

AI Service Providers

Central to the AI revolution are AI service providers, companies that offer AI capabilities as a service, making advanced AI technology accessible to businesses of all sizes. From tech giants to specialized start-ups, these providers are democratizing AI, enabling even small businesses to leverage powerful AI tools. This article explores the landscape of AI service providers and how they are making AI more accessible.

Tech Giants Leading the Charge

- **Google AI Platform:** Google AI Platform offers a comprehensive suite of tools for building, training, and deploying ML models. It provides access to pretrained models and supports custom model development, making it versatile for various AI applications. This platform integrates seamlessly with other Google Cloud services, offering scalability and flexibility for businesses of all sizes.
- **Microsoft Azure AI:** Azure AI provides a wide range of AI services, including prebuilt models for vision, speech, language, and decision making. It also offers tools for building custom models, making it a powerful platform for developing tailored AI solutions. Its integration with Microsoft's cloud infrastructure ensures robust performance and scalability.
- **Amazon Web Services (AWS):** AWS is a fully managed service that enables developers and data scientists to build, train, and deploy ML models quickly. SageMaker offers a range of tools for data labeling, model training, and deployment, making it a comprehensive solution for end-to-end ML workflows. AWS's extensive cloud infrastructure supports the scalability required for large AI projects.
- **IBM Watson Studio:** IBM Watson Studio accelerates ML and deep learning workflows, facilitating AI innovation in businesses. It provides tools for data analysis, model training, and deployment, supporting both code and

no-code model building. Watson Studio's integration with IBM's cloud services ensures a seamless AI development experience.

Specialized Start-Ups Making Waves

- **OpenAI:** OpenAI is renowned for its generative AI models, such as generative pretrained transformer (GPT). These models are capable of generating humanlike text, making them useful for a variety of applications, including content creation, customer support, and more. OpenAI offers its models through APIs, making advanced AI accessible to developers and businesses without requiring extensive AI expertise.
- **Anthropic AI:** Anthropic AI is an AI safety and research company that focuses on developing AI systems that are interpretable and aligned with human intentions. Their AI services are designed to be safe and reliable, making them suitable for critical applications where trust and transparency are paramount. Amazon's significant investment in Anthropic highlights the growing importance of AI safety in the industry.
- **Domino Data Lab:** Domino Data Lab provides an enterprise platform that centralizes data science and AI functions, offering tools for building, using, and managing ML models. The platform supports collaboration among data scientists and integrates with various cloud services, making it a versatile solution for large organizations.
- **Clari AI:** Clari's AI-enabled platform helps companies unify their revenue operations by providing features for forecasting, managing strategy, and data visibility. Businesses across industries use Clari's technology to improve win rates and forecast accuracy, demonstrating the practical applications of AI in business operations.

The Role of AI-as-a-Service (AIaaS)

AIaaS platforms are making AI technology accessible to a broader audience by offering prebuilt AI models and tools that can be easily integrated into existing applications. These platforms reduce the need for extensive in-house AI expertise and infrastructure, allowing businesses to leverage AI capabilities quickly and cost-effectively.

- **Google AI Platform:** Google AI Platform offers a range of AI services, including NLP, image recognition, and predictive analytics. These services can be accessed via APIs, enabling businesses to integrate AI capabilities into their applications without needing to build models from scratch.
- **Microsoft Azure AI:** Azure AI provides prebuilt models for common tasks such as sentiment analysis, anomaly detection, and translation. These models can be easily integrated into applications using Azure's API services, making it simple for businesses to add AI functionality to their products.
- **Amazon SageMaker:** Amazon SageMaker offers a variety of prebuilt models and tools for custom model development. Its user-friendly interface and integration with AWS's cloud infrastructure make it an attractive option for businesses looking to deploy AI solutions quickly and efficiently.

Making AI More Accessible

AI service providers are playing a crucial role in making AI technology accessible to businesses of all sizes. By offering scalable, flexible, and user-friendly AI tools, these providers are democratizing AI, enabling even small businesses to harness the power of AI.

- **Scalability and Flexibility:** Cloud-based AI platforms offer virtually unlimited computing resources, allowing businesses to scale their AI operations as needed. This scalability is essential for handling large datasets and complex models, ensuring that businesses can grow their AI capabilities over time.

- **Cost-Effectiveness:** AIaaS platforms operate on a pay-as-you-go model, allowing businesses to use AI tools without significant upfront investment. This cost-effective approach makes advanced AI technology accessible to start-ups and small businesses, leveling the playing field in the competitive market.

Summary

AI service providers, from tech giants to specialized start-ups, are transforming the AI landscape by making advanced AI technology accessible to businesses of all sizes. Through scalable, flexible, and cost-effective AI tools, these providers are democratizing AI, enabling even small businesses to leverage powerful AI capabilities.

As AI technology continues to evolve, these service providers will play an increasingly important role in driving innovation and growth across industries.[††]

[††] ***AI Service Providers***

CNBC
"FOMO Drives Tech Heavyweights to Invest Billions in Generative AI," www.cnbc.com/2024/03/30/fomo-drives-tech-heavyweights-to-invest-billions-in-generative-ai-.html.

Built In
"92 Artificial Intelligence Companies to Know," https://builtin.com/artificial-intelligence/ai-companies-roundup.

Predictive Analytics Today
"Top 18 Artificial Intelligence Platforms in 2024," www.predictiveanalyticstoday.com/artificial-intelligence-platforms/.

PART 2

Harnessing AI Across Business Functions

This section explores some business applications in detail, providing insights and case studies that illustrate the transformative power of AI in each business function. By understanding and implementing AI strategies, businesses can unlock new levels of efficiency, innovation, and competitive advantage.

In the rapidly evolving landscape of AI, businesses are discovering transformative opportunities across various functions. Part 2 of this book delves into the practical applications of AI, showcasing how it can revolutionize key areas within an organization. From enhancing customer engagement to optimizing operational efficiency, AI is becoming an indispensable tool for modern enterprises.

Chapter 4 Covers Marketing and Sales

AI is reshaping marketing and sales by enabling personalized customer experiences, predictive analytics, and automated customer service. Businesses can leverage AI to analyze consumer behavior, tailor marketing campaigns, and streamline sales processes, ultimately driving growth and customer satisfaction.

Chapter 5 Covers Operations and Supply Chain

In operations and supply chain management, AI offers solutions for demand forecasting, inventory optimization, and logistics planning. By integrating AI, companies can achieve greater efficiency, reduce costs, and enhance supply chain resilience, ensuring timely delivery and improved service levels.

Chapter 6 Covers Finance and Accounting

AI is transforming finance and accounting through automated data entry, fraud detection, and financial forecasting. These advancements allow finance professionals to focus on strategic decision making, improve accuracy, and enhance financial transparency.

Chapter 7 Covers Human Resources

AI applications in human resources include talent acquisition, employee engagement, and performance management. AI-powered tools can streamline recruitment processes, provide insights into employee satisfaction, and support personalized career development plans, fostering a more productive and motivated workforce.

Chapter 8 Covers the Health Care Industry

In health care, AI is driving innovations in diagnostics, treatment planning, and patient care. From predictive analytics that identify potential health risks to AI-assisted surgeries, the integration of AI in health care promises improved patient outcomes and operational efficiencies.

Chapter 9 Covers the Entertainment Industry

AI is revolutionizing the entertainment industry by enabling content personalization, enhancing creative processes, and optimizing distribution strategies. Whether through recommendation algorithms or AI-generated content, the entertainment sector is leveraging AI to captivate audiences and drive engagement.

CHAPTER 4

AI for Marketing and Sales

Revolutionizing Customer Engagement and Business Growth

In the rapidly evolving landscape of marketing and sales, AI has emerged as a game-changing force, transforming how businesses interact with customers, analyze data, and make strategic decisions.

This chapter explores four key areas where AI is making significant impacts: predictive analytics for marketing campaigns, conversational AI and chatbots, customer segmentation and personalization, and sales forecasting.

Predictive Analytics for Marketing Campaigns

Predictive analytics harnesses the power of AI to analyze historical data, identify patterns, and forecast future outcomes. In marketing, this technology enables businesses to optimize their campaigns by predicting customer behavior, identifying the most effective channels, and determining the optimal timing for communications. By leveraging ML algorithms, marketers can now make data-driven decisions that significantly improve campaign performance and return on investment (ROI).

In marketing, AI tools can analyze consumer behavior and predict trends, enabling marketers to create more targeted and effective campaigns. By augmenting human capabilities, AI allows employees to make better-informed decisions and achieve higher levels of productivity.

Conversational AI and Chatbots

The rise of conversational AI and chatbots has revolutionized customer service and engagement. These AI-powered tools provide instant, 24/7 support to customers, handling inquiries, resolving issues, and even facilitating purchases. As NLP capabilities continue to advance, chatbots are becoming increasingly sophisticated, offering personalized interactions that closely mimic human conversation. This technology not only enhances customer experience but also frees up human resources (HR) for more complex tasks.

AI for Customer Segmentation and Personalization

AI's ability to process and analyze vast amounts of data has taken customer segmentation and personalization to new heights. ML algorithms can identify intricate patterns in customer behavior, preferences, and demographics, allowing businesses to create highly targeted marketing strategies. This level of personalization extends beyond simple demographic groupings, enabling companies to deliver tailored content, product recommendations, and offers that resonate with individual customers on a deeper level.

Sales Forecasting With AI

Accurate sales forecasting is crucial for business planning and resource allocation. AI-powered sales forecasting tools use historical data, market trends, and external factors to predict future sales with remarkable accuracy. These systems can account for complex variables and seasonality, providing sales teams and executives with valuable insights for strategic decision making. By reducing human bias and incorporating a wider range of data points, AI enhances the reliability and precision of sales projections.

The following sections delve deeper into each of these areas, exploring the technologies behind them, their practical applications, and the benefits they bring to modern marketing and sales strategies. By navigating through these topics, it will become clear how AI is not just an add-on to existing practices, but a fundamental shift in how businesses approach customer engagement and revenue generation.

What Is Predictive Analytics

In today's fast-paced digital world, marketers are always looking for ways to make their campaigns more effective. One powerful tool they are using is predictive analytics, which uses AI to help make better marketing decisions.

This section explores how predictive analytics works and why it is so valuable for marketing campaigns.

Predictive analytics is like having a crystal ball for your marketing efforts. It uses AI to analyze data from past marketing campaigns and customer behaviors to make educated guesses about what might happen in the future. This is not just random guessing—it is based on complex calculations and pattern recognition that only computers can do quickly and accurately.

How Does Predictive Analytics Work

- **Gathering Data:** The first step is collecting information. This can include data from previous marketing campaigns, customer purchases, website visits, social media interactions, and more.
- **Analyzing Patterns:** AI algorithms then sift through this data to find patterns. For example, they might notice that customers who buy one product often buy another related product within a month.
- **Making Predictions:** Based on these patterns, AI can make predictions about future customer behavior or campaign performance.
- **Continuous Learning:** As new data comes in, the AI keeps learning and improving its predictions.

Now, let us examine how marketers use predictive analytics to make their campaigns better:

Predicting Customer Behavior

Predictive analytics can help guess what a customer might do next.

For example:

- It might predict that a customer who just bought a new phone is likely to buy a phone case soon.
- It could identify customers who are at risk of leaving for a competitor.

With these insights, marketers can create targeted campaigns to encourage desired behaviors or prevent customer loss.

Finding the Best Marketing Channels

Not all marketing channels work equally well for every campaign. Predictive analytics can help figure out which channels (such as email, social media, or TV ads) are likely to perform best for different types of campaigns or customer groups.

Timing Is Everything

Predictive analytics can also suggest the best times to reach out to customers. It might show that some customers are more likely to open emails in the morning while others tend to make purchases on weekends. By timing messages just right, marketers can increase the chances of customers seeing and responding to their campaigns.

Making Data-Driven Decisions

One of the biggest benefits of predictive analytics is that it helps marketers make decisions based on data rather than gut feelings. This leads to the following:

- **Better Resource Allocation:** Marketers can invest more in campaigns that are predicted to perform well.

- **Personalized Marketing:** By understanding individual customer preferences, marketers can create more personalized and relevant messages.
- **Improved Customer Experience:** When marketing is more relevant and timely, customers are likely to have a better experience with the brand.
- **Higher Return on Investment:** By focusing efforts on the most promising opportunities, companies can get more value from their marketing budgets.

Real-World Examples

To bring this to life, let us look at a couple of examples:

- **Ecommerce Website:** An online store uses predictive analytics to recommend products to customers based on their browsing and purchase history. This leads to more sales and happier customers who find what they need more easily.
- **Email Marketing:** A software company uses predictive analytics to determine the best time to send upgrade offers to their customers. By timing these emails when customers are most likely to be considering an upgrade, they see a significant increase in conversions.

Challenges and Considerations

While predictive analytics is powerful, it is not without challenges:

- **Data Quality:** The predictions are only as good as the data used. Ensuring high-quality, accurate data is crucial.
- **Privacy Concerns:** With increased data collection and analysis, companies must be careful to respect customer privacy and comply with data protection regulations.
- **Overreliance on Predictions:** While predictive analytics is valuable, it shouldn't completely replace human judgment and creativity in marketing.

The Future of Predictive Analytics in Marketing

As AI technology continues to advance, predictive analytics will become even more powerful and accessible. One can expect to see:

- More accurate predictions as algorithms improve.
- Easier-to-use tools that make predictive analytics accessible to smaller businesses.
- Integration with other marketing technologies for seamless campaign optimization.

Implementing Predictive Analytics

Small businesses can implement predictive analytics without a large budget by taking a strategic and focused approach. Here are some key ways to get started:

- **Start Small and Focus:** Begin with a specific, high-impact area of your business where predictive analytics could provide clear value, rather than trying to implement it across the entire organization at once. This allows you to test the waters and demonstrate ROI before scaling up.
- **Leverage Existing Data:** Use the data you already have from your current systems and processes as a starting point. This could include customer information, sales data, website analytics, or operational metrics. You don't need to invest in expensive new data collection methods right away.
- **Utilize Affordable or Free Tools:** There are several low-cost or free predictive analytics tools available that are suitable for small businesses. These include the following::
    - **Google Analytics** (free) https://marketingplatform.google.com/about/analytics/
    - **RapidMiner** (free version) https://altair.com/altair-rapidminer
    - **KNIME** (open-source) www.knime.com/knime-analytics-platform
    - **Orange** (open-source) https://opensource.orange.com/en/open-source-orange/

- **Cloud-Based Solutions:** Consider cloud-based predictive analytics services, which often have more affordable pricing models for small businesses compared to on-premises software.
- **Invest in Learning:** Educate yourself and your team about predictive analytics through online courses, webinars, and tutorials. This can help you make the most of the tools you choose without needing to hire expensive experts.
- **Focus on Clear Objectives:** Define specific goals for your predictive analytics efforts, such as improving customer retention or optimizing inventory management. This helps ensure that your efforts are targeted and measurable.
- **Start with Simple Models:** Begin with basic predictive models that are easier to implement and understand, such as linear regression or decision trees. As you gain experience, you can move to more complex models.
- **Collaborate with Local Universities:** Partner with local universities or colleges that have data science programs. Students or faculty might be interested in working on real-world projects, providing you with expertise at a lower cost.
- **Use What You Know:** Once you have predictions, act on them. Modify your business plans and strategies based on the insights you gain. This is crucial for deriving value from your efforts.
- **Iterate and Improve:** Treat predictive analytics as an ongoing process. Start with a proof of concept, learn from it, and gradually expand and refine your approach as you see results.

The goal is to make data-driven decisions that improve your business outcomes. Even with a limited budget, small businesses can gain valuable insights from predictive analytics by starting small, focusing on high-impact areas, and leveraging affordable tools and existing data. As you see positive results, you can gradually expand your use of predictive analytics across more areas of your business.

Summary

Predictive analytics is transforming the way marketers plan and execute their campaigns. By harnessing the power of AI to analyze past data and predict future outcomes, businesses can create more effective, efficient, and personalized marketing efforts. As this technology continues to evolve, it will play an increasingly important role in helping companies connect with their customers and achieve their marketing goals.*

---

* ***Predictive Analytics***

Geeks for Growth
"Harnessing Predictive Analytics for Small Businesses and Startups," https://geeksforgrowth.com/blog/predictive-analytics-or-small-businesses-and-startups/.

Logility
"Step-by-Step Guide to Implementing Predictive Analytics in Your Company," www.logility.com/blog/how-to-implement-predictive-analytics-into-your-company/.

Podium
"Optimizing Small Business Operations With Predictive Analytics," www.podium.com/article/analytics-for-small-business/.

Conversational AI and Chatbots

In the digital age, customer service and engagement have been transformed by the advent of conversational AI and chatbots. These AI-powered tools provide instant, 24/7 support to customers, handling inquiries, resolving issues, and even facilitating purchases.

This section explores how conversational AI and chatbots have revolutionized customer service, their capabilities, and the benefits they offer to both businesses and customers.

Instant, 24/7 Customer Support

One of the most significant advantages of conversational AI and chatbots is their ability to provide round-the-clock customer support. Unlike human agents, chatbots do not require breaks or sleep, ensuring that customers can receive assistance at any time of the day or night. This constant availability helps businesses cater to a global audience and meet the expectations of today's always-connected consumers.

For instance, customers visiting an ecommerce website at midnight can still get answers to their questions, track their orders, or even process returns without waiting for business hours. This immediate response capability enhances customer satisfaction and loyalty, as customers appreciate the convenience and efficiency of getting their issues resolved promptly.

Handling Inquiries and Resolving Issues

Conversational AI chatbots are designed to handle a wide range of customer inquiries and resolve common issues. They can answer frequently asked questions (FAQs), provide product information, assist with troubleshooting, and offer solutions to common problems. By doing so, chatbots reduce the workload on human customer service agents, allowing them to focus on more complex and sensitive issues that require human intervention.

For example, a chatbot can guide a customer through the process of resetting a password, checking the status of an order, or finding a specific product on a website. This automation not only speeds up the resolution process but also ensures consistency in the responses provided to customers.

Facilitating Purchases

Beyond answering questions and resolving issues, chatbots can also facilitate purchases, making the buying process smoother and more efficient. They can recommend products based on customer preferences and past behavior, assist with the checkout process, and even handle payment transactions. This capability turns chatbots into powerful sales tools that can drive revenue growth.

Imagine a customer browsing an online store and receiving personalized product recommendations from a chatbot. The chatbot can suggest complementary items, provide information about ongoing promotions, and help the customer complete their purchase seamlessly. This personalized shopping experience can significantly enhance customer satisfaction and increase sales.

Advancements in Natural Language Processing

As NLP capabilities continue to advance, chatbots are becoming increasingly sophisticated. Modern chatbots can understand and interpret human language more accurately, allowing them to engage in more natural and meaningful conversations with customers. They can recognize the context and sentiment of customer inquiries, providing responses that are not only relevant but also empathetic.

For instance, a chatbot equipped with advanced NLP can detect when a customer is frustrated and respond with a more empathetic tone, offering reassurance and solutions to address their concerns. This level of sophistication helps create a more humanlike interaction, making customers feel understood and valued.

Enhancing Customer Experience

The use of conversational AI and chatbots significantly enhances the overall customer experience. By providing quick, accurate, and personalized responses, chatbots help create a seamless and enjoyable interaction for customers. This improved experience can lead to higher customer satisfaction, increased loyalty, and positive word-of-mouth referrals. Moreover, chatbots can handle multiple customer interactions simultaneously, ensuring that no customer has to wait in line for assistance. This efficiency is particularly valuable during peak times when the volume of customer inquiries can overwhelm human agents.

Freeing up Human Resources

One of the key benefits of implementing chatbots is that they free up HR for more complex tasks. By automating routine and repetitive inquiries, chatbots allow human agents to focus on issues that require critical thinking, empathy, and problem-solving skills. This not only improves the efficiency of the customer service team but also enhances job satisfaction for human agents, as they can engage in more meaningful and challenging work.

For example, while a chatbot handles basic inquiries about store hours or return policies, human agents can dedicate their time to resolving escalated issues, providing personalized support, and building stronger relationships with customers.

Summary

The rise of conversational AI and chatbots has revolutionized customer service and engagement, offering businesses a powerful tool to enhance customer experience and operational efficiency. By providing instant, 24/7 support, handling inquiries, resolving issues, and facilitating purchases, chatbots have become indispensable in the modern customer service landscape. This technology not only improves customer satisfaction but also allows businesses to optimize their resources, ultimately driving growth and success.*See Endnote References*[†]

---

† ***Conversational AI and Chatbots***

The CX Lead
"Top AI Chatbots for Enhancing Customer Service in 2024," https://thecxlead.com/tools/best-ai-customer-service-software/.

Dialpad
"A Comprehensive Guide to Conversational AI for Customer Service," www.dialpad.com/blog/conversational-ai-for-customer-service/.

Intercom
"Understanding Conversational AI: Transforming Customer Service," www.intercom.com/learning-center/conversational-ai-for-customer-service.

AI-Powered Customer Segmentation and Personalization

In today's digital age, businesses have access to more customer data than ever before. However, the sheer volume of this data can be overwhelming. This is where AI comes in, revolutionizing how companies understand and interact with their customers. AI's ability to process and analyze vast amounts of data has taken customer segmentation and personalization to new heights, allowing businesses to create highly targeted marketing strategies that resonate with individual customers on a deeper level.

The Power of AI in Customer Segmentation

Traditional customer segmentation often relied on broad demographic categories such as age, gender, or location. While useful, these groupings could miss important nuances in customer behavior and preferences. AI-powered segmentation goes far beyond these basic categories, using ML algorithms to identify intricate patterns in customer data.

How AI Analyzes Customer Data

AI systems can process and analyze various types of customer data, including:

- Purchase history
- Browsing behavior on websites and apps
- Social media interactions
- Customer service interactions
- Survey responses
- Demographic information

By examining this data, AI can identify patterns that humans might miss.

For example, an AI system might notice that customers who buy a certain product often make another specific purchase within three months, or that customers who engage with certain types of content are more likely to respond to email marketing.

Creating Microsegments

With its ability to analyze complex data patterns, AI can create highly specific customer segments, often called microsegments. These microsegments group customers based on a combination of factors, such as:

- Purchasing behavior
- Brand preferences
- Life stage
- Interests and hobbies
- Communication preferences
- Price sensitivity

For instance, instead of simply targeting "women aged 25 to 35," a clothing retailer might identify a microsegment of "eco-conscious professional women in their early 30s who prefer minimalist styles and shop primarily on mobile devices."

Personalization: Beyond Basic Segmentation.

While segmentation groups customers with similar characteristics, personalization takes this a step further by tailoring marketing efforts to individual customers. AI-powered personalization can create unique experiences for each customer, based on their specific behaviors, preferences, and needs.

Tailored Content

AI can analyze a customer's past interactions with a brand to determine what type of content they find most engaging. This could include the following:

- Blog posts or articles on topics they've shown interest in
- Videos that match their viewing preferences
- Social media posts that align with their engagement patterns

For example, a fitness brand might show workout videos to one customer who frequently watches video content, while sending blog posts about nutrition to another who prefers reading articles.

Product Recommendations

One of the most common applications of AI in personalization is product recommendations. By analyzing a customer's browsing and purchase history, AI can suggest products that are likely to interest them. These recommendations can be incredibly specific, taking into account factors such as:

- Past purchases
- Items viewed but not purchased
- Seasonal trends
- Complementary products

For instance, an online bookstore might recommend a new mystery novel to a customer who has previously purchased books in that genre, while also suggesting related nonfiction books about true crime.

Personalized Offers

AI can also help businesses create personalized offers and promotions. By analyzing a customer's purchase history and behavior, AI can determine:

- What types of discounts motivate them to buy
- Which products they might be interested in trying
- When they're most likely to make a purchase

This allows businesses to send the right offer to the right customer at the right time. For example, a coffee shop might send a loyal customer a discount on their favorite drink on their birthday, or offer a free trial of a new flavor based on their past preferences.

Benefits of AI-Powered Segmentation and Personalization

The use of AI in customer segmentation and personalization offers several key benefits:

- **Improved Customer Experience:** By receiving relevant content, recommendations, and offers, customers feel understood and valued by the brand.
- **Increased Engagement:** Personalized marketing efforts are more likely to capture customers' attention and encourage interaction with the brand.
- **Higher Conversion Rates:** When customers receive offers that align with their interests and needs, they're more likely to make a purchase.
- **Enhanced Customer Loyalty:** Personalized experiences can strengthen the relationship between customers and brands, leading to increased loyalty.
- **More Efficient Marketing:** By targeting the right customers with the right messages, businesses can reduce wasted marketing efforts and improve ROI.

Challenges and Considerations

While AI-powered segmentation and personalization offer significant benefits, there are also challenges to consider:

- **Data Privacy:** Businesses must ensure that they're collecting and using customer data ethically and in compliance with regulations.
- **Data Quality:** The effectiveness of AI depends on the quality of the data it is working with. Ensuring accurate and comprehensive data is crucial.
- **Balancing Personalization and Privacy:** While customers appreciate personalized experiences, they may also be concerned about how much a company knows about them.

- **Avoiding Overpersonalization:** There's a fine line between helpful personalization and feeling "creepy" to customers. Businesses need to find the right balance.

Summary

AI has transformed customer segmentation and personalization, allowing businesses to understand and interact with their customers in more meaningful ways. By leveraging ML algorithms to analyze vast amounts of data, companies can create highly targeted marketing strategies that resonate with individual customers on a deeper level. This level of personalization, extending far beyond simple demographic groupings, enables businesses to deliver tailored content, product recommendations, and offers that truly speak to each customer's unique preferences and needs.

As AI technology continues to advance, one can expect even more sophisticated and effective personalization strategies in the future, further enhancing the customer experience and driving business success.[‡]

---

‡ ***AI-Powered Customer Segmentation and Personalization***

ZS

Future of customer segmentation: AI in hyper-personalization. www.zs.com/insights/ai-driven-customer-segmentation.

IBM

AI Personalization. www.ibm.com/think/topics/ai-personalization.

Mailchimp

AI Customer Segmentation Strategies. https://mailchimp.com/resources/ai-customer-segmentation/.

The Importance of Accurate Sales Forecasting

Sales forecasting is a critical component of business planning and resource allocation. Accurate predictions about future sales help make informed decisions, manage resources efficiently, and set realistic business goals. In recent years, AI-powered sales forecasting tools have revolutionized this process, offering unprecedented accuracy and insights.

This section explores why accurate sales forecasting is essential and how AI technologies are transforming the way businesses predict their sales.

Why Accurate Sales Forecasting Matters

Accurate sales forecasting is crucial for several reasons:

- **Resource Allocation:** Knowing how much product will be sold helps businesses manage inventory, staff, and finances. Overestimating sales can lead to excess inventory and wasted resources while underestimating can result in stockouts and missed opportunities.
- **Financial Planning:** Accurate forecasts enable better budgeting and financial planning. Companies can predict revenue streams, manage cash flow, and plan for investments or cost-cutting measures.
- **Goal Setting:** Realistic sales targets motivate sales teams and align their efforts with the company's strategic objectives. Unrealistic goals can lead to frustration and decreased morale.
- **Strategic Decision Making:** Sales forecasts inform strategic decisions such as market expansion, product development, and marketing campaigns. Accurate predictions help businesses capitalize on opportunities and mitigate risks.

How AI-Powered Sales Forecasting Works

AI-powered sales forecasting tools use advanced algorithms to analyze a wide range of data and predict future sales with remarkable accuracy. Here's how they work:

Historical Data Analysis

AI systems start by analyzing historical sales data. This includes past sales figures, customer behavior, and transaction details. By examining this data, AI can identify patterns and trends that are likely to continue in the future.

- **Market Trends**
  In addition to historical data, AI tools consider current market trends. This includes changes in consumer preferences, economic indicators, and industry developments. By incorporating these trends, AI can adjust its predictions to reflect the current market environment.
- **External Factors**
  AI-powered tools also account for external factors that can impact sales. These factors might include seasonality, weather conditions, competitor actions, and even geopolitical events. By considering these variables, AI can provide a more comprehensive and accurate forecast.
- **Accounting for Complex Variables and Seasonality**
  One of the strengths of AI in sales forecasting is its ability to handle complex variables and seasonality:

Complex Variables

AI algorithms can process vast amounts of data and identify relationships between different variables. For example, an AI system might recognize that sales of a particular product increase when a specific marketing campaign is run, or those sales dip during certain economic conditions. By understanding these relationships, AI can make more accurate predictions.

Seasonality

Seasonal trends are a significant factor in many industries. AI systems can analyze past sales data to identify seasonal patterns and adjust forecasts accordingly. For instance, a retailer might see higher sales during the holiday season, while a travel company might experience peaks during summer vacations. AI can account for these patterns and provide more precise forecasts.

- **Reducing Human Bias and Enhancing Reliability**
  Human judgment is inherently biased and can be influenced by various factors such as personal experiences, emotions, and cognitive biases. AI-powered sales forecasting tools help reduce these biases by relying on data-driven analysis.
- **Data-Driven Decisions**
  AI systems base their predictions on objective data rather than subjective opinions. This reduces the risk of overoptimism or undue pessimism, leading to more reliable forecasts.
- **Incorporating a Wider Range of Data Points**
  AI can analyze a broader range of data points than a human analyst could manage. This includes not only sales data but also external factors such as social media trends, economic indicators, and competitor activities. By considering a wider array of information, AI provides a more holistic view of future sales.

Valuable Insights for Strategic Decision Making

AI-powered sales forecasting tools offer valuable insights that can guide strategic decision making:

- **Identifying Opportunities:** By analyzing market trends and customer behavior, AI can identify new growth opportunities. This might include emerging markets, untapped customer segments, or potential product innovations.
- **Risk Management:** Accurate forecasts help businesses anticipate potential challenges and plan accordingly. For example, if a forecast predicts a downturn in sales, a company can take proactive measures to mitigate the impact.
- **Performance Monitoring:** AI tools can continuously monitor sales performance and compare it to forecasts.

This allows businesses to track progress, identify deviations, and make necessary adjustments in real time.

AI Sales Forecasting Tools

AI sales forecasting tools can incorporate various types of external data to improve prediction accuracy. Based on the search results here are some key types of external data commonly used:

- **Market Trends:** AI tools analyze broader industry and market trends that could impact sales.
- **Economic Indicators:** Factors such as GDP growth, inflation rates, and consumer spending patterns are often incorporated.
- **Competitor Data:** Information on competitors' activities, pricing, and market share can be used to refine forecasts.
- **Weather Data:** For businesses affected by seasonal patterns, weather forecasts can be valuable inputs.
- **Social Media Trends:** AI can analyze social media sentiment and trends related to products or brands.
- **Web Traffic Data:** Information on website visits, engagement metrics, and online behavior can inform predictions.
- **News and Events:** Major news stories or events that could impact consumer behavior or the business environment.
- **Geopolitical Factors:** For global businesses, geopolitical events and trends in different regions may be considered.
- **Demographic Data:** Population trends, income levels, and other demographic shifts can influence forecasts.
- **Technological Changes:** Advancements or technology disruptions that could affect the market.
- **Regulatory Changes:** New laws or regulations that might impact sales or operations.

By incorporating these diverse external data sources, AI forecasting tools can provide a more comprehensive and accurate picture of future sales trends. The ability to process and analyze large volumes of varied data gives AI an advantage over traditional forecasting methods in capturing complex market dynamics.

Summary

Accurate sales forecasting is essential for effective business planning and resource allocation. AI-powered sales forecasting tools leverage historical data, market trends, and external factors to provide highly accurate predictions. By accounting for complex variables and seasonality, these tools offer valuable insights that help businesses make informed decisions, manage resources efficiently, and set realistic goals.

By reducing human bias and incorporating a wider range of data points, AI enhances the reliability and precision of sales projections, ultimately driving business success.[§]

---

§ ***Sales Forecasting***

eWeek
"AI Sales Forecasting: Benefits and How-To Guide," www.eweek.com/artificial-intelligence/ai-sales-forecasting/.

JustCall Blog
"Sales Forecasting With AI: A How-To Guide," https://justcall.io/blog/sales-forecasting-with-ai.html.

Xactly Blog
"The Impact of AI on Forecasting Sales," www.xactlycorp.com/blog/ai-sales-forecasting.

CHAPTER 5

AI in Operations and Supply Chain

Transforming Business Efficiency and Resilience

In the rapidly evolving landscape of modern business, AI has emerged as a transformative force in operations and supply chain management. Organizations are increasingly integrating AI into their operations to stay competitive. This integration involves not only adopting AI technologies but also rethinking business processes and organizational structures.

The rise of AI has led to the creation of new roles focused on AI development, implementation, and oversight. Data scientists, ML engineers, and AI ethicists are now essential parts of many organizations. These professionals are responsible for developing AI models, ensuring their accuracy, and addressing ethical concerns related to AI use.

Additionally, roles such as AI trainers and explainability experts are emerging. AI trainers help improve AI systems by providing them with high-quality data and feedback, while explainability experts ensure that AI decisions are transparent and understandable to stakeholders.

This chapter explores how AI is revolutionizing key aspects of these critical business functions, enhancing efficiency, reducing costs, and improving overall performance.

The chapter delves into five key areas where AI is making significant impacts:

- **Predictive Maintenance**
  AI-powered predictive maintenance is changing how businesses approach equipment upkeep and reliability.

By analyzing vast amounts of sensor data and historical performance records, AI algorithms can predict when machinery is likely to fail, allowing for proactive maintenance that minimizes downtime and extends equipment life.

- **Demand Forecasting**
  The ability to accurately predict future demand is crucial for effective supply chain management. AI is dramatically improving demand forecasting by processing complex datasets, including historical sales data, market trends, and even external factors such as weather and social media sentiment. This leads to more accurate predictions and better-informed business decisions.
- **Inventory Optimization**
  AI is helping businesses strike the perfect balance between overstocking and stockout. By analyzing sales patterns, lead times, and market conditions, AI systems can recommend optimal inventory levels, reducing carrying costs while ensuring product availability.
- **Intelligent Logistics**
  The logistics sector is transformed by AI, with intelligent systems optimizing everything from warehouse operations to last-mile delivery. AI-powered robots and automated guided vehicles are increasing efficiency in warehouses, while ML algorithms are improving route planning and load optimization.
- **Routing**
  AI is revolutionizing route planning and optimization, whether for delivery vehicles, supply chain logistics, or internal factory processes. By considering multiple variables simultaneously, AI can determine the most efficient routes, reducing transportation costs, delivery times, and environmental impact.

The following sections explore each of these areas in depth, examining the technologies behind them, their practical applications, and the benefits they bring to modern operations and supply chain management.

By navigating through these topics, it will become clear how AI is not just enhancing existing practices, but fundamentally reshaping how businesses approach operations and supply chain challenges in the 21st century.

Predictive Maintenance: Revolutionizing Equipment Upkeep

Predictive maintenance powered by AI is transforming the way businesses approach equipment reliability and upkeep. This innovative approach leverages advanced algorithms to analyze vast amounts of data, predicting potential failures before they occur and enabling proactive maintenance strategies.

Let us dive deeper into this topic:

How AI Predictive Maintenance Works

- **Data Collection:** Sensors installed on machinery continuously collect data on various parameters such as temperature, vibration, pressure, and performance metrics.
- **Data Analysis:** AI algorithms, often using ML techniques, analyze this data along with historical performance records.
- **Pattern Recognition:** The AI identifies patterns and anomalies that may indicate potential future failures.
- **Failure Prediction:** Based on these patterns, the system predicts when and how a piece of equipment is likely to fail.
- **Maintenance Recommendations:** The AI suggests optimal times for maintenance, often before any noticeable issues occur.

Benefits of AI Predictive Maintenance

- **Minimized Downtime:** By predicting failures in advance, maintenance can be scheduled during planned downtimes, reducing unexpected breakdowns.
- **Extended Equipment Life:** Regular, timely maintenance based on actual equipment conditions helps extend the operational life of machinery.

- **Cost Savings:** Predictive maintenance reduces the need for emergency repairs, which are often more expensive than planned maintenance.
- **Improved Safety:** By preventing equipment failures, workplace safety is enhanced.
- **Optimized Maintenance Scheduling:** Resources can be allocated more efficiently, focusing on equipment that truly needs attention.
- **Enhanced Production Quality:** Well-maintained equipment is more likely to produce consistent, high-quality output.

Real-World Applications

- **Manufacturing:** Predictive maintenance on production line equipment can prevent costly halts in manufacturing processes.
- **Energy Sector:** Power plants use AI to predict maintenance needs for turbines and other critical equipment, ensuring a consistent energy supply.
- **Transportation:** Airlines employ predictive maintenance for aircraft, improving safety and reducing flight delays.
- **Telecommunications:** Network providers use AI to predict and prevent outages in their infrastructure.

Challenges and Considerations

- **Data Quality:** The effectiveness of predictive maintenance relies heavily on the quality and quantity of data available.
- **Initial Investment:** Implementing AI-powered systems and sensors can require significant upfront costs.
- **Integration With Existing Systems:** Businesses may need to update or replace legacy systems to fully benefit from AI predictive maintenance.
- **Skilled Personnel:** Operating and interpreting AI systems often requires specialized skills.

Future Trends

- **Edge Computing:** Processing data closer to its source for faster, more efficient analysis.
- **Digital Twins:** Creating virtual replicas of physical assets for more accurate simulations and predictions.
- **Augmented Reality (AR):** Using AR to guide maintenance technicians in real time, improving efficiency and accuracy.

Summary

AI-powered predictive maintenance represents a significant leap forward in equipment management. Enabling businesses to anticipate and prevent failures not only reduces costs and downtime but also extends equipment life and improves overall operational efficiency.

As AI technology continues to advance, one can expect even more sophisticated and effective predictive maintenance solutions in the future, further enhancing the reliability and performance of industrial equipment across various sectors. AI-powered predictive maintenance is revolutionizing how businesses manage their equipment and assets.*

---

* ***Predictive maintenance***

Artificial Intelligence for Predictive Maintenance Applications
Key Components, Trustworthiness, and Future Trends: This paper review recent developments in AI-based predictive maintenance, focusing on key components, trustworthiness, and future trends. www.mdpi.com/2076-3417/14/2/898.

Artificial Intelligence in Predictive Maintenance
A Systematic Literature Review on Review Papers: This systematic literature review identifies the AI revolution in predictive maintenance and focuses on the next stages available in the literature. https://link.springer.com/chapter/10.1007/978-3-031-39619-9_18.

Deep Learning Models for Predictive Maintenance
This survey gathers information from various electronic databases to provide insights into the use of deep learning models for predictive maintenance. https://link.springer.com/article/10.1007/s10489-021-03004-y.

Demand Forecasting: Revolutionizing Supply Chain Management

In the world of business, knowing what customers will want and when they'll want it is like having a crystal ball. This ability to predict future demand is crucial for effective supply chain management. It helps businesses make smart decisions about how much inventory to keep, how many products to make, and how to plan their operations. In recent years, AI has dramatically improved the way companies forecast demand, leading to more accurate predictions and better-informed business decisions.

Why Accurate Demand Forecasting Matters

Before diving into how AI is changing the game, let us understand why accurate demand forecasting is so important:

- **Inventory Management:** Predicting demand helps businesses keep the right amount of stock. Too much inventory ties up money and can lead to waste, especially for perishable goods. Too little can result in lost sales and unhappy customers.
- **Production Planning:** Manufacturers use demand forecasts to plan their production schedules, ensuring that they make enough products without overproducing.
- **Resource Allocation:** Accurate forecasts help companies allocate resources efficiently, from raw materials to labor.
- **Financial Planning:** Predicting future sales helps businesses make financial plans, set budgets, and make investment decisions.
- **Customer Satisfaction:** Having the right products available when customers want them leads to higher satisfaction and loyalty.

How AI Is Improving Demand Forecasting

AI is taking demand forecasting to new levels of accuracy and sophistication. Here's how:

Processing Complex Datasets

AI can analyze vast amounts of data quickly and accurately. This includes:

- **Historical Sales Data:** AI can identify patterns and trends in past sales that humans might miss.
- **Market Trends:** AI can keep track of broader industry trends and how they might affect demand.
- **External Factors:** Things such as weather, economic indicators, and even social media sentiment can be factored into AI predictions.

For example, an ice cream company might use AI to analyze not just past sales but also weather forecasts, local events, and social media buzz about new flavors to predict demand for the coming summer.

Real-Time Analysis

Unlike traditional forecasting methods that might update monthly or quarterly, AI systems can continuously analyze data and update predictions in real time. This means businesses can respond quickly to changing conditions.

Pattern Recognition

AI excels at recognizing complex patterns that might not be obvious to human analysts. For instance, it might be noticed that sales of a particular product spike not just during obvious seasons but also concerning specific events or trends.

Handling Uncertainty

AI models can account for uncertainty and provide a range of possible outcomes, helping businesses prepare for different scenarios.

Practical Applications of AI in Demand Forecasting

Let us look at some real-world examples of how AI is improving demand forecasting:

- **Retail:** A clothing retailer uses AI to predict demand for different styles and sizes across various locations. The AI considers factors such as local weather, fashion trends, and even social media influencer activity to make its predictions.
- **Food and Beverage:** A restaurant chain uses AI to forecast demand for ingredients, considering factors such as local events, weather, and even trending diets to ensure that they have the right stock without waste.
- **Manufacturing:** An electronics manufacturer uses AI to predict demand for components, considering global supply chain issues, consumer tech trends, and even geopolitical factors that might affect demand.
- **Ecommerce:** Online retailers use AI to predict not just overall demand but also which products individual customers are likely to want, enabling personalized marketing and inventory planning.

Benefits of AI-Powered Demand Forecasting

The improvements brought by AI lead to several key benefits:

- **Reduced Costs:** More accurate forecasts mean less wasted inventory and more efficient resource use.
- **Improved Customer Satisfaction:** Having the right products available when customers want them leads to happier customers and fewer lost sales.
- **Better Decision Making:** With more accurate and timely information, businesses can make better strategic decisions.

- **Increased Agility:** Real-time forecasting allows businesses to respond quickly to changing market conditions.
- **Competitive Advantage:** Companies that can better predict and meet customer demand have a significant edge over their competitors.

Challenges and Considerations

While AI offers tremendous benefits for demand forecasting, there are some challenges to consider:

- **Data Quality:** AI systems are only as good as the data they're fed. Ensuring high-quality, comprehensive data is crucial.
- **Integration:** Implementing AI forecasting systems often requires integration with existing business systems, which can be complex.
- **Skill Requirements:** Utilizing AI forecasting tools effectively often requires new skills within the organization.
- **Balancing AI and Human Insight:** While AI is powerful, it is important to combine its insights with human expertise and intuition for the best results.

The Future of AI in Demand Forecasting

As AI technology continues to advance, one can expect even more sophisticated and accurate demand forecasting capabilities. Future trends might include the following:

- **Increased Personalization:** AI might predict demand not just for broad customer segments but also for individual customers.
- **Autonomous Supply Chains:** AI could potentially manage entire supply chains, automatically adjusting orders and production based on predicted demand.
- **Cross-Industry Insights:** AI systems might draw insights from seemingly unrelated industries to improve forecasts.

Summary

AI is dramatically improving demand forecasting by processing complex datasets, identifying intricate patterns, and providing real-time insights. This leads to more accurate predictions and better-informed business decisions. As companies continue to adopt and refine AI-powered forecasting tools, one can expect to see more efficient, responsive, and customer-focused supply chains across industries.

Whereas challenges exist, the benefits of AI in demand forecasting are clear, offering businesses a powerful tool to navigate the complexities of modern markets and meet customer needs more effectively than ever before.[†]

[†] ***Demand Forecasting Using AI***

Predicting the Future of Demand
How Amazon is Reinventing Forecasting with Machine Learning : This article discusses how Amazon uses machine learning to predict future demand for millions of products globally. www.forbes.com/sites/amazonwebservices/2021/12/03/predicting-the-future-of-demand-how-amazon-is-reinventing-forecasting-with-machine-learning/.

Predictive Big Data Analytics for Supply Chain Demand Forecasting
Methods, Applications, and Research Opportunities: This survey paper explores various methods and applications of big data analytics in supply chain demand forecasting. https://journalofbigdata.springeropen.com/articles/10.1186/s40537-020-00329-2.

Demand Prediction in Retail
This book provides a comprehensive overview of the process of predicting demand for retailers, including data collection, evaluation, and visualization of prediction results. https://link.springer.com/book/10.1007/978-3-030-85855-1.

AI-Powered Inventory Optimization: Striking the Perfect Balance

In the world of business, managing inventory is like walking a tightrope. On one side, you have the risk of overstocking—tying up money in excess inventory that might not sell quickly. On the other side, there's the danger of stockouts—running out of products and disappointing customers. AI is now helping businesses find the perfect balance, ensuring that they have just the right amount of inventory at all times.

The Inventory Challenge

Before diving into how AI is changing the game, understanding why inventory optimization is so crucial:

- **Carrying Costs:** Storing inventory costs money. There's the cost of warehouse space, insurance, and the risk of products becoming obsolete or damaged.
- **Cash Flow:** Money tied up in inventory can't be used for other business needs.
- **Customer Satisfaction:** Running out of stock can lead to lost sales and unhappy customers.
- **Perishability:** For businesses dealing with perishable goods, having too much stock can lead to waste.

Traditionally, businesses have relied on historical data and human judgment to manage inventory. But this approach often leads to either overstocking or stockouts, especially in today's fast-paced, unpredictable markets.

How AI Is Revolutionizing Inventory Management

AI is transforming inventory management by analyzing vast amounts of data and making real-time recommendations. Here's how:

Analyzing Complex Datasets

AI systems can process and analyze huge amounts of data, including:

- **Sales History:** Past sales patterns across different products, locations, and periods.
- **Lead Times:** How long does it take to replenish stock from suppliers?
- **Market Trends:** Current and predicted market conditions that might affect demand.
- **External Factors:** Things such as weather, local events, or economic indicators that could impact sales.

For example, an AI system might notice that sales of umbrellas spike not just during rainy seasons but also when certain weather patterns are forecast, allowing the business to adjust inventory accordingly.

Predictive Analytics

AI doesn't just look at past data; it uses this information to predict future trends. This predictive capability allows businesses to anticipate changes in demand before they happen.

Real-Time Adjustments

Unlike traditional inventory systems that might update weekly or monthly, AI systems can continuously analyze data and adjust recommendations in real time. This means businesses can respond quickly to sudden changes in demand or supply.

Multivariable Optimization

AI can consider multiple factors simultaneously to find the optimal inventory level. It might balance the cost of storage against the risk of stockouts, while also considering factors such as bulk purchase discounts or upcoming promotions.

Practical Applications of AI in Inventory Optimization

Let us look at some real-world examples of how AI is improving inventory management:

- **Retail:** A clothing retailer uses AI to optimize inventory across multiple stores and its online platform. The AI considers factors such as local fashion trends, weather, and upcoming events to recommend stock levels for each location.
- **Grocery Stores:** AI helps grocery chains manage perishable goods by predicting demand based on factors such as local events, weather, and even social media trends about food.
- **Manufacturing:** A car manufacturer uses AI to optimize the inventory of parts, considering global supply chain issues, production schedules, and predicted demand for different models.
- **Pharmaceuticals:** AI helps pharmacies manage the inventory of medications, considering factors such as local health trends, prescription patterns, and even flu season predictions.

Benefits of AI-Powered Inventory Optimization

The improvements brought by AI lead to several key benefits:

- **Reduced Carrying Costs:** By maintaining optimal inventory levels, businesses can significantly reduce the costs associated with storing excess stock.
- **Improved Cash Flow:** Less money tied up in inventory means more cash available for other business needs.
- **Higher Customer Satisfaction:** With the right products in stock at the right time, businesses can meet customer demands more effectively.
- **Reduced Waste:** Especially important for perishable goods, AI helps minimize the amount of stock that goes to waste.

- **Increased Sales:** By ensuring popular items are always in stock, businesses can maximize sales opportunities.
- **Better Supplier Relationships:** More accurate ordering can lead to more consistent and predictable orders from suppliers.

Challenges and Considerations

While AI offers tremendous benefits for inventory optimization, there are some challenges to consider:

- **Data Quality:** AI systems rely on accurate and comprehensive data. Ensuring data quality is crucial for effective inventory optimization.
- **Integration With Existing Systems:** Implementing AI often requires integration with existing inventory management and point-of-sale systems, which can be complex.
- **Initial Costs:** While AI can lead to significant savings over time, there may be substantial upfront costs for implementation.
- **Staff Training:** Employees need to understand how to work with and interpret AI recommendations.

The Future of AI in Inventory Optimization

As AI technology continues to advance, one can expect even more sophisticated inventory management capabilities:

- **Autonomous Ordering:** AI systems might eventually place orders automatically, adjusting to demand in real time without human intervention.
- **Predictive Maintenance for Inventory:** AI could predict when products in storage might degrade or become obsolete, allowing for proactive management.
- **Cross-Industry Insights:** AI systems might draw insights from seemingly unrelated industries to improve inventory predictions.

Summary

AI is revolutionizing inventory optimization by helping businesses strike the perfect balance between overstocking and stockouts. By analyzing complex datasets including sales patterns, lead times, and market conditions, AI systems can recommend optimal inventory levels with unprecedented accuracy. This not only reduces carrying costs but also ensures product availability, leading to improved customer satisfaction and overall business performance.

While challenges exist in implementation, the benefits of AI in inventory management are clear, offering businesses a powerful tool to navigate the complexities of modern markets and meet customer needs more effectively than ever before.

As businesses continue to adopt and refine AI-powered inventory optimization tools, one can expect to see more efficient, responsive, and profitable operations across various industries.[‡]

[‡] ***AI-Powered Inventory Optimization***

Applications of Artificial Intelligence in Inventory Management: A Systematic Review of the Literature: This article provides a comprehensive review of AI applications in inventory management, focusing on research articles published between 2012 and 2022. https://link.springer.com/article/10.1007/s11831-022-09879-5.

Material Requirements Planning with SAP S/4 HANA, 2nd Edition by Caetano Almeida: This book covers various aspects of material requirements planning, including AI-powered methods. https://ijettjournal.org/archive/ijett-v71i8p202.

Machine Learning Applications for Demand Driven in Supply Chain: Literature Review: This chapter provides insights into machine learning applications for demand-driven inventory management. www.odoo.com/app/inventory.

AI Revolutionizes Logistics: The Rise of Smart Warehouses

The logistics sector is undergoing a dramatic transformation, thanks to the power of AI. From warehouse operations to last-mile delivery, AI is optimizing every step of the logistics process, making it faster, more efficient, and more cost-effective. Let us explore how AI is reshaping the logistics landscape and what this means for businesses and consumers alike.

Warehouses are the heart of logistics operations, and AI is making them smarter than ever before.

AI-Powered Robots

Gone are the days when warehouses relied solely on human workers for picking and packing. Today, AI-powered robots are taking center stage:

- **Automated Picking:** Robots equipped with computer vision can identify and pick items with incredible speed and accuracy. They don't get tired, don't make mistakes due to fatigue, and can work 24/7.
- **Inventory Management:** AI-powered drones and robots can continuously scan shelves, updating inventory in real time. This ensures accurate stock levels and helps prevent stockouts or overstocking.
- **Collaborative Robots (Cobots):** These robots work alongside human workers, assisting with tasks such as lifting heavy items or reaching high shelves, improving efficiency and worker safety.

Automated Guided Vehicles (AGVs)

AGVs are transforming how goods move within warehouses:

- **Efficient Movement:** These self-driving vehicles can navigate warehouse floors, moving goods from one area to another without human intervention.

- **Optimized Routes:** AI algorithms help AGVs determine the most efficient routes, reducing travel time and increasing productivity.
- **Safety:** AGVs are equipped with sensors to detect obstacles, ensuring safe operation around human workers.

Intelligent Storage Systems

AI is even changing how goods are stored:

- **Dynamic Slotting:** AI analyzes order patterns and predicts future demand, automatically reorganizing warehouse layouts to place fast-moving items in easily accessible locations.
- **Vertical Storage:** AI-powered vertical lift modules can maximize warehouse space, retrieving items quickly and efficiently.

AI's impact extends far beyond the warehouse walls, revolutionizing how goods are transported and delivered:

Route Planning and Optimization

ML algorithms are taking route planning to new levels of efficiency:

- **Real-Time Adjustments:** AI can analyze traffic patterns, weather conditions, and even social media data to predict and avoid delays, dynamically adjusting routes in real time.
- **Multistop Optimization:** For delivery vehicles making multiple stops, AI can calculate the most efficient order of deliveries, considering factors such as time windows, vehicle capacity, and driver breaks.
- **Predictive Maintenance:** AI can predict when vehicles are likely to need maintenance, schedule servicing before breakdowns occur, and minimize disruptions.

Load Optimization

AI is helping logistics companies make the most of their cargo space:

- **3D Load Planning:** AI algorithms can calculate the optimal way to pack items of different shapes and sizes into trucks or containers, maximizing space utilization and reducing the number of trips needed.
- **Weight Distribution:** AI ensures that loads are balanced properly, improving fuel efficiency and safety.
- **Multimodal Planning:** For shipments that involve multiple modes of transport (e.g., truck, rail, and ship), AI can optimize the entire journey, considering factors such as cost, speed, and environmental impact.

Last-Mile Delivery

The final step of delivery is often the most challenging and expensive, but AI is helping to streamline this process:

- **Delivery Time Prediction:** AI analyzes historical data and current conditions to provide accurate delivery time estimates, improving customer satisfaction.
- **Autonomous Vehicles:** While still in development, self-driving delivery vehicles and drones powered by AI promise to revolutionize last-mile delivery in the future.
- **Smart Lockers:** AI-powered locker systems can optimize pickup locations and times, reducing failed deliveries and improving efficiency.

The Benefits of AI in Logistics

The integration of AI into logistics operations offers numerous benefits:

- **Increased Efficiency:** AI-powered systems can work faster and more accurately than humans, significantly boosting productivity.
- **Cost Reduction:** By optimizing routes, reducing errors, and improving resource utilization, AI helps cut operational costs.
- **Improved Customer Satisfaction:** Faster, more reliable deliveries and accurate tracking lead to happier customers.

- **Enhanced Safety:** AI can help prevent accidents in warehouses and on the road, improving worker safety.
- **Sustainability:** By optimizing routes and loads, AI can help reduce fuel consumption and emissions, making logistics operations more environmentally friendly.

Challenges and Considerations

While the benefits of AI in logistics are clear, there are challenges to consider:

- **Initial Investment:** Implementing AI systems can be expensive, requiring significant upfront costs.
- **Data Quality:** AI systems rely on high-quality data to function effectively. Ensuring data accuracy and consistency can be challenging.
- **Workforce Adaptation:** As AI takes over more tasks, the logistics workforce will need to adapt and acquire new skills.
- **Ethical Considerations:** The use of AI raises questions about job displacement and data privacy that need to be addressed.

The Future of AI in Logistics

As AI technology continues to advance, one can expect even more innovations in the logistics sector:

- **Predictive Logistics:** AI might predict demand before orders are even placed, allowing for proactive inventory management and shipping.
- **Blockchain Integration:** Combining AI with blockchain could provide unprecedented transparency and security in supply chains.
- **Augmented Reality (AR):** AI-powered AR systems could assist warehouse workers and delivery drivers, providing real-time information and guidance.

Summary

In summary, AI is transforming the logistics sector from warehouse operations to last-mile delivery. By leveraging intelligent systems, robots, and ML algorithms, logistics companies can achieve new levels of efficiency, accuracy, and customer satisfaction. While challenges exist, the potential benefits of AI in logistics are too significant to ignore. As technology continues to evolve, one can expect AI to play an increasingly central role in shaping the future of logistics.[§]

---

§ ***AI Revolutionizes Logistics***

ThroughPut World
"Accelerating Supply Chain Success With AI: Key Benefits and Use Cases," https://throughput.world/blog/ai-in-supply-chain-and-logistics/.

LeewayHertz
"Transforming Logistics and Supply Chain With AI: Applications and Implementation," www.leewayhertz.com/ai-in-logistics-and-supply-chain/.

Consumer Goods Technology
"The Future of AI in Logistics: Trends and Predictions," https://consumergoods.com/what-future-ai-logistics.

AI Routing: Paving the Way for Efficiency

In today's fast-paced world, getting things from point A to point B quickly, cheaply, and efficiently is more important than ever. Whether it is delivering packages to customers, moving materials through a supply chain, or managing the flow of products within a factory, route planning plays a crucial role. This is where AI comes in, revolutionizing how one approaches route planning and optimization.

The Challenge of Route Planning

Before diving into how AI is changing the game, let us understand why route planning is so complex:

- **Multiple Destinations:** Planning routes often involves multiple stops, and finding the best order to visit these locations is not straightforward.
- **Time Constraints:** Some deliveries or processes have specific time windows, adding another layer of complexity.
- **Variable Conditions:** Traffic, weather, and other external factors can affect travel times and route efficiency.
- **Resource Limitations:** There are often constraints on vehicle capacity, driver hours, or available equipment.
- **Cost Considerations:** Different routes may have different costs associated with them, such as toll roads or fuel consumption.

Traditionally, route planning relied heavily on human expertise and simple algorithms. However, as the complexity of logistics operations has grown, these methods have become increasingly inadequate.

How AI Transforms Route Planning

AI brings a new level of sophistication to route planning, considering multiple variables simultaneously and finding optimal solutions in ways that humans simply can't match. Here's how:

Processing Vast Amounts of Data

AI systems can analyze huge volumes of data in real time, including:

- Historical traffic patterns
- Current road conditions
- Weather forecasts
- Vehicle capacity and capabilities
- Driver schedules and preferences
- Delivery time windows
- Fuel costs and toll charges

By considering all these factors together, AI can create routes that are optimized for efficiency, cost, and timeliness.

Dynamic Route Adjustment

Unlike traditional static route planning, AI can adjust routes on the fly:

- If traffic conditions change, the AI can recalculate the route instantly.
- If a new delivery is added to the schedule, the AI can seamlessly incorporate it into the existing route.
- If a vehicle breaks down, the AI can quickly redistribute its deliveries among other vehicles.

This dynamic capability ensures that routes remain optimal even as conditions change throughout the day.

Predictive Analytics

AI doesn't just react to current conditions; it can predict future scenarios:

- By analyzing historical data, AI can predict when traffic is likely to be heaviest on certain routes.
- It can anticipate seasonal changes in demand and adjust routing strategies accordingly.

- AI can even predict when vehicles are likely to need maintenance, allowing for proactive scheduling that minimizes disruptions.

Multiobjective Optimization

AI can balance multiple, sometimes competing, objectives:

- Minimizing total distance traveled
- Reducing fuel consumption
- Meeting delivery time windows
- Maximizing vehicle utilization
- Minimizing overtime for drivers

By considering all these factors simultaneously, AI can find solutions that best meet the overall goals of the organization.

Real-World Applications

Let us look at how AI-powered route optimization is applied in different contexts:

Delivery Services

For companies such as FedEx or Amazon, AI route optimization can:

- Reduce delivery times by finding the most efficient routes between multiple stops.
- Decrease fuel consumption by minimizing unnecessary travel.
- Improve customer satisfaction by providing more accurate delivery time estimates.

Supply Chain Logistics

In complex supply chains, AI can optimize routes across multiple modes of transportation:

- Determining the best combination of truck, rail, and ship transport for long-distance freight.
- Optimizing the flow of materials among suppliers, manufacturers, and distributors.
- Reducing inventory holding costs by timing deliveries more precisely.

Factory Operations

Within factories, AI can optimize the movement of materials and products:

- Planning the most efficient routes for AGVs moving materials between workstations.
- Optimizing the sequence of operations to minimize bottlenecks and maximize throughput.
- Coordinating the movement of multiple robots to avoid collisions and maximize efficiency.

Benefits of AI-Powered Route Optimization

The advantages of using AI for route planning are significant:

- **Cost Reduction:** By minimizing travel distances and optimizing vehicle utilization, AI can significantly reduce transportation costs.
- **Time Savings:** More efficient routes mean faster deliveries and shorter production times.
- **Improved Customer Satisfaction:** Faster, more reliable deliveries lead to happier customers.
- **Environmental Impact:** By reducing unnecessary travel and optimizing fuel consumption, AI-powered routing can lower carbon emissions.
- **Better Resource Utilization:** AI can help companies make the most of their vehicles, equipment, and personnel.
- **Scalability:** AI systems can handle routing problems of any size, from small local operations to global supply chains.

Challenges and Considerations

While the benefits are clear, there are challenges to implementing AI-powered route optimization:

- **Data Quality:** AI systems rely on accurate, up-to-date data. Ensuring data quality can be a significant challenge.
- **Integration With Existing Systems:** Implementing AI often requires integration with existing logistics and tracking systems.
- **Initial Costs:** While AI can lead to long-term savings, there may be significant upfront costs for implementation and training.
- **Human Factors:** Drivers and operators need to trust and be willing to follow AI-generated routes, which may require a cultural shift.

The Future of AI in Route Optimization

As AI technology continues to advance, one can expect even more sophisticated routing capabilities:

- **Autonomous Vehicle Integration:** As self-driving vehicles become more common, AI will play a crucial role in coordinating their movements.
- **Drone Delivery Optimization:** AI will be essential in planning and coordinating drone delivery routes, considering factors such as battery life and airspace regulations.
- **Sustainability Focus:** Future AI systems may place even greater emphasis on minimizing environmental impact, and finding routes that balance efficiency with sustainability.

Summary

In summary, AI is revolutionizing route planning and optimization across various industries, from delivery services to supply chain logistics and factory operations. By considering multiple variables simultaneously, AI can determine the most efficient routes, reducing transportation costs, delivery times, and environmental impact. While challenges exist in implementation, the potential benefits of AI in route optimization are too significant to ignore.

As technology continues to evolve, one can expect AI to play an increasingly central role in shaping the future of logistics and operations management.[¶]

[¶] ***AI Route Optimization***

AI Route Optimization and Route Planning Guide
This guide from FarEye explains how AI technologies, including machine learning and predictive analytics, are used to optimize routing decisions. It covers the benefits of AI in route optimization, such as efficiency, dynamic adaptability, and environmental considerations. https://fareye.com/resources/blogs/ai-route-optimization.

AI Route Optimization: Everything You Need to Know in 2024
This blog by Upper Inc. provides an in-depth look at AI route optimization, discussing its fundamentals, challenges, and key features. It also explains how AI algorithms collect and analyze data to generate optimal routes. www.upperinc.com/blog/ai-route-optimization/.

The Power of AI and Machine Learning in Route Planning
This resource from RouteSmart explores how AI and machine learning are transforming parcel and postal delivery by making route planning more efficient and data-driven. It highlights the use of predictive analytics and dynamic routing. www.routesmart.com/resource/the-power-of-ai-and-machine-learning-in-route-planning/.

CHAPTER 6

AI in Finance and Accounting

AI is revolutionizing the finance and accounting industries, transforming core processes, and enabling new capabilities. This chapter explores four key areas where AI is making a significant impact:

AI for Fraud Detection: Advanced ML algorithms are dramatically improving the ability to detect fraudulent activities in real time. By analyzing vast amounts of transactional and behavioral data, AI systems can identify subtle patterns and anomalies that may indicate fraud, allowing financial institutions to respond swiftly and minimize losses.

Intelligent Process Automation: AI-powered automation is streamlining routine financial and accounting tasks, from data entry and reconciliation to report generation. This not only improves efficiency and reduces errors but also frees up human workers to focus on higher value strategic activities.

Financial Forecasting and Risk Analysis: Predictive AI models are enhancing the accuracy of financial forecasts and providing deeper insights into potential risks. By processing historical data alongside real-time market information, these systems can project future trends and highlight areas of concern with greater precision than traditional methods.

AI Investment Strategies: ML algorithms are deployed to optimize investment portfolios and develop sophisticated trading strategies. These AI systems can rapidly analyze market conditions, identify opportunities, and execute trades at speeds impossible for human traders.

This section examines the underlying technologies, explore real-world applications, and assess both the opportunities and the challenges presented by AI in finance and accounting. The transformative potential of AI in this sector is immense, promising to enhance decision making, improve operational efficiency, and unlock new sources of value for businesses and investors alike.

AI for Fraud Detection

In the fast-paced world of finance and accounting, the ability to detect fraudulent activities swiftly and accurately is crucial. Fraud can result in significant financial losses, damage to reputation, and legal consequences for businesses. Traditional methods of fraud detection, which often rely on manual reviews and predefined rules, are increasingly outpaced by sophisticated fraudsters. This is where advanced ML algorithms come into play, offering a powerful tool to enhance fraud detection capabilities in real time.

ML is a subset of AI that enables computers to learn from data and make predictions or decisions without explicitly programming for each task. In the context of fraud detection, ML algorithms are trained on vast datasets that include both legitimate and fraudulent transactions. By analyzing this data, the algorithms learn to recognize patterns and behaviors associated with fraud.

Analyzing Transactional Data

Transactional data refers to the records of financial transactions, such as purchases, transfers, and withdrawals. Each transaction contains various attributes, including the amount, date, time, location, and the parties involved. ML is a subset of AI that enables computers to learn from data and make predictions or decisions without explicitly programming for each task. In the context of fraud detection, ML algorithms are trained on vast datasets that include both legitimate and fraudulent transactions.

By analyzing this data, the algorithms learn to recognize patterns and behaviors associated with fraud.

For example, consider a credit card transaction that occurs in a different country just minutes after a purchase was made locally. This sudden location change is a red flag that traditional systems might miss. However, an ML algorithm can quickly flag this transaction as potentially fraudulent based on the anomaly in the user's spending behavior.

Behavioral Data Analysis

In addition to transactional data, ML algorithms also analyze behavioral data, which includes information about how users interact with financial systems. This can encompass login patterns, device usage, and even typing speed. By building a profile of normal behavior for each user, the system can detect deviations that may suggest fraud.

For instance, if a user typically logs in from the same device and suddenly accesses their account from a new device with a different IP address, the system can flag this as suspicious. Similarly, if the user's typing speed or mouse movements differ significantly from their usual patterns, it could indicate that someone else is attempting to access the account.

Identifying Subtle Patterns and Anomalies

One of the key strengths of ML algorithms is their ability to identify subtle patterns and anomalies that might be missed by human analysts or rule-based systems. Fraudsters often try to mimic legitimate behavior to avoid detection, but ML algorithms can detect even minor discrepancies.

For example, a fraudster might make multiple small transactions to avoid triggering alerts for large purchases. An ML algorithm can recognize this pattern of behavior as unusual for the user and flag it for further investigation. Additionally, the algorithm can compare the transaction against a broader dataset to identify similarities with known fraudulent activities.

Real-Time Detection and Swift Response

The real-time capabilities of ML algorithms are particularly valuable in fraud detection. Traditional methods often involve batch processing, where transactions are reviewed after they occur. This delay can give fraudsters time to complete their schemes and disappear.

In contrast, ML algorithms can analyze transactions as they happen, allowing financial institutions to respond immediately.

For instance, if a transaction is flagged as potentially fraudulent, the system can automatically trigger actions such as temporarily freezing the account, sending an alert to the user, or requiring additional authentication. This swift response helps to minimize losses and prevent further fraudulent activities.

Continuous Learning and Adaptation

Fraudsters are constantly evolving their tactics, which means that fraud detection systems must also continuously adapt. ML algorithms excel in this area because they can be retrained with new data to improve their accuracy over time. As new fraud patterns emerge, the algorithms learn from these examples and update their models accordingly.

Moreover, ML algorithms can incorporate feedback from human analysts. When a transaction is flagged as fraudulent and confirmed by an analyst, the system uses this information to refine its detection criteria. This iterative process ensures that the system remains effective in identifying new and evolving fraud schemes.

Summary

Advanced ML algorithms are revolutionizing fraud detection in finance and accounting by analyzing vast amounts of transactional and behavioral data. These algorithms can identify subtle patterns and anomalies that may indicate fraud, allowing financial institutions to respond swiftly and minimize losses. With their ability to learn and adapt continuously, ML algorithms provide a robust and dynamic defense against the ever-changing landscape of financial fraud.

As technology continues to advance, the role of AI in fraud detection will only become more critical, helping to safeguard the integrity and security of financial systems worldwide.*

* ***AI for Fraud Detection***

Understanding AI Fraud Detection and Prevention Strategies
This article from DigitalOcean explores the mechanics of AI fraud detection, the benefits and challenges of using it, and best practices for building a strategy that leverages this technology. www.credo.ai/solutions/financial-services.

AI for Fraud Detection: Techniques and Implementation
This blog by RapidCanvas discusses various AI techniques like machine learning, deep learning, and natural language processing used in fraud detection. It also covers implementation strategies and the benefits of AI in combating financial crime. www.digitalocean.com/resources/article/ai-fraud-detection.

Generative AI for Fraud Detection—Mechanisms and Real-World Examples
This article from Master of Code explains how generative AI can be used to analyze patterns in data and identify potential risk factors, providing real-world examples of its application. https://masterofcode.com/blog/generative-ai-for-fraud-detection.

AI-Powered Automation in Finance and Accounting

The world of finance and accounting is often filled with repetitive and time-consuming tasks. These tasks, while essential, can be prone to human error and can take up a significant amount of time that could be better spent on more strategic activities. This is where AI-powered automation comes in, transforming the way financial and accounting professionals work by streamlining routine tasks, improving efficiency, and reducing errors.

What Is AI-Powered Automation?

AI-powered automation refers to the use of AI technologies to perform tasks that traditionally require human intervention. In finance and accounting, this involves using AI to handle processes such as data entry, reconciliation, and report generation. By automating these tasks, businesses can save time, reduce errors, and allow their employees to focus on more valuable work.

Streamlining Data Entry

Data entry is one of the most basic yet critical tasks in finance and accounting. It involves inputting financial data into systems for further processing and analysis. Traditionally, this task has been done manually, which can be slow and error-prone. AI-powered automation can significantly improve this process.

For example, AI systems can automatically extract data from invoices, receipts, and other financial documents using optical character recognition (OCR) technology. This data is then accurately entered into the relevant systems without the need for manual input. Not only does this speed up the process but it also reduces the risk of errors that can occur when data is entered by hand.

Enhancing Reconciliation

Reconciliation is the process of ensuring that financial records match up with actual transactions. This is crucial for maintaining accurate financial statements and identifying any discrepancies. Manual reconciliation can be a tedious and time-consuming task, often involving cross-checking large volumes of data.

AI-powered automation can streamline reconciliation by automatically comparing transaction records from different sources, such as bank statements and internal financial records. The AI system can quickly identify any discrepancies and flag them for further review. This not only speeds up the reconciliation process but also ensures greater accuracy, reducing the likelihood of errors going unnoticed.

Simplifying Report Generation

Generating financial reports is another essential task in finance and accounting. These reports provide valuable insights into a company's financial health and are used for decision making by management, investors, and other stakeholders. However, creating these reports can be a complex and time-consuming process.

AI-powered automation can simplify report generation by automatically compiling data from various sources and generating accurate and comprehensive reports. For instance, AI systems can pull data from accounting software, spreadsheets, and other databases to create financial statements, budget reports, and performance analyses. This not only saves time but also ensures that reports are consistent and error-free.

Improving Efficiency and Reducing Errors

One of the most significant benefits of AI-powered automation is its ability to improve efficiency and reduce errors. By automating routine tasks, businesses can complete them much faster than if they were done manually. This increased efficiency can lead to cost savings and allow businesses to operate more smoothly.

Moreover, AI systems are less prone to errors compared to humans. For example, an AI system can process thousands of transactions with a high degree of accuracy, whereas a human might make mistakes due to fatigue or oversight. By reducing errors, businesses can maintain more accurate financial records and avoid costly mistakes.

Freeing up Human Workers for Strategic Activities

Perhaps, one of the most exciting aspects of AI-powered automation is its potential to free up human workers to focus on higher value strategic activities. When routine tasks are automated, employees have more time to engage in work that requires critical thinking, creativity, and decision making.

For instance, instead of spending hours on data entry or reconciliation, financial professionals can focus on analyzing financial data to identify trends and opportunities. They can also work on developing strategic plans, improving financial models, and advising management on important financial decisions. By shifting their focus to these higher value activities, employees can contribute more significantly to the growth and success of the business.

Summary

AI-powered automation is transforming the finance and accounting industries by streamlining routine tasks, improving efficiency, and reducing errors. From data entry and reconciliation to report generation, AI is making these processes faster, more accurate, and less labor-intensive. As a result, human workers are freed up to focus on higher value strategic activities that can drive business growth and innovation.

The adoption of AI-powered automation is not just a technological advancement; it is a strategic move that can enhance the overall performance and competitiveness of financial and accounting functions in any organization.[†]

[†] ***AI-Powered Automation in Finance and Accounting***

Artificial Intelligence in Finance: A Comprehensive Review
This article provides a detailed overview of AI applications in finance, including predictive systems, classification, and big data analytics. It covers various AI applications in stock markets, trading models, portfolio management, and more. https://link.springer.com/article/10.1007/s43546-023-00618-x.

Artificial Intelligence in Finance and Accounting
Opportunities and Challenges: This conference paper discusses the transformative impact of AI on finance and accounting, highlighting opportunities for increased efficiency and improved decision making, as well as challenges related to data quality, bias, and regulatory compliance. https://link.springer.com/chapter/10.1007/978-981-99-5652-4_17.

Modernize Your Finance Operations With AI-Powered Automation
This resource explores how modern finance teams are leveraging AI-driven automation to streamline operations, improve accuracy, and reduce costs. https://link.springer.com/content/pdf/10.1007/s43546-023-00618-x.pdf.

AI-Powered Financial Forecasting and Risk Analysis

In the dynamic world of finance and accounting, the ability to accurately predict future trends and identify potential risks is crucial for making informed decisions. Traditional forecasting and risk analysis methods, while valuable, often struggle to keep pace with the complexity and speed of modern financial markets. This is where predictive AI models come into play, offering enhanced accuracy in financial forecasts and deeper insights into potential risks.

Understanding Predictive AI Models

Predictive AI models are sophisticated computer programs that use AI and ML techniques to analyze data and make predictions about future events. In finance and accounting, these models process vast amounts of historical data alongside real-time market information to forecast financial trends and identify potential risks.

Enhancing Financial Forecasts

Financial forecasting is the process of estimating future financial outcomes for a business or investment. Traditionally, this has been done using statistical methods and expert judgment. While these approaches are still valuable, AI-powered predictive models can significantly enhance their accuracy and reliability.

Processing Historical Data

AI models can analyze years of historical financial data, including sales figures, economic indicators, and market trends. By identifying patterns and relationships within this data, the models can understand how different factors have influenced financial outcomes in the past.

For example, an AI model might recognize that a company's sales tend to increase during certain seasons or in response to specific economic conditions. This understanding forms the foundation for more accurate predictions.

Incorporating Real-Time Information

One of the key advantages of AI models is their ability to rapidly process and incorporate real-time market information. This could include current stock prices, exchange rates, news events, and social media sentiment.

By combining historical patterns with up-to-the-minute data, AI models can make forecasts that are both grounded in past trends and responsive to current market conditions. This results in predictions that are more accurate and relevant than those based solely on historical data.

Projecting Future Trends

Using the insights gained from historical and real-time data, AI models can project future financial trends with greater precision than traditional methods. These projections can cover a wide range of financial metrics, from revenue and profit forecasts to stock price predictions and market share estimates.

For instance, an AI model might predict how a company's revenue is likely to change over the next quarter, taking into account factors such as seasonal trends, current economic conditions, and recent company announcements.

Highlighting Areas of Concern Providing Deeper Insights Into AI Potential Risks

In addition to enhancing financial forecasts, predictive AI models are particularly valuable for identifying and analyzing potential risks. Risk analysis is crucial in finance and accounting, as it helps businesses and investors understand and prepare for potential challenges.

Identifying Risk Factors

AI models can process vast amounts of data to identify factors that may pose risks to a business or investment. This could include economic indicators, market trends, regulatory changes, or company-specific issues.

For example, an AI model might flag a potential risk if it detects a correlation between rising interest rates and decreased profitability in a particular industry.

Assessing Probability and Impact

Once potential risks are identified, AI models can assess both the probability of these risks occurring and their potential impact. This is done by analyzing historical instances of similar risks and their outcomes, as well as considering current market conditions. This allows businesses and investors to prioritize risks based on their likelihood and potential severity, enabling more effective risk management strategies.

Stress Testing and Scenario Analysis

AI models excel at performing complex stress tests and scenario analyses. These processes involve simulating various potential future scenarios to understand how they might affect financial outcomes.

For instance, an AI model could simulate the impact of a sudden economic downturn on a company's financial performance, helping the business prepare for such a possibility. By processing all this information, AI models can highlight areas of concern with greater precision than traditional methods. This might involve flagging unusual patterns in financial data that could indicate fraud, identifying potential cash flow issues before they become critical, or spotting early warning signs of market volatility.

AI Advantages Over Traditional Methods

While traditional forecasting and risk analysis methods remain valuable, AI-powered approaches offer several key advantages:

- **Speed:** AI models can process vast amounts of data and generate forecasts much faster than human analysts.
- **Objectivity:** AI models are not influenced by human biases or emotions, leading to more objective analyses.

- **Complexity:** AI can handle much more complex relationships between variables than traditional statistical methods.
- **Adaptability:** AI models can quickly adapt to changing market conditions and new data, continuously improving their accuracy.

Summary

By processing historical data alongside real-time market information, these systems can project future trends and highlight areas of concern with greater precision than traditional methods. This enhanced accuracy and depth of insight enable businesses and investors to make more informed decisions, better manage risks, and stay ahead in the fast-paced world of finance.

As AI technology continues to advance, one can expect even more sophisticated and accurate predictive models in the future. However, it is important to remember that while AI is a powerful tool, it should be used in conjunction with human expertise and judgment for the best results in financial decision making.[‡]

---

‡ ***Financial Forecasting and Risk Analysis***

Artificial Intelligence in Finance: a Comprehensive Review
This article provides an extensive overview of AI applications in finance, including predictive systems, classification, and big data analytics. It covers various AI applications in stock markets, trading models, portfolio management, and more. https://link.springer.com/article/10.1007/s43546-023-00618-x.

Artificial Intelligence in Finance Sector for Risk Prediction
This chapter from Springer discusses how AI enhances risk assessment, management, and decision making in the finance industry. It includes a model for predicting loan defaults using AI techniques. https://link.springer.com/chapter/10.1007/978-3-031-63451-2_17.

Applications of Explainable Artificial Intelligence in Finance
This systematic literature review explores the importance of explainable AI (XAI) in finance, highlighting current research and applications in risk analysis and financial forecasting. https://link.springer.com/article/10.1007/s11301-023-00320-0.

AI-Driven Investment Strategies in Finance and Accounting

In the ever-evolving world of finance and accounting, making smart investment decisions is crucial for maximizing returns and minimizing risks. Traditionally, investment strategies have relied on human expertise and manual analysis. However, the advent of AI and ML is transforming the landscape, enabling the development of sophisticated trading strategies and optimized investment portfolios. This chapter explores how ML algorithms are revolutionizing investment management by rapidly analyzing market conditions, identifying opportunities, and executing trades at speeds far beyond human capabilities.

ML is a branch of AI that allows computers to learn from data and make decisions without explicitly programmed for each task. In investment management, ML algorithms analyze vast amounts of financial data to uncover patterns, predict market movements, and optimize investment strategies.

Optimizing Investment Portfolios

An investment portfolio is a collection of assets, such as stocks, bonds, and other securities, that an investor holds. The goal of portfolio optimization is to maximize returns while minimizing risks. ML algorithms play a crucial role in achieving this balance.

Analyzing Historical Data

ML algorithms can process extensive historical data, including past performance of assets, economic indicators, and market trends. By examining this data, the algorithms identify patterns and relationships that inform investment decisions.

For example, an ML algorithm might analyze the historical performance of various stocks and determine that certain combinations of assets tend to perform well together. This insight helps in constructing a diversified portfolio that balances risk and reward.

Predicting Future Performance

One of the strengths of ML algorithms is their ability to predict future performance based on historical data. By recognizing patterns and trends, these algorithms can forecast how different assets are likely to perform under various market conditions.

For instance, an ML algorithm might predict that a particular stock is likely to increase in value based on recent market trends and historical performance. This prediction helps investors make informed decisions about which assets to include in their portfolios.

Continuous Optimization

Markets are dynamic, and asset performance can change rapidly. ML algorithms continuously monitor market conditions and adjust investment portfolios accordingly. This ongoing optimization ensures that portfolios remain aligned with the investor's goals and risk tolerance.

For example, if an ML algorithm detects that a particular asset is underperforming, it can recommend reallocating funds to more promising investments. This proactive approach helps in maintaining an optimal balance between risk and return.

Developing Sophisticated Trading Strategies

Trading strategies involve buying and selling assets to capitalize on market opportunities. ML algorithms excel at developing and executing sophisticated trading strategies by rapidly analyzing market conditions and identifying profitable opportunities.

Rapid Market Analysis

ML algorithms can process vast amounts of real-time market data, including stock prices, trading volumes, and news events. This rapid analysis allows them to identify market trends and opportunities much faster than human traders.

For example, an ML algorithm might analyze real-time stock prices and detect a pattern indicating that a particular stock is undervalued.

The algorithm can then recommend buying the stock before the market corrects itself, potentially leading to significant profits.

Identifying Opportunities

ML algorithms use various techniques, such as pattern recognition and anomaly detection, to identify trading opportunities. These opportunities might include undervalued stocks, market inefficiencies, or emerging trends.

For instance, an ML algorithm might identify a temporary market inefficiency where a stock's price does not reflect its true value. By exploiting this inefficiency, the algorithm can execute trades that capitalize on the price discrepancy.

Speed and Precision

One of the most significant advantages of ML algorithms in trading is their speed and precision. These algorithms can execute trades in milliseconds, far faster than any human trader. This speed is crucial in high-frequency trading, where even a slight delay can result in missed opportunities.

For example, an ML algorithm might detect a sudden price movement in a stock and execute a trade within milliseconds to take advantage of the change. This rapid response can lead to substantial profits that would be impossible to achieve with manual trading.

Benefits of AI-Driven Investment Strategies

The deployment of ML algorithms in investment management offers several key benefits:

- **Enhanced Accuracy:** ML algorithms can analyze vast amounts of data and identify patterns that humans might miss, leading to more accurate predictions and better investment decisions.
- **Increased Efficiency:** By automating data analysis and trade execution, ML algorithms save time and reduce the workload for human traders and analysts.

- **Reduced Risk:** Continuous monitoring and optimization of investment portfolios help in managing risks more effectively, ensuring that portfolios remain aligned with the investor's goals.
- **Competitive Advantage:** The speed and precision of ML algorithms provide a competitive edge in the fast-paced world of trading, allowing investors to capitalize on opportunities before others.

Summary

ML algorithms are revolutionizing investment management by optimizing portfolios and developing sophisticated trading strategies. These AI systems can rapidly analyze market conditions, identify opportunities, and execute trades at speeds impossible for human traders. By leveraging the power of ML, investors can achieve enhanced accuracy, increased efficiency, reduced risk, and a competitive advantage in the financial markets.

As AI technology continues to advance, its role in investment management will only grow, offering new possibilities for maximizing returns and managing risks.[§]

---

§ ***AI-Driven Investment Strategies in Finance and Accounting***

Artificial Intelligence in Finance: A Comprehensive Review
This article provides an extensive overview of AI applications in finance, including predictive systems, classification, and big data analytics. It covers various AI applications in stock markets, trading models, portfolio management, and more. https://link.springer.com/article/10.1007/s43546-023-00618-x.

Artificial Intelligence in Finance Sector for Risk Prediction
This chapter from Springer discusses how AI enhances risk assessment, management, and decision making in the finance industry. It includes a model for predicting loan defaults using AI techniques. https://link.springer.com/chapter/10.1007/978-3-031-63451-2_17.

Applications of Explainable Artificial Intelligence in Finance
This systematic literature review explores the importance of explainable AI (XAI) in finance, highlighting current research and applications in risk analysis and financial forecasting. https://link.springer.com/article/10.1007/s11301-023-00320-0.

CHAPTER 7

AI for Human Resources

AI is revolutionizing various aspects of HR, transforming traditional practices into more efficient, data-driven processes. This chapter delves into the multifaceted applications of AI in HR, focusing on four key areas: Talent Acquisition and Hiring, Employee Training and Development, Workforce Analytics and Planning, and Improving Employee Engagement.

AI is transforming the business landscape, redefining the division of labor between humans and machines. As AI systems become more sophisticated, they are increasingly integrated into business operations to augment human capabilities, automate routine tasks, and create new roles centered on AI development and oversight.

This chapter explores these changing dynamics and how organizations are adapting to this new reality.

AI's ability to process vast amounts of data and perform complex calculations at high speed is shifting the traditional roles of human workers. Tasks that were once labor-intensive and time-consuming can now be automated, allowing humans to focus on more strategic and creative aspects of their jobs.

The Changing Dynamics of the AI–Human Workforce

AI for Talent Acquisition and Hiring

AI is significantly enhancing talent acquisition by automating repetitive tasks such as resume screening and candidate shortlisting. Traditional recruitment processes are often time-consuming and prone to human error, but AI-powered tools can analyze large volumes of resumes efficiently, matching candidates' skills and experiences with job requirements.

This not only saves recruiters' time but also improves the quality of hires by ensuring a more objective and data-driven selection process. Companies adopting AI in recruitment have reported increased performance, higher revenue per employee, and reduced turnover rates.

Employee Training and Development With AI

AI is also transforming employee training and development by providing personalized learning experiences. AI-driven platforms can analyze individual learning styles and career goals to recommend tailored training programs. This personalization helps employees acquire new skills more effectively and aligns their development with organizational needs. Additionally, AI can track progress and provide real-time feedback, making the training process more interactive and engaging.

AI for Workforce Analytics and Planning

Workforce analytics powered by AI enables HR professionals to make informed decisions based on data. AI can analyze various data points, such as employee performance metrics, turnover rates, and engagement levels, to provide insights into workforce trends and potential issues. This predictive capability helps organizations plan their workforce more strategically, ensuring that they have the right talent in place to meet future demands. By leveraging AI for workforce planning, companies can optimize resource allocation, improve productivity, and reduce costs.

AI for Improving Employee Engagement

Employee engagement is crucial for organizational success, and AI offers innovative solutions to enhance it. AI can analyze employee feedback, sentiment, and interaction patterns to identify factors affecting engagement. By understanding these factors, HR can implement targeted interventions to improve the work environment and employee satisfaction. AI-driven chatbots and virtual assistants also provide employees with instant support and information, fostering a more connected and responsive workplace.

In summary, AI is reshaping HR by automating routine tasks, providing personalized development opportunities, offering deep analytical insights, and enhancing employee engagement. As organizations continue to integrate AI into their HR practices, they can expect to see significant improvements in efficiency, effectiveness, and employee satisfaction.*

---

* ***AI for HR***

An Introduction to AI-First Recruiting
https://pages.eightfold.ai/rs/278-NXO-307/images/TTL_Provider_Insights-An_Introduction_to_AI-First_Recruiting.pdf.

Simple AI for Recruiting: A Comprehensive Guide
https://ideal.com/ebook-simple-ai-for-recruiting-guide/.

The Rise of Artificial Intelligence in Talent Acquisition
www.researchgate.net/publication/352247209_The_Rise_of_Artificial_Intelligence_in_Talent_Acquisition.

Enhancing Talent Acquisition With AI: A Game Changer for HR

In today's fast-paced business world, finding the right talent quickly and efficiently has become more critical than ever. HR departments are constantly seeking ways to improve their recruitment processes to attract the best candidates. One of the most significant advancements in this area is the use of AI. AI is revolutionizing talent acquisition by automating repetitive tasks such as resume screening and candidate shortlisting, making the hiring process faster, more efficient, and more effective.

Automating Resume Screening

Traditionally, resume screening is a time-consuming task that involves manually reviewing each applicant's resume to determine if they meet the job requirements. This process can be overwhelming, especially when there are hundreds or even thousands of applicants for a single position. AI-powered tools can automate this task, saving recruiters a considerable amount of time and effort.

These AI tools use NLP and ML algorithms to analyze resumes. They can quickly scan through large volumes of resumes, extracting relevant information such as skills, experience, education, and other qualifications. By doing so, they can match candidates' profiles with the job requirements more accurately and efficiently than a human recruiter could.

Matching Skills and Experiences

One of the key benefits of using AI in talent acquisition is its ability to match candidates' skills and experiences with job requirements. AI algorithms can be trained to understand the specific needs of a job role and identify candidates who possess the necessary qualifications. This ensures that only the most suitable candidates are shortlisted for further evaluation.

For example, if a company is looking for a software developer with expertise in Python and experience in ML, the AI tool can filter out resumes that do not meet these criteria. It can also rank candidates based on how closely their skills and experiences align with the job requirements. This helps recruiters focus their efforts on the best candidates, increasing the chances of making a successful hire.

Saving Time and Improving Quality

By automating repetitive tasks, AI-powered tools save recruiters a significant amount of time. Instead of spending hours or even days sifting through resumes, recruiters can rely on AI to do the heavy lifting. This allows them to focus on more strategic aspects of the hiring process, such as interviewing candidates and assessing their cultural fit with the organization.

Moreover, AI brings a level of objectivity to the recruitment process that is difficult to achieve with manual screening. Human recruiters can be influenced by unconscious biases, leading to unfair hiring decisions. AI, on the other hand, evaluates candidates based on data and predefined criteria, reducing the risk of bias. This results in a more objective and fair selection process, improving the overall quality of hires.

Reducing Turnover Rates

Hiring the right candidate is not just about filling a position; it is about finding someone who will thrive in the role and stay with the company for the long term. High turnover rates can be costly and disruptive for organizations. By improving the quality of hires, AI can help reduce turnover rates.

AI tools can analyze historical data on employee performance and retention to identify patterns and factors that contribute to successful hires. They can then use this information to predict which candidates are likely to perform well and stay with the company. This predictive capability enables recruiters to make more informed hiring decisions, increasing the likelihood of long-term employee retention.

Summary

AI is transforming talent acquisition by automating repetitive tasks such as resume screening and candidate shortlisting. AI-powered tools can efficiently analyze large volumes of resumes, matching candidates' skills and experiences with job requirements. This not only saves recruiters' time but also improves the quality of hires by ensuring a more objective and data-driven selection process. Additionally, by enhancing the accuracy of candidate matching, AI can help reduce turnover rates, leading to more stable and productive workforces.

As organizations continue to embrace AI in their recruitment processes, they can expect to see significant improvements in efficiency, effectiveness, and overall hiring outcomes. AI is indeed a game-changer for HR, paving the way for a more streamlined and successful talent acquisition process.[†]

---

† ***Enhancing Talent Acquisition With AI***

The Impact of AI on Talent Acquisition and Recruitment: This article from SHRM explores how AI is redefining recruitment strategies, increasing efficiency, and improving the candidate experience. www.shrm.org/executive-network/insights/the-impact-of-ai-on-talent-acquisition-and-recruitment.

Strategic AI Adoption in Talent Acquisition Today: Mercer provides insights into the strategic role of AI in talent acquisition, including overcoming barriers and future possibilities. www.shrm.org/executive-network/insights/the-impact-of-ai-on-talent-acquisition-and-recruitment.

AI in Talent Acquisition: Role, Benefits, and Challenges: Pocket HRMS discusses how AI can streamline various talent acquisition processes, from candidate sourcing to predictive analytics. www.mercer.com/en-us/insights/talent-and-transformation/attracting-and-retaining-talent/strategic-ai-adoption-in-talent-acquisition-today/.

AI in Employee Training and Development: Personalizing the Learning Experience

In the modern workplace, continuous learning and development are crucial for both employees and organizations. As industries evolve and new technologies emerge, employees need to keep their skills up-to-date. Traditional training methods, however, often fall short of meeting the diverse needs of individual learners. This is where AI comes into play. AI is transforming employee training and development by providing personalized learning experiences, making the process more effective and engaging.

Personalized Learning Experiences

One of the most significant advantages of AI in training and development is its ability to create personalized learning experiences. AI-driven platforms can analyze various data points about employees, such as their learning styles, career goals, and past performance. By understanding these individual characteristics, AI can recommend tailored training programs that suit each employee's unique needs.

For instance, some employees may prefer visual learning, while others might benefit more from hands-on practice. AI can identify these preferences and suggest the most suitable training materials, whether they are videos, interactive simulations, or written content. This ensures that employees receive the type of training that resonates best with them, enhancing their learning experience.

Aligning Development With Organizational Needs

Personalized training not only benefits employees but also aligns their development with organizational needs. AI can analyze the skills required for various roles within the company and identify gaps in the current workforce. By recommending targeted training programs, AI helps employees acquire the skills that are most relevant to their job roles and the organization's strategic goals.

For example, if a company is looking to expand its digital marketing efforts, AI can identify employees who have the potential to excel in this area and recommend specific courses or certifications. This targeted approach ensures that the organization builds a workforce with the right skills to achieve its objectives, leading to improved performance and competitiveness.

Tracking Progress and Providing Real-Time Feedback

Another way AI enhances employee training is by tracking progress and providing real-time feedback. Traditional training programs often lack mechanisms for continuous assessment and feedback, making it difficult for employees to gauge their progress. AI addresses this issue by monitoring employees' learning activities and performance in real time.

AI-driven platforms can track various metrics, such as completion rates, quiz scores, and time spent on different modules. Based on this data, AI can provide instant feedback, highlighting areas where employees excel and areas that need improvement. This continuous feedback loop helps employees stay on track and make adjustments to their learning strategies as needed.

Making Training Interactive and Engaging

AI also makes the training process more interactive and engaging. Interactive elements such as quizzes, simulations, and gamified learning experiences can be integrated into training programs. AI can adapt these elements based on employees' progress and preferences, ensuring that the training remains challenging yet achievable.

For instance, AI can introduce more complex scenarios as employees master basic concepts, keeping them engaged and motivated. Additionally, AI-powered chatbots and virtual assistants can provide instant support and answer questions, creating a more dynamic and responsive learning environment.

Summary

AI is revolutionizing employee training and development by providing personalized learning experiences. By analyzing individual learning styles and career goals, AI-driven platforms can recommend tailored training programs that help employees acquire new skills more effectively. This personalization aligns employees' development with organizational needs, ensuring that the workforce is equipped with the right skills to achieve strategic goals.

Moreover, AI's ability to track progress and provide real-time feedback makes the training process more interactive and engaging. Employees receive continuous support and can adjust their learning strategies based on instant feedback, leading to better learning outcomes.

As organizations continue to integrate AI into their training and development programs, they can expect to see significant improvements in employee performance, satisfaction, and overall organizational success. AI is indeed a powerful tool for creating a more effective and engaging learning environment, paving the way for a more skilled and adaptable workforce.[‡]

---

‡ ***Employee Training and Development With AI***

AI in L&D: How to Implement AI in Employee Training
Empuls provides insights into integrating AI in learning and development, including content generation and learner data analysis. https://blog.empuls.io/ai-in-learning-and-development/.

Artificial Intelligence and Its Role in Employee Training and Development
Business Tech Weekly discusses the role of AI in training, coaching, and performance management. https://time.ly/blog/ai-in-training-and-development-20-practical-applications/.

AI in Learning and Development: Transforming Employee Training
Inkling highlights how AI can automate administrative tasks and improve talent development strategies. www.inkling.com/blog/2023/09/ai-learning-and-development/.

AI-Powered Workforce Analytics: Transforming HR Decision Making

In today's data-driven business world, HR departments are increasingly turning to AI to gain deeper insights into their workforce. AI-powered workforce analytics is revolutionizing how HR professionals make decisions, plan for the future, and optimize their human capital. This chapter explores how AI enables data-based decision making in HR and its impact on strategic workforce planning.

Making Informed Decisions With AI

Traditionally, HR decisions were often based on intuition and experience. While these factors are still valuable, AI brings a new level of precision and objectivity to HR decision making. AI-powered workforce analytics tools can process vast amounts of data from various sources, including employee records, performance reviews, and even external market data. By analyzing this information, AI can uncover patterns and trends that might be invisible to the human eye.

For example, AI can analyze employee performance metrics, turnover rates, and engagement levels to provide a comprehensive view of the workforce. This analysis can reveal insights such as:

- Which departments have the highest turnover rates and why?
- What factors contribute to high employee performance?
- How engagement levels correlate with productivity?
- Which skills are most critical for the organization's success?

Armed with these insights, HR professionals can make more informed decisions about hiring, training, and retention strategies.

Predicting Workforce Trends and Issues

One of the most powerful capabilities of AI in workforce analytics is its ability to predict future trends and potential issues. By analyzing historical data and current patterns, AI can forecast:

- Future skill gaps in the organization
- Likely turnover in specific roles or departments

- Upcoming recruitment needs
- Potential impacts of organizational changes

This predictive capability allows HR to be proactive rather than reactive. Instead of scrambling to fill unexpected vacancies or address sudden skill shortages, HR can plan and implement strategies to mitigate these challenges before they become critical issues.

Strategic Workforce Planning

AI's predictive capabilities are particularly valuable for strategic workforce planning. By analyzing current workforce data and future business projections, AI can help organizations ensure that they have the right talent in place to meet future demands.

For instance, if AI predicts a growing need for data science skills in the next few years, HR can start developing training programs or adjust their recruitment strategies accordingly. This forward-thinking approach helps organizations stay competitive and adaptable in rapidly changing markets.

Optimizing Resource Allocation

AI-powered workforce analytics can also help companies optimize their resource allocation. By analyzing productivity data, skill sets, and project requirements, AI can suggest the most efficient ways to allocate HRs across different teams and projects.

For example, AI might identify that certain employees with specific skill combinations are particularly effective on certain types of projects. This information can be used to assign employees to projects where they're likely to have the greatest impact, improving overall productivity and job satisfaction.

Improving Productivity

By providing insights into what drives employee performance and engagement, AI can help organizations implement targeted strategies to improve productivity. For instance, if AI identifies that flexible working hours correlate with higher productivity in certain roles, HR can consider expanding flexible work options.

Moreover, AI can help identify early signs of employee burnout or disengagement, allowing HR to intervene before these issues impact productivity. This proactive approach can lead to a more satisfied and productive workforce.

Reducing Costs

Effective use of AI in workforce analytics can lead to significant cost savings for organizations. By improving hiring decisions, reducing turnover, and optimizing resource allocation, companies can minimize the costs associated with recruitment, training, and lost productivity.

For example, if AI predicts that certain employees are at high risk of leaving, HR can take preventive measures to retain these valuable team members, saving on the costs of hiring and training replacements.

Summary

AI-powered workforce analytics is transforming how HR professionals make decisions and plan for the future. By analyzing various data points, AI provides valuable insights into workforce trends and potential issues. This predictive capability enables organizations to plan their workforce more strategically, ensuring that they have the right talent to meet future demands.

By leveraging AI for workforce planning, companies can optimize resource allocation, improve productivity, and reduce costs. As AI technology continues to advance, its role in HR decision making is likely to grow, leading to more data-driven, efficient, and effective HR management.

However, it is important to remember that while AI is a powerful tool, it should complement rather than replace human judgment. The most effective approach combines AI's analytical capabilities with HR professionals' experience and understanding of human factors. This balanced approach can lead to better decision making and more successful workforce strategies.[§]

[§] ***AI-Powered Workforce Analytics***

AI in HR: How AI Is Transforming the Future of HR
Gartner provides a comprehensive guide on implementing AI in HR, including workforce analytics and its impact on talent management. https://boomi.com/content/report/gartner-flex-report-how-to-pilot-generative-ai/.

Workforce Optimization: Staff Scheduling With AI
McKinsey explores how AI-driven schedule optimization can enhance workforce planning and efficiency. www.mckinsey.com/capabilities/operations/our-insights/smart-scheduling-how-to-solve-workforce-planning-challenges-with-ai.

AI in HR: 2024 Guide to Opportunities and Applications in HR
AIHR discusses how AI analytics platforms can uncover trends, predict turnover, and identify skills gaps. www.aihr.com/blog/ai-in-hr/.

Enhancing Employee Engagement With AI: A New Frontier in HR

Employee engagement is a critical factor in organizational success. Engaged employees are more productive, innovative, and loyal to their companies. They contribute to a positive work culture and help drive business growth. However, maintaining high levels of employee engagement can be challenging, especially in large organizations or those with remote workforces. This is where AI comes in, offering innovative solutions to enhance employee engagement and create a more connected workplace.

The Importance of Employee Engagement

Before diving into how AI can help, it is crucial to understand why employee engagement matters. Engaged employees:

- Are more productive and efficient
- Provide better customer service
- Are more likely to stay with the company, reducing turnover costs
- Contribute to a positive work culture
- Are more innovative and creative in problem-solving

Given these benefits, it is clear that improving employee engagement can have a significant positive impact on an organization's success.

AI's Role in Analyzing Employee Engagement

One of the most powerful ways AI enhances employee engagement is through its ability to analyze vast amounts of data to identify factors affecting engagement. AI can process and analyze various types of data, including:

- Employee feedback from surveys and reviews
- Sentiment analysis from internal communications
- Interaction patterns in collaboration tools
- Performance metrics
- Attendance and leave patterns

By analyzing these data points, AI can uncover patterns and trends that might be invisible to human observers. For example, AI might identify that employees in a particular department have lower engagement scores and higher turnover rates. It could then correlate this with factors such as workload, management style, or lack of growth opportunities.

Identifying Factors Affecting Engagement

AI's ability to process and analyze large volumes of data allows it to identify specific factors that impact employee engagement. These might include the following:

- Work–life balance issues
- Lack of recognition or feedback
- Limited career growth opportunities
- Poor communication from management
- Inadequate resources or tools

By pinpointing these factors, AI provides HR professionals with actionable insights they can use to improve the work environment and boost employee satisfaction.

Implementing Targeted Interventions

Once AI has identified the factors affecting engagement, HR can implement targeted interventions to address these issues. For example:

- If AI identifies that lack of recognition is a key factor, HR might implement a new recognition program.
- If work–life balance is an issue, the company might introduce more flexible working options.
- If career growth is a concern, HR could develop new training and development programs.

These targeted interventions are more likely to be effective because they address specific issues identified through data analysis, rather than generic, one-size-fits-all solutions.

AI-Driven Chatbots and Virtual Assistants

Another way that AI enhances employee engagement is through AI-driven chatbots and virtual assistants. These tools can provide employees with instant support and information, fostering a more connected and responsive workplace. For example:

- HR chatbots can answer common questions about policies, benefits, and procedures, providing quick and accurate information to employees.
- Virtual assistants can help employees schedule meetings, manage their calendars, and set reminders, improving productivity and reducing stress.
- AI-powered learning platforms can recommend personalized training content based on an employee's role, skills, and career goals.

By providing instant, personalized support, these AI tools can significantly improve the employee experience and engagement.

Creating a More Connected Workplace

AI can also foster a more connected workplace by facilitating better communication and collaboration. For instance:

- AI can analyze communication patterns to identify teams or departments that might be siloed and suggest ways to improve cross-functional collaboration.
- AI-powered tools can match employees with mentors or peers based on skills, interests, and career goals, fostering a culture of learning and development.
- Virtual assistants can help remote workers feel more connected by facilitating virtual coffee chats or team-building activities.

Continuous Improvement Through Real-Time Feedback

One of the key advantages of using AI for employee engagement is the ability to gather and analyze real-time feedback. Traditional annual surveys provide only a snapshot of employee sentiment, but AI can continuously monitor engagement levels through various data points. This allows organizations to:

- Identify and address issues quickly before they become major problems.
- Track the effectiveness of engagement initiatives in real time.
- Make data-driven decisions about HR policies and practices.

Summary

AI offers innovative solutions to enhance employee engagement, a crucial factor in organizational success. By analyzing employee feedback, sentiment, and interaction patterns, AI can identify factors affecting engagement and help HR implement targeted interventions. AI-driven chatbots and virtual assistants provide instant support and information, fostering a more connected and responsive workplace. As organizations continue to leverage AI in their HR practices, they can expect to see improvements in employee satisfaction, productivity, and retention. However, it is important to remember that AI should complement, not replace, human interaction. The most effective approach combines AI's analytical capabilities with HR professionals' empathy and interpersonal skills.

By embracing AI-powered solutions for employee engagement, organizations can create a more satisfying work environment, leading to happier, more productive employees and ultimately, greater business success.[¶]

[¶] ***Enhancing Employee Engagement With AI***

Artificial Intelligence at Work: Enhancing Employee Engagement and Business Success
This article from Harvard Business Review explores how AI solutions like ChatGPT and predictive analytics are being used to boost employee engagement and business outcomes. https://boomi.com/content/report/gartner-flex-report-how-to-pilot-generative-ai.

AI in Employee Engagement: The Complete Guide
Qualtrics provides a comprehensive guide on how AI can be used to improve employee engagement through data-driven decision making and predictive analytics. https://hbr.org/sponsored/2024/01/artificial-intelligence-at-work-enhancing-employee-engagement-and-business-success.

How to Use AI to Improve Employee Engagement and Retention
Calibr.ai discusses the use of AI algorithms to analyze employee data and predict retention risks, helping organizations proactively engage and retain their workforce. https://hbr.org/sponsored/2024/01/artificial-intelligence-at-work-enhancing-employee-engagement-and-business-success.

CHAPTER 8

AI in the Health Care Industry

The integration of AI into the health care industry is revolutionizing the way medical professionals diagnose, treat, and monitor patients. This chapter explores the transformative impact of AI across several critical areas in health care: Health Care Analytics, Medical Imaging, Surgical Robots, and Patient Monitoring.

Health Care Analytics

AI in health care analytics is enabling the analysis of vast amounts of clinical data to identify patterns and trends that inform better decision making. By leveraging ML algorithms, health care providers can predict potential health risks, personalize treatment plans, and improve patient outcomes. AI's ability to process and analyze data from electronic health records (EHRs), clinical trials, and patient feedback allows for more accurate diagnoses and effective treatments.

Medical Imaging

AI is making significant strides in medical imaging by enhancing the accuracy and speed of image analysis. AI-powered tools can detect anomalies in radiological images, such as tumors or fractures, with greater precision than traditional methods. This capability not only aids in early disease detection but also reduces the workload on radiologists, allowing them to focus on more complex cases. The integration of AI in medical imaging is paving the way for more reliable and timely diagnoses, ultimately improving patient care.

Surgical Robots

The advent of surgical robots powered by AI is transforming surgical procedures. These robots assist surgeons with precision and control that surpass human capabilities. AI-driven surgical systems can perform minimally invasive surgeries with high accuracy, reducing recovery times and minimizing complications. The use of AI in surgery enhances the surgeon's ability to execute complex procedures, leading to better patient outcomes and increased surgical success rates.

Patient Monitoring

AI is also revolutionizing patient monitoring by providing real-time insights into patient health. AI-driven monitoring systems can continuously track vital signs, detect abnormalities, and alert health care providers to potential issues before they become critical. This proactive approach to patient care ensures timely interventions and reduces the risk of complications. Additionally, AI-powered wearables and remote monitoring devices enable patients to manage their health more effectively, promoting better long-term health outcomes.

In summary, the application of AI in health care is driving significant advancements in health care analytics, medical imaging, surgical procedures, and patient monitoring. As AI technology continues to evolve, its role in health care will become increasingly vital, offering new opportunities to enhance patient care, improve efficiency, and reduce costs.

This chapter delves into these exciting developments, highlighting the potential of AI to transform the health care industry and improve health outcomes for patients worldwide.*

---

* ***AI in Healthcare***

ForeSee Medical: Artificial Intelligence in Healthcare
Transforming Patient Care and Outcomes, www.foreseemed.com/artificial-intelligence-in-healthcare.

NCBI
The Potential for Artificial Intelligence in Healthcare, www.ncbi.nlm.nih.gov/pmc/articles/PMC6616181/.

IBM: AI Healthcare Benefits
Enhancing Efficiency and Patient Care, www.ibm.com/think/insights/ai-healthcare-benefits.

AI in Health Care Analytics: Transforming Patient Care Through Data-Driven Insights

AI is revolutionizing health care analytics, enabling health care providers to harness the power of vast amounts of clinical data to improve patient care and outcomes. By leveraging advanced ML algorithms, AI is helping to identify patterns and trends that were previously hidden, leading to better decision making, more accurate diagnoses, and personalized treatment plans.

Analyzing Vast Amounts of Clinical Data

One of the most significant advantages of AI in health care analytics is its ability to process and analyze enormous volumes of data quickly and accurately. Traditional methods of data analysis are often time-consuming and limited in scope, but AI can sift through millions of data points in a fraction of the time it would take a human analyst.

This capability allows health care providers to:

- Identify trends across large patient populations
- Detect subtle patterns that might indicate emerging health issues
- Compare treatment outcomes across different patient groups
- Analyze the effectiveness of various interventions and medications

By processing data from EHRs, clinical trials, and patient feedback, AI can provide a comprehensive view of patient health and treatment efficacy.

Predicting Potential Health Risks

One of the most promising applications of AI in health care analytics is its ability to predict potential health risks. By analyzing a patient's medical history, lifestyle factors, and genetic information, AI algorithms can identify individuals who may be at higher risk for certain conditions.

For example:

- AI can analyze a patient's EHR to predict the likelihood of developing chronic diseases such as diabetes or heart disease.
- ML models can identify patients at risk of hospital readmission, allowing for proactive interventions.
- AI can detect early signs of cancer or other serious illnesses by analyzing medical imaging data and patient symptoms.

This predictive capability enables health care providers to implement preventive measures and early interventions, potentially saving lives and reducing health care costs.

Personalizing Treatment Plans

AI is also playing a crucial role in personalizing treatment plans for patients. By analyzing data from similar cases and considering individual patient characteristics, AI can help health care providers tailor treatments to each patient's unique needs.

This personalization can lead to:

- More effective treatments with fewer side effects
- Improved patient adherence to treatment plans
- Better management of chronic conditions
- Optimized medication dosages based on individual patient responses

For instance, in oncology, AI can analyze a patient's genetic profile and cancer type to recommend the most effective combination of treatments, potentially improving outcomes and reducing unnecessary side effects.

Improving Patient Outcomes

The ultimate goal of AI in health care analytics is to improve patient outcomes. By providing health care providers with more accurate and timely information, AI enables better decision making throughout the care process.

Some ways AI is improving patient outcomes

- Reducing medical errors by flagging potential drug interactions or contraindications.
- Identifying patients who may benefit from specific clinical trials or experimental treatments.
- Monitoring patient progress in real time and alerting providers to potential complications.
- Facilitating more efficient and effective care coordination among different health care providers.

More Accurate Diagnoses and Effective Treatments

AI's ability to process and analyze data from various sources, including EHRs, clinical trials, and patient feedback, is leading to more accurate diagnoses and effective treatments. By considering a broader range of information than a human physician could feasibly process, AI can help identify rare conditions or complex combinations of symptoms that might otherwise be missed.

For example:

- AI can analyze medical imaging data to detect subtle abnormalities that human radiologists might overlook.
- NLP algorithms can extract relevant information from unstructured clinical notes, providing a more comprehensive view of a patient's health history.
- AI can compare a patient's symptoms and test results against vast databases of medical knowledge to suggest potential diagnoses and appropriate treatment options.

Challenges and Considerations

While the potential of AI in health care analytics is immense, it is important to note that there are challenges and considerations to address:

- Data privacy and security concerns must be carefully managed to protect patient information.
- The "black box" nature of some AI algorithms can make it difficult to explain how certain summaries were reached.
- There's a need for ongoing validation and testing of AI models to ensure their accuracy and reliability.
- Health care providers need training to effectively interpret and use AI-generated insights.

Summary

AI in health care analytics is transforming the way health care providers analyze data, make decisions, and treat patients. By enabling the analysis of vast amounts of clinical data, AI is helping to identify patterns and trends that inform better decision making. Through ML algorithms, health care providers can predict potential health risks, personalize treatment plans, and ultimately improve patient outcomes. As AI technology continues to advance, one can expect even more sophisticated applications in health care analytics. This ongoing evolution promises to bring us closer to a future of truly personalized, data-driven health care that can significantly improve patient care and outcomes.

See Endnote References[†]

---

† ***AI in Healthcare Analytics***

ForeSee Medical
Artificial Intelligence in Healthcare: Transforming Patient Care and Outcomes, www.foreseemed.com/artificial-intelligence-in-healthcare.

Tiga Healthcare
Data-Driven Health: AI and Healthcare Analytics for Patient Carehttps, www.tigahealth.com/data-driven-health-ai-and-healthcare-analytics-for-patient-care/.

Medical Economics
Artificial Intelligence and Analytics in Health Care: Bringing Back Humanity with Technology, www.medicaleconomics.com/view/artificial-intelligence-and-analytics-in-health-care-bringing-back-humanity-with-technology.

AI in Medical Imaging: Enhancing Accuracy and Speed

AI is making significant strides in the field of medical imaging, transforming how radiological images are analyzed and interpreted. This technological advancement is enhancing the accuracy and speed of image analysis, leading to earlier disease detection, reduced workload for radiologists, and ultimately, improved patient care.

Enhancing Accuracy in Image Analysis

One of the most remarkable capabilities of AI in medical imaging is its ability to detect anomalies with greater precision than traditional methods. AI-powered tools use advanced algorithms to analyze radiological images, such as X-rays, MRIs, and CT scans, to identify abnormalities such as tumors, fractures, and other conditions.

For example, AI can be trained to recognize the subtle differences between benign and malignant tumors in mammograms. By analyzing thousands of images, AI algorithms learn to detect patterns that might be missed by the human eye. This leads to more accurate diagnoses and fewer false positives or negatives. Studies have shown that AI can match or even surpass the diagnostic accuracy of experienced radiologists in certain cases, such as detecting lung cancer nodules or identifying early signs of diabetic retinopathy.

Speeding up the Diagnostic Process

In addition to enhancing accuracy, AI significantly speeds up the diagnostic process. Traditional image analysis can be time-consuming, requiring radiologists to meticulously examine each image. AI-powered tools can analyze images in a fraction of the time, providing quick and reliable results.

For instance, an AI system can process a chest X-ray in seconds, flagging potential issues for further review by a radiologist. This rapid analysis is particularly beneficial in emergencies where timely diagnosis is critical. By quickly identifying patients who need urgent care, AI helps ensure that they receive the necessary treatment without delay.

Reducing Radiologists' Workload

The integration of AI in medical imaging also reduces the workload on radiologists, allowing them to focus on more complex cases. Radiologists often face high volumes of images to review, which can lead to fatigue and increased risk of errors. AI can handle the initial screening of images, identifying those that require closer examination.

This not only improves the efficiency of radiological departments but also enhances the quality of care. Radiologists can dedicate more time and attention to cases that need their expertise, leading to better patient outcomes. Moreover, by automating routine tasks, AI helps alleviate the burden on radiologists, reducing burnout and improving job satisfaction.

Early Disease Detection

One of the most significant benefits of AI in medical imaging is its potential for early disease detection. Early detection is crucial for the successful treatment of many conditions, such as cancer and cardiovascular diseases. AI's ability to analyze images with high precision means that it can identify early signs of disease that might be overlooked in manual reviews.

For example, AI can detect microscopic changes in tissue that indicate the early stages of cancer. By catching these changes early, health care providers can initiate treatment sooner, improving the chances of successful outcomes. Early detection also means that less invasive treatments may be possible, reducing the overall burden on patients.

Improving Patient Care

The integration of AI in medical imaging is paving the way for more reliable and timely diagnoses, ultimately improving patient care. By enhancing the accuracy and speed of image analysis, AI ensures that patients receive the correct diagnosis and appropriate treatment as quickly as possible.

In addition, AI can help personalize patient care. By analyzing a patient's imaging data alongside their medical history and genetic information, AI can provide insights into the most effective treatment options. This personalized approach leads to better treatment outcomes and improved patient satisfaction.

Summary

AI is revolutionizing the field of medical imaging by enhancing the accuracy and speed of image analysis. AI-powered tools can detect anomalies in radiological images with greater precision than traditional methods, aiding in early disease detection and reducing the workload on radiologists. This capability not only ensures more reliable and timely diagnoses but also improves overall patient care.

As AI technology continues to advance, its role in medical imaging will become increasingly vital. The integration of AI in medical imaging is not just about improving efficiency; it is about transforming health care delivery to provide better outcomes for patients. By leveraging the power of AI, the health care industry can move toward a future where diagnoses are more accurate, treatments are more effective, and patient care is significantly enhanced.[‡]

---

‡ ***AI in Medical Imaging***

TIME
How AI Is Changing Medical Imaging, https://time.com/6227623/ai-medical-imaging-radiology/.

Stanford AIMI Center
Center for Artificial Intelligence in Medicine and Imaging, https://aimi.stanford.edu/.

Google Health
AI Imaging and Diagnostics, https://health.google/health-research/imaging-and-diagnostics/.

AI-Powered Surgical Robots: Transforming Modern Surgery

The advent of surgical robots powered by AI is revolutionizing the field of surgery, bringing unprecedented precision, control, and efficiency to operating rooms worldwide. These advanced systems are transforming surgical procedures, enhancing surgeons' capabilities, and improving patient outcomes.

Precision and Control Beyond Human Capabilities

AI-powered surgical robots are designed to assist surgeons in performing complex procedures with a level of precision and control that surpasses human capabilities. These robots are equipped with highly sensitive instruments and advanced imaging systems that provide surgeons with enhanced visualization of the surgical site.

For example, the da Vinci Surgical System, one of the most widely used surgical robots, features robotic arms that can rotate 360 degrees and move in ways that human hands cannot. This increased range of motion allows surgeons to operate in tight spaces and perform intricate maneuvers with greater ease and accuracy.

Moreover, AI algorithms can filter out natural hand tremors, ensuring that every movement of the robotic instruments is smooth and precise. This level of control is particularly beneficial in delicate procedures, such as neurosurgery or microsurgery, where even the slightest tremor could have significant consequences.

Minimally Invasive Surgeries With High Accuracy

One of the most significant advantages of AI-driven surgical systems is their ability to perform minimally invasive surgeries with high accuracy. Traditional open surgeries often require large incisions, leading to longer recovery times and increased risk of complications. In contrast, robotic systems allow surgeons to operate through small incisions, using tiny instruments and a camera inserted into the patient's body.

AI enhances these minimally invasive techniques by providing real-time analysis of the surgical site. For instance, AI algorithms can process images from the camera, highlighting important structures and potential risks. This augmented reality-like view helps surgeons navigate complex anatomies with greater confidence and precision.

The result is a significant reduction in recovery times and postoperative complications. Patients undergoing robot-assisted surgeries often experience less pain, smaller scars, and faster return to normal activities compared to traditional surgical methods.

Enhancing Surgeons' Abilities in Complex Procedures

AI in surgery doesn't replace surgeons; instead, it enhances their abilities, especially in complex procedures. These systems act as an extension of the surgeon's skills, providing additional capabilities that complement human expertise.

For example, AI can analyze preoperative imaging data to create detailed 3D models of a patient's anatomy. During surgery, this model can be overlaid on the live view of the surgical site, helping surgeons navigate around critical structures with greater accuracy. This is particularly valuable in procedures such as tumor removals, where preserving healthy tissue is crucial.

Additionally, AI can provide real-time recommendations based on vast databases of surgical procedures and outcomes. By analyzing the current state of the surgery and comparing it to similar past cases, AI can suggest optimal next steps or alert surgeons to potential complications before they occur.

Improved Patient Outcomes and Surgical Success Rates

The combination of increased precision, minimally invasive techniques, and enhanced surgical capabilities leads to significantly improved patient outcomes and higher surgical success rates.

Studies have shown that robot-assisted surgeries often result in:

- Reduced blood loss during surgery
- Lower risk of surgical site infections
- Shorter hospital stays
- Faster recovery and return to normal activities
- Reduced postoperative pain and need for pain medication

Moreover, the consistency and precision of robotic systems can help standardize surgical procedures, reducing variability in outcomes between different surgeons or hospitals.

Continuous Learning and Improvement

One of the most exciting aspects of AI in surgery is its ability to learn and improve continuously. Every surgery performed with these systems generates data that can be analyzed to refine surgical techniques and improve outcomes.

ML algorithms can identify patterns and best practices across thousands of procedures, providing insights that can benefit surgeons worldwide. This collective learning accelerates the advancement of surgical techniques and contributes to ongoing improvements in patient care.

Challenges and Future Directions

While the benefits of AI-powered surgical robots are significant, there are challenges to address. These include the following:

- High initial costs of robotic systems
- Need for specialized training for surgeons and operating room staff
- Ensuring data privacy and security
- Addressing potential technical malfunctions during surgery

Despite these challenges, the future of AI in surgery looks promising. Ongoing research is focused on developing more autonomous systems, improving haptic feedback for surgeons, and integrating advanced imaging technologies for even greater precision.

Summary

AI-powered surgical robots are transforming modern surgery by providing unprecedented precision, control, and efficiency. These systems enable minimally invasive procedures with high accuracy, enhance surgeons' abilities to perform complex operations, and lead to improved patient outcomes and increased surgical success rates.

As technology continues to advance, one can expect AI to play an increasingly significant role in surgery, pushing the boundaries of what's possible in medical care. While challenges remain, the potential benefits for patients and health care providers are immense, promising a future where surgeries are safer, less invasive, and more effective than ever before.[§]

[§] ***AI-Powered Surgical Robots***

AI Is Poised to "Revolutionize" Surgery—This article from the American College of Surgeons discusses how AI is transforming surgical care and its potential to revolutionize the field. www.facs.org/for-medical-professionals/news-publications/news-and-articles/bulletin/2023/june-2023-volume-108-issue-6/ai-is-poised-to-revolutionize-surgery/.

Clinical Applications of Artificial Intelligence in Robotic Surgery—This review article from *Journal of Robotic Surgery* outlines recent contributions of AI to robotic surgery, focusing on intraoperative enhancements and ethical considerations. https://link.springer.com/article/10.1007/s11701-024-01867-0.

Advancements in Healthcare: The Impact of AI on Robotic Surgery Systems—This article explores the future applications of AI in robotic surgery, including real time decision making and postoperative care optimization. https://aiupbeat.com/advancements-in-healthcare-the-impact-of-ai-on-robotic-surgery-systems/.

AI in Patient Monitoring: Revolutionizing Health Care With Real-Time Insights

AI is transforming the way health care providers monitor patients, offering real-time insights into patient health that were previously unimaginable. AI-driven monitoring systems continuously track vital signs, detect abnormalities, and alert health care providers to potential issues before they become critical. This proactive approach ensures timely interventions, reduces the risk of complications, and promotes better long-term health outcomes.

Continuous Tracking of Vital Signs

One of the most significant advancements in patient monitoring is the ability of AI to continuously track vital signs. Traditional monitoring methods often involve periodic checks by health care staff, which can miss important changes in a patient's condition. AI-driven systems, on the other hand, can monitor vital signs such as heart rate, blood pressure, respiratory rate, and oxygen levels round the clock.

These systems use sensors and wearable devices to collect data in real time. For example, a patient in a hospital might wear a wristband that continuously monitors their heart rate and sends the data to an AI system for analysis. This constant stream of information allows health care providers to have a comprehensive view of the patient's health status at all times.

Detecting Abnormalities and Early Warning Systems

AI excels at detecting abnormalities in the data it collects. By analyzing patterns and trends, AI can identify signs of potential health issues long before they become critical. For instance, an AI system might detect subtle changes in a patient's heart rate that suggest the early stages of a cardiac event. It can then alert health care providers to take preventive action.

These early warning systems are crucial in preventing complications. In many cases, early detection and intervention can mean the difference between a minor issue and a life-threatening emergency. For example, in patients with chronic conditions such as diabetes or heart disease, AI can monitor blood sugar levels or heart rhythms and alert doctors to any concerning changes, allowing for timely adjustments in treatment.

Proactive Patient Care

The proactive approach enabled by AI-driven monitoring systems ensures that health care providers can intervene before a patient's condition worsens. This is particularly important in critical care settings, where rapid response to changes in a patient's condition can save lives.

For example, in an intensive care unit (ICU), AI can monitor multiple vital signs simultaneously and provide real-time alerts to medical staff if any parameter deviates from the norm. This allows for immediate action, such as administering medication or adjusting ventilator settings, to stabilize the patient.

Reducing the Risk of Complications

By providing continuous monitoring and early detection of potential issues, AI helps reduce the risk of complications. This is especially beneficial for patients with chronic illnesses or those recovering from surgery. Continuous monitoring ensures that any deviations from expected recovery patterns are quickly identified and addressed.

For instance, after a surgical procedure, AI can monitor a patient's vital signs to detect early signs of infection or other complications. By catching these issues early, health care providers can intervene promptly, reducing the likelihood of severe complications and improving recovery outcomes.

AI-Powered Wearables and Remote Monitoring Devices

AI-powered wearables and remote monitoring devices are extending the benefits of continuous monitoring beyond the hospital setting. These devices enable patients to manage their health more effectively from the comfort of their homes.

Wearable devices, such as smartwatches and fitness trackers, can monitor various health metrics, including heart rate, physical activity, and sleep patterns. These devices use AI algorithms to analyze the data and provide personalized health insights and recommendations. For example, a smartwatch might alert a user to irregular heart rhythms and suggest seeking medical advice.

Remote monitoring devices, such as home blood pressure monitors and glucose meters, can transmit data to health care providers in real time. This allows doctors to monitor patient's conditions remotely and make informed decisions about their care. For instance, a patient with hypertension can use a home blood pressure monitor that sends readings to their doctor, who can then adjust medication as needed.

Promoting Better Long-Term Health Outcomes

The continuous, real-time monitoring enabled by AI-powered devices promotes better long-term health outcomes. Patients can take a more active role in managing their health, leading to improved adherence to treatment plans and healthier lifestyles.

For example, a patient with diabetes can use a continuous glucose monitor (CGM) that tracks blood sugar levels throughout the day. The AI system can analyze the data and provide insights into how different foods and activities affect blood sugar levels. This information empowers the patient to make informed decisions about their diet and exercise, leading to better blood sugar control and reduced risk of complications.[5]

---

[5] ***AI in Patient Monitoring***

Patient Safety and Artificial Intelligence in Clinical Care
This article discusses the potential benefits and risks of AI in clinical settings, including patient monitoring. https://jamanetwork.com/journals/jama-health-forum/fullarticle/2815239.

A Deep Dive Into Remote Patient Monitoring
This blog post explores the impact of AI on remote patient monitoring, highlighting its revolutionary effects on health outcomes. https://kms-healthcare.com/blog/the-impact-of-ai-on-healthcare-a-deep-dive-into-remote-patient-monitoring/.

AI in Remote Patient Monitoring—Five Real-Life Examples
This article provides real-life examples of how AI is being used in remote patient monitoring to create personalized healthcare plans. https://bing.com/search?q=AI+in+Patient+Monitoring.

AI-Powered Patient Education Videos

AI-powered patient education videos can address challenges such as ineffective education, poor health literacy, and limited access to reliable information. These videos offer tailored, engaging, and easily understandable content personalized to each patient's needs. They could improve postdischarge outcomes, reduce readmission rates, lower health care costs, and enhance patient satisfaction. They could also address linguistic diversity and low health literacy, making critical health information accessible in vernacular languages and tailored to cultural contexts. These topics are presented hereafter in point form for clarity.

Challenges in Patient Education:

- Ineffective patient education
- Poor health literacy
- Limited access to reliable health information

Potential of AI-Powered Videos:

- Tailored, engaging, and easily understandable content
- Personalized to each patient's unique needs, concerns, and preferences

Impact on Health Care Delivery:

- Improved postdischarge outcomes
- Reduced readmission rates
- Lower health care costs
- Enhanced patient satisfaction and engagement

Impact of Cultural Backgrounds:

- Addressing linguistic diversity and low health literacy
- Making critical health information accessible in vernacular languages
- Tailoring content to specific cultural and socioeconomic contexts

Global Health Organizations' Initiatives:

- WHO's S.A.R.A.H (Smart AI Resource Assistant for Health)**
- Provides information on major health topics
- Communicates in eight languages
- Available on any device
- WHO's Access Initiative for Quitting Tobacco
- NIH's Bridge2AI program

Challenges and Considerations:

- Ensuring accuracy, reliability, and safety of AI-generated content
- Rigorous testing, validation, and ongoing monitoring
- Data privacy, security, and ethical use of patient information
- Equitable access to AI-powered technologies
- Investments in digital infrastructure, device accessibility, and digital literacy programs

Future of Patient-Centered Care:

- Integration of generative AI and personalized video content
- Tailoring care to individual needs, preferences, and circumstances
- Overcoming logistical challenges of creating customized content at scale
- Collaborative efforts to ensure responsible deployment and address challenges

** **The Smart AI Resource Assistant for Health, or S.A.R.A.H.**, is an AI-powered digital health promoter developed by the World Health Organization (WHO). S.A.R.A.H. uses generative AI to provide health information on various topics, including mental health, cancer, heart disease, lung disease, and diabetes. S.A.R.A.H. is available 24/7 in eight languages and can interact with users via video or text. She offers tips on destressing, eating right, quitting tobacco, and more. However, S.A.R.A.H. is not designed to give medical advice.

Global health organizations such as WHO and NIH have initiatives to support AI-powered education, such as WHO's S.A.R.A.H and Access Initiative for Quitting Tobacco, and NIH's Bridge2AI program.[††] Challenges include ensuring accuracy, reliability, safety, data privacy, and equitable access.

The future of patient-centered care involves integrating generative AI and personalized video content, overcoming logistical challenges, and ensuring responsible deployment.

Summary

AI is revolutionizing patient monitoring by providing real-time insights into patient health. AI-driven monitoring systems continuously track vital signs, detect abnormalities, and alert health care providers to potential issues before they become critical. This proactive approach ensures timely interventions, reduces the risk of complications, and promotes better long-term health outcomes.

Additionally, AI-powered wearables and remote monitoring devices enable patients to manage their health more effectively, extending the benefits of continuous monitoring beyond the hospital setting. As AI technology continues to advance, its role in patient monitoring will

---

[††] **The NIH's Bridge2AI program** is an initiative designed to accelerate the use of artificial intelligence in biomedical and behavioral research. The program aims to create high-quality, ethically sourced datasets that are ready for AI analysis. Key goals of the Bridge2AI program include:

- Generating new flagship biomedical and behavioral datasets that are trustworthy and well-defined.
- Developing software and standards to unify data attributes across multiple sources.
- Creating automated tools to create FAIR (Findable, Accessible, Interoperable, and Reusable) datasets.
- Providing resources for data dissemination, ethical principles, tools, and best practices.
- Offering training materials and activities to bridge the AI, biomedical, and behavioral research communities.

become increasingly vital, leading to more personalized, proactive, and effective health care. This transformation promises a future where patients receive the care they need when they need it, ultimately improving health outcomes and quality of life.‡‡

‡‡ ***AI-Powered Patient Education Video***

ChatGPT in Medical Education: Generative AI and the Future of Artificial Intelligence in Health Care
This article discusses how generative AI is being integrated into medical education and its potential impact on patient care. www.ama-assn.org/practice-management/digital/chatgpt-medical-education-generative-ai-and-future-artificial.

How Can Artificial Intelligence Advance Medical Education and Research to Transform Patient Care?
This piece from Yale School of Medicine explores how AI is being used to improve medical education and research, ultimately benefiting patient care. https://medicine.yale.edu/news-article/artificial-intelligence-medical-education-research-patient-care/.

Role of Artificial Intelligence in Patient Education and Clinical Care
This article highlights how AI offers personalized educational materials, virtual consultations, and language translation tools to enhance patient education. https://bing.com/search?q=AI-Powered+Patient+Education.

Harnessing the Power of AI and Personalized Videos: A New Era in Patient Education and Clinical Care
This article discusses the use of AI-powered personalized videos to create content tailored to each patient's unique needs. www.cureus.com/articles/253597.

JAMA's AI in Clinical Practice

The JAMA Network's "AI in Clinical Practice" channel explores how AI is transforming medical practice, training, research, and publishing. It features interviews with clinicians and AI experts discussing various topics, such as:

- **Diagnostic Accuracy**: AI tools for estimating gestational age from ultrasound sweeps.
- **Wearables and Mobile Devices**: The future of patient care using these technologies.
- **Ethics and Bias**: Addressing automation bias and ethical considerations in clinical AI models.
- **Medical Education**: How AI is changing medical education and training.

The channel provides insights into the potential and challenges of integrating AI into health care, aiming to improve patient care and outcomes. Investments in digital infrastructure and literacy programs are essential.[§§]

[§§] ***JAMA's AI in Clinical Practice***

JAMANetwork
The Promise and Pitfalls of AI in the Complex World of Diagnosis, Treatment, and Disease Management, https://jamanetwork.com/journals/jama/article-abstract/2810236.

JAMANetwork
https://jamanetwork.com/channels/ai-in-clinical-practice/pages/podcast (see below).

- Large Language Model–Based Responses to Patients' In-Basket Messages *JAMA Network Open | Audio | July 16,* 2024
- The Future of Wearables and Mobile Devices for Patient Care *JAMA | Audio | July 5,* 2024
- AI and Clinical Practice: Using AI to Increase Access to Reliable Health Information

  JAMA | Audio | April 5, 2024

CHAPTER 9

AI in the Entertainment Industry

AI is making a profound impact across various industries, and the entertainment sector is no exception. This chapter explores the transformative role of AI in the entertainment industry, focusing on three key areas: Film and TV, Gaming, and AR. Each of these domains is experiencing significant advancements due to AI, enhancing creativity, efficiency, and user experience.

AI in Film and TV

AI is revolutionizing the Film and TV industry by automating various aspects of production and postproduction, improving content creation, and enhancing viewer experiences. AI-powered tools can analyze scripts to predict box office success, optimize shooting schedules, and even assist in editing by identifying the best takes from raw footage. Additionally, AI algorithms can personalize content recommendations ensuring viewers find shows and movies that match their preferences. This not only enhances viewer satisfaction but also increases engagement and retention for streaming platforms.

AI in Gaming

The gaming industry is leveraging AI to create more immersive and interactive experiences. AI-driven game design allows for the development of adaptive and intelligent nonplayer characters (NPCs) that can learn and evolve based on player actions, providing a more dynamic and engaging gameplay experience. Procedural content generation, powered by AI, enables the creation of vast, unique game worlds that keep players entertained for longer periods. Furthermore, AI is used in game testing to identify bugs and optimize performance, ensuring a smoother and more enjoyable gaming experience.

AI in Augmented Reality

AR is another area where AI is making significant strides. AI enhances AR applications by improving object recognition, tracking, and interaction. This allows for a more seamless integration of digital elements into the real world, creating more realistic and engaging AR experiences. In entertainment, AI-powered AR can be used for interactive storytelling, immersive gaming, and even live events, where digital content can be overlaid with the physical environment in real time. This fusion of AI and AR opens up new possibilities for creative expression and audience engagement.

In summary, AI is transforming the entertainment industry by enhancing the production and consumption of content in Film and TV, Gaming, and AR. These advancements are not only improving efficiency and creativity but also providing more personalized and immersive experiences for audiences.

As AI technology continues to evolve, its impact on the entertainment industry will only grow, paving the way for even more innovative and engaging forms of entertainment.*

---

* ***AI in the Entertainment Industry***

World Economic Forum
This article discusses six ways AI is likely to disrupt the entertainment industry, including the creation of synthetic voices and digital avatars. www.weforum.org/agenda/2023/08/hollywood-strike-synthetic-voice-digital-avatar-ai-entertainment/.

MIT Sloan Management Review
This piece explores the impact of generative AI on Hollywood, including its potential to create scripts, marketing campaigns, and even movie backdrops. https://sloanreview.mit.edu/article/the-impact-of-generative-ai-on-hollywood-and-entertainment/.

DataForest
This blog post provides a comprehensive overview of how AI is transforming media and entertainment, from content creation to distribution and engagement. https://dataforest.ai/blog/a-handbook-on-ai-in-media-and-entertainment-influence.

AI in Film and TV: Revolutionizing Production and Enhancing Viewer Experience

AI is transforming the Film and TV industry in unprecedented ways, automating various aspects of production and postproduction, improving content creation, and enhancing viewer experiences. This chapter explores how AI-powered tools are revolutionizing the industry, from script analysis to personalized content recommendations.

Automating Production and Postproduction

AI is making significant strides in automating many labor-intensive tasks in film and television production. One of the key areas where AI is having a profound impact is script analysis. AI-powered tools can analyze scripts to predict box office success by examining factors such as plot structure, character development, and dialogue. These tools use ML algorithms to compare new scripts with historical data from successful films, providing producers with valuable insights into a script's potential performance.

In addition to script analysis, AI is optimizing shooting schedules. Traditional scheduling is a complex process that involves coordinating the availability of actors, crew, and locations. AI algorithms can streamline this process by analyzing various constraints and generating the most efficient shooting schedule. This not only saves time but also reduces production costs.

AI is also revolutionizing the editing process. AI-driven systems can review raw footage and identify the best takes, significantly speeding up the editing process. These systems use advanced pattern recognition to detect elements such as facial expressions, lighting, and camera angles, ensuring that the final cut is of the highest quality. By automating these tasks, AI allows editors to focus on the creative aspects of their work, enhancing the overall production quality.

Enhancing Content Creation

AI is not just about automation; it is also enhancing the creative process in film and television. AI-powered tools can assist writers and directors in developing more compelling stories. For instance, AI can analyze audience preferences and trends to suggest plot twists or character arcs that are likely to resonate with viewers. This data-driven approach to storytelling ensures that content is engaging and relevant to the target audience.

Moreover, AI is used to create realistic visual effects. AI algorithms can generate lifelike animations and special effects, reducing the need for expensive and time-consuming manual work. This technology is particularly useful in creating complex scenes that would be difficult to achieve with traditional methods.

Personalizing Viewer Experiences

One of the most visible impacts of AI in the Film and TV industry is the personalization of viewer experiences. Streaming platforms such as Netflix and Amazon Prime use AI algorithms to analyze viewer data and recommend content tailored to individual preferences. These algorithms consider factors such as viewing history, ratings, and even the time of day a user is watching to suggest shows and movies that match their tastes.

This personalization not only enhances viewer satisfaction but also increases engagement and retention. When viewers find content that resonates with them, they are more likely to spend more time on the platform and remain loyal subscribers. This, in turn, boosts the platform's revenue and market share.

Improving Viewer Satisfaction and Engagement

AI's ability to personalize content recommendations is a game-changer for streaming platforms. By understanding viewer preferences, AI can curate a personalized viewing experience that keeps audiences engaged. For example, if a viewer enjoys romantic comedies, the AI algorithm will prioritize recommending similar movies and shows. This targeted approach ensures that viewers always have something they are interested in watching, reducing the likelihood of them switching to a competitor.

Furthermore, AI can analyze viewer feedback and sentiment to improve content quality. By monitoring social media and online reviews, AI can gauge audience reactions to new releases and provide filmmakers with insights into what worked and what didn't. This feedback loop allows creators to refine their content and deliver what the audiences want.

Summary

AI is revolutionizing the Film and TV industry by automating various aspects of production and postproduction, improving content creation, and enhancing viewer experiences. AI-powered tools can analyze scripts to predict box office success, optimize shooting schedules, and assist in editing by identifying the best takes from raw footage. Additionally, AI algorithms can personalize content recommendations, ensuring that viewers find shows and movies that match their preferences. This not only enhances viewer satisfaction but also increases engagement and retention for streaming platforms.

The future of entertainment is here, and AI is at the forefront, transforming how one creates, consumes, and enjoys films and television shows.

As AI technology continues to evolve, its impact on the Film and TV industry will only grow, paving the way for even more innovative and engaging content.[†]

[†] ***AI in Film and TV: Revolutionizing Production and Enhancing Viewer Experience***

AI in Film
Revolutionizing Movie Production, www.alltalent.com/article/ai-in-film-revolutionising-movie-production.

Video Production With AI
Changing the Film Industry, www.gopoint.com/artificial-intelligence-changing-film/.

The Role of AI in Transforming the Magic of Film and Video Production
https://blog.emb.global/the-role-of-ai-in-transforming-production/.

AI in Gaming: Creating Immersive and Interactive Experiences

The gaming industry is transforming, thanks to the integration of AI. AI is enhancing the gaming experience by making it more immersive and interactive. This chapter explores how AI-driven game design allows for the development of adaptive and intelligent NPCs, the creation of vast, unique game worlds through procedural content generation, and the optimization of game testing to ensure a smoother and more enjoyable gaming experience.

Adaptive and Intelligent NPCs

One of the most exciting applications of AI in gaming is the development of adaptive and intelligent NPCs. Traditionally, NPCs followed preprogrammed behaviors, making their actions predictable and often repetitive. AI changes this by enabling NPCs to learn and evolve based on player actions, creating a more dynamic and engaging gameplay experience.

For example, in a stealth game, an AI-driven NPC might learn from previous encounters with the player. If the player consistently uses a particular hiding spot, the NPC can adapt by checking that spot more frequently. This adaptability makes the game more challenging and realistic, as players must continually adjust their strategies.

AI-powered NPCs can also exhibit more lifelike behaviors. They can interact with the game environment and other characters in ways that make the game world feel more alive. For instance, NPCs in a role-playing game might have their daily routines, react to changes in the environment, and remember past interactions with the player. This level of sophistication adds depth to the game, making it more immersive and enjoyable.

Procedural Content Generation

AI is also revolutionizing the way game worlds are created through procedural content generation. This technique uses algorithms to generate game content automatically, rather than having developers create every detail manually. AI-powered procedural generation can create vast, unique game worlds that keep players entertained for longer periods.

For example, in open-world games, AI can generate diverse landscapes, from sprawling forests to bustling cities, each with its unique features and challenges. This not only saves developers time but also ensures that no two playthroughs are the same, providing endless replayability.

AI can also generate quests, characters, and storylines, making each player's experience unique. In a fantasy game, AI might create a quest involving a dragon attack on a village, complete with NPCs who have their backstories and motivations. This dynamic content keeps the game fresh and engaging, as players never know what to expect next.

Optimizing Game Testing

Game testing is a crucial part of the development process, ensuring that games are free of bugs and perform well on various devices. Traditionally, this process involves extensive manual testing, which can be time-consuming and costly. AI is streamlining this process by automating many aspects of game testing.

AI algorithms can simulate thousands of gameplay scenarios in a fraction of the time it would take human testers. These algorithms can identify bugs, performance issues, and balance problems, providing developers with detailed reports on what needs to be fixed. This allows for quicker iterations and improvements, leading to a more polished final product.

Moreover, AI can analyze player behavior data to identify areas where players might struggle or lose interest. By understanding these pain points, developers can make adjustments to improve the overall gameplay experience. For example, if AI detects that players frequently abandon a game at a particular level, developers can investigate and make the level more engaging or easier to navigate.

Enhancing Player Experience

AI's impact on gaming goes beyond development and testing; it also enhances the player experience in real time. AI can personalize gameplay by adjusting difficulty levels based on the player's skill. For instance, if a player is struggling with a particular section of a game, AI can dynamically lower the difficulty to prevent frustration. Conversely, if a player is breezing through the game, AI can introduce new challenges to keep them engaged.

AI can also provide real-time assistance to players. Virtual assistants or AI-driven hints can offer guidance when players are stuck, helping them progress without spoiling the experience. This support makes games more accessible to a wider audience, including those who might be new to gaming.

Summary

AI is revolutionizing the gaming industry by creating more immersive and interactive experiences. AI-driven game design allows for the development of adaptive and intelligent NPCs that learn and evolve based on player actions, providing a dynamic and engaging gameplay experience. Procedural content generation, powered by AI, enables the creation of vast, unique game worlds that keep players entertained for longer periods. Additionally, AI optimizes game testing by identifying bugs and performance issues, ensuring a smoother and more enjoyable gaming experience.

The future of gaming is bright, with AI at the forefront, transforming how games are developed, played, and experienced.

As AI technology continues to advance, its role in gaming will only grow, leading to even more innovative and engaging games.[‡]

---

‡ ***AI in Gaming***

Forbes
"The Gaming Industry's Edge in the Artificial Intelligence Revolution," www.forbes.com/sites/forbesbooksauthors/2024/03/27/the-gaming-industrys-edge-in-the-artificial-intelligence-revolution/.

Columbia Engineering
"AI in Video Games: Transforming the Gaming Industry," https://ai.engineering.columbia.edu/ai-applications/ai-video-games/.

Engati
"AI for Gaming: Enhancing Gameplay with Intelligent Systems," www.engati.com/blog/ai-for-gaming.

AI and Augmented Reality: Transforming Entertainment Experiences

AR is rapidly evolving as a technology, and AI is playing a crucial role in its advancement. This fusion of AI and AR is opening up new possibilities for creative expression and audience engagement in the entertainment industry. From interactive storytelling to immersive gaming and live events, AI-powered AR is creating more realistic and engaging experiences by seamlessly integrating digital elements into the real world.

Enhancing AR Applications With AI

AI is significantly improving AR applications by enhancing three key areas: object recognition, tracking, and interaction. These advancements allow for a more seamless integration of digital elements into the real world, resulting in more realistic and engaging AR experiences.

Object Recognition

AI-powered object recognition enables AR applications to identify and understand real-world objects in real time. This capability is crucial for creating contextually relevant AR experiences. For example, in an AR game, AI can recognize a table in the user's environment and use it as a surface for placing virtual game elements. This level of understanding of the physical world allows for more natural and immersive AR experiences.

Tracking

AI algorithms improve the tracking capabilities of AR applications, allowing digital elements to maintain their position and orientation relative to the real world, even as the user moves around. This enhanced tracking creates a more stable and believable AR experience. For instance, in an AR art exhibition, AI-powered tracking ensures that virtual artworks remain fixed in their designated spaces as viewers move through the gallery.

Interaction

AI enables more natural and intuitive interactions between users and AR content. By analyzing user behavior and gestures, AI can predict user intent and respond accordingly. This capability allows for more engaging and interactive AR experiences. For example, in an AR educational app, AI can recognize when a user is pointing at a specific part of a virtual model and provide relevant information or animations.

AI-Powered AR in Entertainment

The combination of AI and AR is revolutionizing various aspects of the entertainment industry, creating new forms of engagement and immersion.

Interactive Storytelling

AI-powered AR is enabling new forms of interactive storytelling. By understanding the user's environment and actions, AR applications can adapt stories in real time, creating personalized narratives. For example, an AR storybook might use AI to recognize objects in a child's room and incorporate them into the story, making each reading experience unique and engaging.

Immersive Gaming

AR gaming is reaching new levels of immersion with AI integration. AI can generate dynamic game elements that respond to the player's real-world environment, creating more challenging and engaging gameplay. For instance, an AR treasure hunt game might use AI to analyze the player's surroundings and generate hidden clues and puzzles that blend seamlessly with the real world.

Live Events

AI-powered AR is transforming live events by overlaying digital content onto the physical environment in real time. This technology can enhance concerts, sports events, and theatrical performances. For example, at a music concert, AR could display lyrics, visual effects, or even virtual band members that interact with the real performers, all powered by AI that responds to the music and crowd reactions.

Creative Expression and Audience Engagement

The fusion of AI and AR is opening up new possibilities for creative expression and audience engagement. Artists and content creators can now design interactive experiences that blur the line between the digital and physical worlds.

Interactive Art Installations

AI-powered AR enables artists to create dynamic, responsive art installations. These installations can change and evolve based on audience interaction, time of day, or even data from external sources such as social media. For example, an AR mural could use AI to analyze pedestrian traffic and change its appearance throughout the day, creating a constantly evolving piece of public art.

Personalized Entertainment Experiences

AI can analyze user preferences and behavior to create personalized AR experiences. This capability allows entertainment companies to tailor content to individual users, increasing engagement and satisfaction. For instance, a theme park could use AR to provide personalized experiences for each visitor, with AI adjusting the virtual elements based on the visitor's age, interests, and previous interactions.

Enhanced Social Interactions

AI-powered AR can facilitate new forms of social interaction in entertainment settings. By recognizing users and their relationships, AR applications can create shared experiences that enhance social connections. For example, at a sporting event, AR could display personalized stats and replays for fans, while also facilitating virtual high-fives between friends watching from different locations.

Summary

The integration of AI and AR is transforming the entertainment industry, creating more immersive, interactive, and personalized experiences.

From enhancing AR applications with improved object recognition, tracking, and interaction, to enabling new forms of storytelling, gaming, and live events, AI-powered AR is opening up exciting possibilities for creative expression and audience engagement.

The fusion of AI and AR has the potential to revolutionize how one consumes and interacts with entertainment, blurring the lines between the digital and physical worlds in various ways.

As these technologies continue to evolve, one can expect to see even more innovative applications in the entertainment industry.[§]

[§] ***AI and Augmented Reality***

Using AI to Create Better Virtual Reality Experiences
This article from Stanford Report discusses how AI is being used to improve 3D displays for virtual and augmented reality technologies. https://news.stanford.edu/stories/2021/11/using-ai-create-better-virtual-reality-experiences.

AR and AI: The Role of AI in Augmented Reality
GeeksforGeeks explores the crucial role AI plays in creating and advancing augmented reality experiences. www.geeksforgeeks.org/ar-and-ai-the-role-of-ai-in-augmented-reality/.

AR and AI: The Role of AI in Augmented Reality
Analytics Vidhya examines how AI and AR can be used together to create more efficient and immersive experiences. www.analyticsvidhya.com/blog/2023/09/ar-and-ai/.

PART 3

Implementing AI Responsibly

As AI continues to revolutionize industries and transform our lives and work, it is imperative to address the ethical, governance, and security challenges that accompany its rapid development.

This section, "Implementing AI Responsibly," delves into the critical aspects of AI ethics and governance, as well as AI data privacy and cybersecurity, to ensure that AI technologies are developed and deployed in a manner that is both ethical and secure.

AI Ethics and Governance

AI ethics and governance are foundational to the responsible implementation of AI. Ethical considerations encompass a wide range of issues, including fairness, transparency, accountability, and the prevention of bias. It is essential to establish robust governance frameworks that guide the ethical development and use of AI systems. These frameworks should include clear guidelines, standards, and best practices to ensure that AI technologies are aligned with societal values and human rights.

AI Data Privacy and Cybersecurity

Data privacy and cybersecurity are paramount in the age of AI, where vast amounts of data are collected, processed, and analyzed. Protecting sensitive information and ensuring the security of AI systems are critical to maintaining trust and preventing malicious activities.

By addressing these key topics, "Implementing AI Responsibly" aims to provide a comprehensive understanding of the ethical, governance, and security considerations necessary for the responsible development and deployment of AI technologies. Through thoughtful and informed approaches, one can harness the power of AI while mitigating potential risks and ensuring a positive impact on society.

This section explores the importance of implementing strong data privacy measures, such as data anonymization and encryption, as well as robust cybersecurity practices to safeguard AI systems from threats and vulnerabilities.

CHAPTER 10

AI Ethics and Governance

AI has become an integral part of our society, transforming industries and reshaping businesses. As AI systems become more sophisticated and pervasive, it is crucial to address the ethical implications and governance challenges that arise from their development and deployment. This chapter explores the critical aspects of AI Ethics and Governance, focusing on four key areas: Ethical AI Principles, Mitigating AI Bias and Discrimination, AI Governance Frameworks, and Explainable AI.

Ethical AI Principles

As AI systems increasingly impact our lives, it is essential to establish a set of ethical principles to guide their development and use. These principles aim to ensure that AI technologies are designed and implemented in ways that respect human rights, promote fairness, and contribute positively to society. This section examines various ethical frameworks proposed by organizations and governments worldwide, discussing their commonalities and differences.

Mitigating AI Bias and Discrimination

AI systems, despite their potential for objectivity, can perpetuate and even amplify existing biases present in their training data or design. This section delves into the causes of AI bias, its potential consequences, and strategies for identifying and mitigating these biases. This section explores case studies that highlight the importance of diverse and representative datasets, as well as the need for ongoing monitoring and adjustment of AI systems to ensure fair and equitable outcomes.

AI Governance Frameworks

As AI technologies become more complex and influential, there is a growing need for robust governance frameworks to regulate their development and use. This section examines various approaches to AI governance, including national and international initiatives, industry self-regulation, and multistakeholder collaborations. This section discusses the challenges of creating effective governance structures that balance innovation with responsible development and use of AI.

Explainable AI

The increasing complexity of AI systems often makes it difficult for users and stakeholders to understand how these systems arrive at their decisions. Explainable AI (XAI) aims to make AI systems more transparent and interpretable, allowing humans to understand, trust, and effectively manage AI-driven decisions. This section explores the importance of XAI, various techniques for achieving explainability, and the trade-offs between model performance and interpretability.

Summary

In summary, this chapter provides a comprehensive overview of the ethical and governance challenges posed by AI technologies. Examining these four key areas aims to foster a deeper understanding of the complexities involved in ensuring that AI systems are developed and deployed in ways that are ethical, fair, and beneficial to society as a whole.*

---

* ***AI Ethics and Governance***

Ethics and Governance of AI at Berkman Klein Center
This page from the Berkman Klein Center explores the impact, governance, ethics, and accountability of AI technologies. https://cyber.harvard.edu/topics/ethics-and-governance-ai.

Global AI Ethics and Governance Observatory by UNESCO
UNESCO's platform provides insights, good practices, and tools for ethical and responsible AI governance. www.unesco.org/ethics-ai/en.

Framework for AI Regulation and Governance
This article from Springer develops a conceptual framework for regulating AI, covering all stages of public policy-making. https://link.springer.com/article/10.1007/s10676-021-09593-z.

The Need for Ethical AI Principles

As AI systems increasingly impact our lives, it has become essential to establish ethical principles to guide their development and use. These principles aim to ensure that AI technologies respect human rights, promote fairness, and contribute positively to society. Let us explore why these principles are crucial and examine some of the ethical frameworks proposed by various organizations and governments.

AI technologies are rapidly becoming integrated into many aspects of our daily lives, from health care and education to finance and transportation. While these technologies offer tremendous benefits, they also raise significant ethical concerns. Without proper guidance, AI systems could:

- Perpetuate or amplify existing biases and discrimination
- Infringe on privacy and personal freedoms
- Make decisions that impact human lives without accountability
- Be used for malicious purposes or cause unintended harm

Establishing ethical principles for AI helps address these concerns by providing a framework for responsible development and deployment. These principles serve as a moral compass, ensuring that AI technologies align with human values and societal norms.

Core Objectives of Ethical AI Principles

The fundamental goals of ethical AI principles:

- Respecting human rights and dignity
- Promoting fairness and nondiscrimination
- Ensuring transparency and accountability
- Protecting privacy and data rights
- Prioritizing human well-being societal benefit
- Maintaining human oversight and control

By adhering to these objectives, AI systems can be designed and implemented in ways that contribute positively to society while minimizing potential harm.

Examining Ethical Frameworks Worldwide

Various organizations and governments have proposed ethical frameworks for AI. Let us examine some of the most prominent ones and discuss their commonalities and differences.

UNESCO Recommendation on the Ethics of AI

UNESCO's framework, adopted by 193 countries in 2021, emphasizes four core values:

- Respect, protection, and promotion of human rights and fundamental freedoms
- Environmental and ecosystem flourishing
- Ensuring diversity and inclusiveness
- Living in peaceful, just, and interconnected societies

This framework takes a broad approach, addressing not only individual rights but also environmental concerns and societal harmony.

European Union's Ethics Guidelines for Trustworthy AI

The EU's guidelines focus on seven key requirements:

- Human agency and oversight
- Technical robustness and safety
- Privacy and data governance
- Transparency
- Diversity, nondiscrimination, and fairness
- Societal and environmental well-being
- Accountability

These guidelines emphasize the importance of human control over AI systems and the need for technical reliability.

IEEE Global Initiative on Ethics of Autonomous and Intelligent Systems

The IEEE's framework includes principles such as:

- Human Rights
- Well-Being
- Data Agency
- Effectiveness
- Transparency
- Accountability
- Awareness of Misuse
- Competence

This framework places a strong emphasis on the technical aspects of AI development and the need for competent design and implementation.

OECD AI Principles

The Organization for Economic Cooperation and Development (OECD) has proposed five principles:

- Inclusive growth, sustainable development, and well-being
- Human-centered values and fairness
- Transparency and explainability
- Robustness, security, and safety
- Accountability

The OECD principles focus on the broader societal impacts of AI, including economic growth and sustainable development.

Commonalities and Differences

While these frameworks have distinct approaches, several common themes emerge:

- **Human Rights:** All frameworks emphasize the importance of respecting human rights and dignity.

- **Fairness and Nondiscrimination:** There's a universal recognition of the need to prevent and mitigate bias in AI systems.
- **Transparency and Accountability:** The importance of explainable AI and clear lines of responsibility is consistently highlighted.
- **Privacy Protection:** Safeguarding personal data and respecting privacy rights is a common concern.
- **Human Oversight:** Most frameworks stress the need for human control over AI systems.

However, there are also notable differences:

- **Scope:** Some frameworks, like UNESCO's, take a broader view that includes environmental concerns, while others focus more narrowly on technical and social aspects.
- **Emphasis:** The IEEE framework places more emphasis on technical competence, while the OECD principles highlight economic considerations.
- **Level of Detail:** Some frameworks provide more specific guidelines, while others offer broader principles.
- **Cultural Context:** Different frameworks may reflect the cultural and societal values of the regions they originate from.

Implementing Ethical AI Principles

While establishing ethical principles is crucial, implementing them in practice presents challenges. Organizations and governments are taking various approaches to turn these principles into actionable policies:

- **Legislation and Regulation:** Some jurisdictions are developing laws and regulations to enforce ethical AI practices.
- **Industry Self-Regulation:** Many tech companies are establishing their own ethical guidelines and review processes.
- **Education and Training:** There's a growing emphasis on educating AI developers and users about ethical considerations.

- **Ethics Review Boards:** Some organizations are creating dedicated boards to oversee AI development and deployment.
- **Auditing and Certification:** Efforts are underway to develop auditing processes and certification standards for ethical AI.

Summary

As AI continues to shape our world, establishing and adhering to ethical principles is essential for ensuring that these powerful technologies benefit humanity while minimizing potential harm. The various frameworks proposed by organizations and governments worldwide share common goals of protecting human rights, promoting fairness, and ensuring accountability. While there are differences in emphasis and approach, these frameworks collectively provide a solid foundation for the responsible development and use of AI.

Moving forward, it will be crucial to continue refining these principles, adapting them to new challenges, and most importantly, translating them into practical, enforceable guidelines that shape the AI landscape for the better.

The journey toward ethical AI is ongoing, requiring collaboration between technologists, policy makers, ethicists, and the public.

By working together to uphold these principles, one can harness the full potential of AI while safeguarding the values that are fundamental to society.[†]

[†] ***The Need for Ethical AI Principles***

AI Ethics 1—Governance | Amii Training
A workshop designed to build awareness of best practices in AI standards and governance for organizations. www.amii.ca/ai-literacy/training/ai-ethics-1-governance/.

UNESCO's Recommendation on the Ethics of Artificial Intelligence
UNESCO's global standard on AI ethics, adopted by 193 Member States, guiding ethical AI governance. www.unesco.org/en/artificial-intelligence/recommendation-ethics.

Global AI Ethics and Governance Observatory—UNESCO
A platform offering resources and insights on AI ethics and governance for policy makers, regulators, and academics. www.unesco.org/ethics-ai/en.

AI Bias: Causes, Consequences, and Mitigation Strategies

AI systems have the potential to be objective and unbiased decision makers, free from human prejudices and emotions. However, in reality, AI systems can perpetuate and even amplify existing biases present in their training data or design. This chapter explores the causes of AI bias, its potential consequences, and strategies for identifying and mitigating these biases.

Causes of AI Bias

AI bias can stem from various sources, including:

- **Biased Training Data:** AI systems learn from historical data, which may contain societal biases and prejudices. If this biased data is used to train AI models, the resulting systems can perpetuate and amplify these biases.
- **Lack of Diverse Data:** When training data doesn't represent the full diversity of the population, AI systems may perform poorly for underrepresented groups.
- **Biased Algorithm Design:** The choices made by developers in designing AI algorithms can inadvertently introduce bias. This can include selecting certain features over others or making assumptions about the data.
- **Historical Discrimination:** In some cases, AI systems may accurately reflect historical patterns of discrimination, leading to biased outcomes even when the system is functioning as intended.
- **Feedback Loops:** When AI systems are deployed and start making decisions, they can create feedback loops that reinforce existing biases over time.

Potential Consequences of AI Bias

The consequences of AI bias can be far-reaching and severe:

- **Discrimination:** Biased AI systems can lead to unfair treatment of certain groups in areas such as hiring, lending, criminal justice, and health care.

- **Reinforcement of Stereotypes:** AI systems can perpetuate and amplify harmful stereotypes, leading to further marginalization of certain groups.
- **Economic Disparities:** Biased AI in areas such as credit scoring or job recruitment can exacerbate economic inequalities.
- **Erosion of Trust:** As biases in AI systems are exposed, it can lead to a loss of public trust in AI technologies and the organizations using them.
- **Legal and Regulatory Risks:** Companies using biased AI systems may face legal challenges and regulatory scrutiny.

Case Studies Highlighting AI Bias

Several high-profile cases have brought attention to the issue of AI bias:

- **Amazon's Recruiting Tool:** Amazon developed an AI-based recruiting tool that showed bias against women. The system was trained on resumes submitted to the company over 10 years, most of which came from men. As a result, the AI learned to prefer male candidates and penalize resumes that included the word "women's" or mentioned all-women's colleges.
- **COMPAS Recidivism Algorithm:** The Correctional Offender Management Profiling for Alternative Sanctions (COMPAS) algorithm, used in the U.S. criminal justice system to predict recidivism risk, was found to be biased against Black defendants. It falsely labeled black defendants as future criminals at almost twice the rate as white defendants.
- **Gender Bias in Machine Translation:** Google Translate has been found to exhibit gender bias when translating gender-neutral languages to English. For example, it often defaults to male pronouns for certain professions such as doctor or engineer, while using female pronouns for occupations such as nurse or teacher.
- **Facial Recognition Systems:** Multiple studies have shown that facial recognition systems perform less accurately for women and people with darker skin tones. This bias can lead to serious consequences in areas such as law enforcement and border control.

To address AI bias, organizations and researchers are developing various strategies:

- **Diverse and Representative Datasets:** Ensuring that training data is diverse and representative of all groups is crucial. This may involve collecting additional data from underrepresented groups or using techniques such as data augmentation to balance datasets.
- **Bias Detection Tools:** Developing and using tools that can detect bias in datasets and AI models. These tools can analyze the input data, the model's decision-making process, and its outputs to identify potential biases.
- **Fairness Metrics:** Implementing fairness metrics to evaluate AI systems. These metrics can help quantify whether a system is treating different groups equitably.
- **Explainable AI:** Developing AI systems that can explain their decision-making processes. This transparency can help identify the sources of bias and make it easier to correct them.
- **Diverse Development Teams:** Ensuring diversity in AI development teams can help bring different perspectives and experiences to the design process, potentially catching biases that might otherwise go unnoticed.
- **Ongoing Monitoring and Adjustment:** Regularly monitoring AI systems in real-world use and adjusting them as needed. This includes tracking performance across different demographic groups and updating models when biases are detected.
- **Ethical Guidelines and Governance:** Implementing strong ethical guidelines and governance structures for AI development and deployment. This can include ethics review boards and clear processes for addressing bias when it is detected.
- **Regulatory Compliance:** Staying informed about and complying with emerging regulations related to AI fairness and nondiscrimination.
- **Stakeholder Engagement:** Engaging with diverse stakeholders, including potentially affected communities, to understand their concerns and perspectives on AI systems.

- **Education and Awareness:** Providing education and training on AI bias to developers, users, and decision makers to increase awareness and promote responsible AI development and use.

Summary

AI bias is a complex issue that requires ongoing attention and effort to address. While AI systems have the potential to be more objective than humans, they can also perpetuate and amplify existing biases if not carefully designed and monitored. By understanding the causes of AI bias, recognizing its potential consequences, and implementing strategies to identify and mitigate bias, one can work toward creating AI systems that are fair, equitable, and beneficial for all.

As AI continues to play an increasingly important role in our society, addressing bias in these systems is not just a technical challenge but an ethical imperative. It requires collaboration between technologists, ethicists, policy makers, and diverse stakeholders to ensure that AI systems are developed and deployed in ways that promote fairness and equality.[‡]

[‡] ***AI Bias: Causes, Consequences, and Mitigation Strategies***

AI Governance Frameworks: Mitigating Risks and Ensuring Ethical AI Use | Shelf.io
An exploration of AI governance frameworks, their importance, and how to create and implement them effectively. https://shelf.io/blog/ai-governance-framework/.

Developing an Artificial Intelligence Governance Framework | ISACA
A guide on creating AI governance frameworks to ensure transparency, ethical use, and compliance with regulations. www.isaca.org/resources/news-and-trends/newsletters/atisaca/2022/volume-38/developing-an-artificial-intelligence-governance-framework.

AI Governance Framework | Artificial Intelligence Governance and Auditing
A practice-oriented framework for implementing responsible AI, aligned with the OECD's AI system lifecycle framework. https://ai-governance.eu.

The Growing Need for Robust AI Governance Frameworks

As AI technologies become more complex and influential, the necessity for robust governance frameworks to regulate their development and use has never been more critical. These frameworks aim to ensure that AI systems are developed responsibly, ethically, and in a manner that aligns with societal values. This chapter explores the importance of AI governance, various approaches to implementing it, and the challenges involved in balancing innovation with responsible AI development.

Why AI Governance Is Essential

AI technologies are now integral to many aspects of our lives, from health care and finance to transportation and entertainment. While AI offers significant benefits, it also poses risks, such as bias, discrimination, privacy violations, and the potential for misuse. Without proper governance, these risks can lead to harmful consequences, undermining public trust in AI systems.

AI governance refers to the strategies, policies, and technical guardrails that guide and regulate the development and use of AI. It encompasses ethical considerations, regulatory compliance, and the technical structures that manage data flow and algorithmic decision making. The goal is to ensure that AI technologies are used safely, fairly, and for the public good, balancing innovation with societal needs.

Approaches to AI Governance

Various approaches to AI governance have been proposed and implemented by organizations and governments worldwide. These approaches include national and international initiatives, industry self-regulation, and multistakeholder collaborations.

National and International Initiatives

Governments around the world are developing national strategies and regulatory frameworks to govern AI. For example:

- **European Union:** The European Union has established the Ethics Guidelines for Trustworthy AI, which outline seven key requirements, including human agency, technical robustness, privacy, transparency, diversity, societal well-being, and accountability. These guidelines aim to ensure that AI systems are trustworthy and align with European values.
- **United States:** The United States has developed the National AI Initiative, which focuses on promoting AI innovation while ensuring ethical considerations and regulatory compliance. This initiative includes efforts to develop standards for AI safety, fairness, and transparency.
- **China:** China has implemented comprehensive AI governance policies that emphasize the importance of ethical AI development, data security, and regulatory oversight. These policies aim to position China as a global leader in AI while addressing potential risks.

Industry Self-Regulation

Many tech companies and industry groups are taking proactive steps to self-regulate AI development and use. These efforts include the following:

- **Ethical Guidelines:** Companies such as Google, Microsoft, and IBM have established their ethical guidelines for AI. These guidelines often cover principles such as fairness, transparency, accountability, and privacy.
- **Ethics Review Boards:** Some organizations have created internal ethics review boards to oversee AI projects and ensure that they adhere to ethical standards. These boards typically include experts from diverse fields, such as ethics, law, and technology.

Multistakeholder Collaborations

Effective AI governance often requires collaboration among various stakeholders, including governments, industry, academia, and civil society. Examples of such collaborations:

- **Partnership on AI:** This multistakeholder organization includes members from tech companies, nonprofits, and academic institutions. It aims to promote responsible AI development and address ethical challenges through research, advocacy, and best practices.
- **IEEE Global Initiative on Ethics of Autonomous and Intelligent Systems:** This initiative brings together experts from around the world to develop ethical guidelines and standards for AI. It focuses on ensuring that AI technologies benefit humanity and respect human rights.

Challenges in AI Governance

Creating effective governance structures for AI is challenging due to several factors:

Balancing Innovation and Regulation

One of the primary challenges is finding the right balance between fostering innovation and implementing necessary regulations. Overly restrictive regulations can stifle innovation and hinder the development of beneficial AI technologies. Conversely, insufficient regulation can lead to ethical lapses, privacy violations, and other risks.

Ensuring Global Consistency

AI technologies are developed and deployed globally, making it essential to have consistent governance frameworks across different regions. However, cultural, legal, and political differences can complicate efforts to create universal standards. International cooperation and harmonization of regulations are crucial to addressing this challenge.

Addressing Bias and Discrimination

AI systems can perpetuate and even amplify existing biases present in their training data. Ensuring fairness and nondiscrimination in AI requires continuous monitoring, diverse datasets, and robust bias mitigation strategies. This is an ongoing challenge that requires collaboration between developers, policy makers, and stakeholders.

AI systems, particularly those based on complex ML models, can be difficult to understand and explain. Ensuring transparency and explainability is essential for building trust and accountability. However, achieving this without compromising the performance of AI systems is a technical challenge that requires innovative solutions.

Summary

As AI technologies become more complex and influential, robust governance frameworks are essential to ensure their responsible development and use. Various approaches to AI governance, including national and international initiatives, industry self-regulation, and multistakeholder collaborations, aim to address the ethical, legal, and technical challenges posed by AI. Balancing innovation with responsible AI development is a complex task that requires continuous effort and collaboration among diverse stakeholders.

By establishing and adhering to robust governance frameworks, one can harness the full potential of AI while safeguarding human rights, promoting fairness, and ensuring that AI technologies contribute positively to society.[§]

[§] ***The Growing Need for Robust AI Governance Framework***

Key Elements of a Robust AI Governance Framework
This article explores the essential components of AI governance, focusing on ethical considerations, legal compliance, and balancing innovation with potential risks. https://transcend.io/blog/ai-governance-framework.

AI Governance Framework—Artificial Intelligence Governance and Auditing
This site provides a practice-oriented framework for implementing responsible AI, aligned with the OECD's AI system lifecycle framework and European AI regulations. https://ai-governance.eu.

What Is AI Governance? | IBM
This page explains AI governance, its importance, and how it ensures that AI tools and systems remain safe, ethical, and aligned with societal values. www.ibm.com/topics/ai-governance.

Understanding the Complexity of AI Systems and the Role of Explainable AI

AI systems have become increasingly complex, making it difficult for users and stakeholders to understand how these systems arrive at their decisions. This complexity arises primarily from the advanced algorithms and vast amounts of data that AI systems process.

For instance, deep learning models, which are a subset of ML, consist of multiple layers of neural networks that can process data in ways that are not easily interpretable by humans. These models are often referred to as "black boxes" because their internal workings are opaque even to the engineers who design them.

The black-box nature of these models poses significant challenges. Users and stakeholders, including business leaders, regulators, and the general public, may find it hard to trust AI systems if they cannot understand how decisions are made. This lack of transparency can lead to skepticism and resistance to adopting AI technologies, especially in critical areas such as health care, finance, and criminal justice, where the consequences of decisions can be profound.

Explainable AI (XAI): Making AI Transparent and Interpretable

XAI aims to address these challenges by making AI systems more transparent and interpretable. XAI involves a set of processes and methods that allow human users to comprehend and trust the results produced by ML algorithms. By providing clear explanations of how AI models work and how they arrive at specific decisions, XAI helps build trust and confidence in AI systems.

Importance of XAI

The importance of XAI cannot be overstated. It plays a crucial role in several key areas:

1. **Trust and Accountability:** By making AI decisions understandable, XAI helps build trust among users and stakeholders. This is par-

ticularly important in regulated industries where accountability is paramount.

2. **Compliance and Regulation:** Many industries are subject to regulatory requirements that mandate transparency in decision-making processes. XAI helps organizations comply with these regulations by providing clear explanations of AI decisions.
3. **Bias and Fairness:** XAI can help identify and mitigate biases in AI models. By understanding how decisions are made, developers can detect and address any unfair biases that may exist in the data or algorithms.
4. **Improved Decision Making:** When users understand how AI systems work, they can make better-informed decisions. This is particularly important in high-stakes environments where the consequences of decisions can be significant.

Techniques for Achieving Explainability

Several techniques have been developed to achieve explainability in AI systems. These techniques can be broadly categorized into model-specific and model-agnostic methods.

Model-Specific Techniques

Model-specific techniques are designed for particular types of AI models. For example:

- **Decision Trees:** These models are inherently interpretable because they make decisions based on a series of simple rules. Each decision path can be easily traced and understood by users.
- **Rule-Based Systems**: Similar to decision trees, rule-based systems use predefined rules to make decisions, making them transparent and easy to interpret.

Model-Agnostic Techniques

Model-agnostic techniques can be applied to any type of AI model. Some of the most popular model-agnostic techniques include the following:

- **Local Interpretable Model-Agnostic Explanations (LIME):** LIME explains the predictions of any classifier by approximating it locally with an interpretable model. It generates explanations by perturbing the input data and observing the changes in the output.
- **Shapley Additive exPlanations (SHAP):** SHAP values are based on cooperative game theory and provide a unified measure of feature importance. They explain the output of any ML model by attributing the prediction to each feature.
- **Counterfactual Explanations:** These explanations provide insights by showing how the input data would need to change to achieve a different outcome. This helps users understand the decision boundaries of the model.

Trade-Offs Between Model Performance and Interpretability

One of the significant challenges in implementing XAI is balancing the trade-offs between model performance and interpretability. Highly complex models, such as deep neural networks, often achieve superior performance in terms of accuracy and predictive power. However, their complexity makes them less interpretable.

On the other hand, simpler models, such as linear regression or decision trees, are more interpretable but may not perform as well on complex tasks. Organizations need to weigh these trade-offs carefully. In some cases, it may be acceptable to sacrifice a degree of performance for the sake of transparency and trust. In other scenarios, particularly where accuracy is critical, more complex models may be justified despite their lack of interpretability.

Summary

The increasing complexity of AI systems poses significant challenges for users and stakeholders in understanding how these systems make decisions. XAI addresses these challenges by making AI models more transparent and interpretable. Through various techniques, XAI helps build trust, ensure compliance, mitigate biases, and improve decision making.

However, achieving explainability often involves trade-offs between model performance and interpretability, requiring careful consideration by organizations.

As AI continues to evolve, the role of XAI will become increasingly important in ensuring responsible and ethical AI deployment.[9]

[9] ***Understanding the Complexity of AI Systems and the Role of Explainable***

The Role of Explainable AI in AI Ethics Research
This article presents a systematic mapping study on the role of explainable AI in the field of AI ethics. https://dl.acm.org/doi/10.1145/3599974.

AI Ethics and eXplainable AI (XAI): Much Easier Said Than Done
This blog post discusses the challenges and importance of integrating ethics into AI and the role of explainable AI in building trust. www.isaca.org/resources/news-and-trends/isaca-now-blog/2022/ai-ethics-and-explainable-ai.

Explainable AI: Getting It Right in Business
This article explores the necessity of explainable AI for businesses, highlighting best practices and strategies for implementation. www.mckinsey.com/capabilities/quantumblack/our-insights/why-businesses-need-explainable-ai-and-how-to-deliver-it.

CHAPTER 11

AI Data Privacy and Cybersecurity

AI has revolutionized the way one handles data, bringing both unprecedented opportunities and significant challenges. As AI systems become more integrated into various aspects of our lives, concerns about data privacy and security have become paramount. This chapter delves into the critical topics of Data Privacy Regulations, Securing AI Systems, Federated Learning, and AI Cybersecurity Applications, providing a comprehensive overview of the measures necessary to protect personal information in an AI-driven world.

Data Privacy Regulations

Data privacy regulations are essential for ensuring that personal information is collected, stored, and processed responsibly. Regulations such as the General Data Protection Regulation (GDPR) in the European Union and the California Consumer Privacy Act (CCPA) in the United States set stringent rules for data handling, requiring explicit consent for data usage and giving individuals greater control over their personal information. These regulations mandate transparency in data practices, ensuring that AI systems operate within ethical and legal boundaries. Compliance with these regulations is crucial for organizations to avoid legal repercussions and build trust with users.

Securing AI Systems

Securing AI systems involves implementing robust measures to protect them from cyber threats and unauthorized access. As AI systems often handle sensitive data, they are attractive targets for cybercriminals. Effective security strategies include encryption, access controls, and regular security audits to identify and mitigate vulnerabilities. Additionally, incorporating privacy by design principles ensures that data protection is integrated into the development process of AI systems, rather than an afterthought. By prioritizing security, organizations can safeguard their AI systems against potential breaches and maintain the integrity of the data they handle.

Federated Learning

Federated Learning (FL) is an innovative approach that addresses privacy concerns by allowing AI models to be trained across multiple decentralized devices without sharing raw data. This technique ensures that personal data remains on local devices, reducing the risk of data breaches and enhancing privacy. FL enables organizations to leverage the power of AI while adhering to data privacy regulations and minimizing the exposure of sensitive information. This approach is particularly beneficial in industries such as health care and finance, where data privacy is of utmost importance.

AI Cybersecurity Applications

AI itself can be a powerful tool in enhancing cybersecurity. AI-driven cybersecurity applications can detect and respond to threats in real time, providing a proactive defense against cyberattacks. These applications use ML algorithms to identify patterns and anomalies in network traffic, enabling them to detect potential threats more accurately and quickly than traditional methods. By continuously learning from new data, AI cybersecurity systems can adapt to evolving threats, offering a dynamic and robust defense mechanism. However, it is crucial to ensure that these AI systems are also secure and transparent to prevent them from becoming targets themselves.

Summary

The integration of AI into various sectors brings both opportunities and challenges in terms of data privacy and security. By adhering to data privacy regulations, securing AI systems, leveraging FL, and utilizing AI for cybersecurity, organizations can navigate the complexities of protecting personal information in an AI-driven world.

As technology continues to evolve, ongoing efforts to enhance data privacy and security will be essential in building trust and ensuring the ethical use of AI.*

---

* ***Data Privacy and Cybersecurity***

Artificial Intelligence and Privacy: Issues and Challenges
This resource provides a high-level understanding of AI and its uses in the public sector, highlighting the challenges and opportunities related to information privacy. https://ovic.vic.gov.au/privacy/resources-for-organisations/artificial-intelligence-and-privacy-issues-and-challenges.

AI in Data Privacy and Security
This paper explores the transformative impact of AI on data privacy and security, discussing traditional methodologies, AI applications, and ethical concerns. www.researchgate.net/publication/378288596_AI_in_Data_Privacy_and_Security.

Generative AI Privacy: Issues, Challenges, and How to Protect
This guide explores the intersection of Generative AI and privacy protection, detailing challenges and safeguarding tips for organizations. https://securiti.ai/generative-ai-privacy/.

The Importance of Data Privacy Regulations in AI

As AI systems become more sophisticated and integrated into various aspects of our lives, the need for robust data privacy regulations has never been more critical. These regulations ensure that personal information is collected, stored, and processed responsibly and protect individuals from unauthorized access and misuse. This section explores the significance of data privacy regulations, focusing on the GDPR in the European Union and the CCPA in the United States.

This section discusses how these regulations mandate transparency in data practices, ensuring that AI systems operate within ethical and legal boundaries, and why compliance is crucial for organizations.

Understanding Data Privacy Regulations

Data privacy regulations are designed to govern the responsible handling, protection, and control of individuals' personal information. These laws aim to prevent unauthorized access, misuse, and potential harm that can arise from data breaches. By setting stringent rules for data handling, these regulations ensure that personal information is treated with utmost care and respect.

General Data Protection Regulation (GDPR)

The GDPR, implemented in May 2018, is one of the most comprehensive data privacy regulations globally. It applies to all organizations operating within the European Union, as well as those outside the European Union that offer goods or services to EU residents. The GDPR mandates that organizations obtain explicit consent from individuals before collecting their data. It also grants individuals the right to access, correct, and delete their personal information. The regulation emphasizes transparency, requiring organizations to communicate how they collect, use, and protect personal data.

California Consumer Privacy Act (CCPA)

The CCPA, effective from January 2020, is a landmark data privacy law in the United States. It provides California residents with significant control over their personal information. Similar to the GDPR, the CCPA requires businesses to obtain explicit consent from consumers before collecting their data. It also gives individuals the right to know what personal information is collected, the purpose of collection, and the ability to opt out of the sale of their data. The CCPA aims to enhance transparency and accountability in data practices, ensuring that consumers are informed and empowered.

Mandating Transparency in Data Practices

Both GDPR and CCPA mandate transparency in how organizations handle personal data. This transparency is crucial for several reasons:

1. **Building Trust:** When organizations are transparent about their data practices, it builds trust with consumers. Individuals are more likely to share their personal information if they understand how it will be used and protected. Transparency helps establish a sense of security and confidence in the organization.
2. **Ensuring Accountability:** Transparency ensures that organizations are held accountable for their data practices. By clearly communicating their data handling procedures, organizations can demonstrate their commitment to ethical and responsible data use. This accountability is essential for maintaining public trust and avoiding legal repercussions.
3. **Empowering Individuals:** Transparency empowers individuals by giving them control over their personal information. When individuals are informed about how their data is used, they can make informed decisions about sharing their information. This empowerment is a fundamental aspect of data privacy regulations, ensuring that individuals' rights are protected.

The Importance of Compliance

Compliance with data privacy regulations is crucial for organizations for several reasons:

1. **Avoiding Legal Repercussions:** Noncompliance with data privacy regulations can result in severe legal consequences, including hefty fines and penalties. For example, under the GDPR, organizations can be fined up to 4 percent of their annual global turnover or €20 million, whichever is higher, for noncompliance. Similarly, the CCPA imposes fines for violations, which can be substantial. By complying with these regulations, organizations can avoid these legal repercussions and the associated financial burden.
2. **Building Trust With Users:** Compliance with data privacy regulations helps build trust with users. When organizations demonstrate their commitment to protecting personal information, it fosters a positive relationship with consumers. Trust is a valuable asset for any organization, as it can lead to increased customer loyalty and a positive brand reputation.
3. **Enhancing Data Security:** Data privacy regulations often include provisions for data security, requiring organizations to implement robust security measures to protect personal information. Compliance with these regulations ensures that organizations adopt best practices for data security, reducing the risk of data breaches and unauthorized access. This proactive approach to data security is essential in today's digital landscape, where cyber threats are constantly evolving.
4. **Promoting Ethical AI:** Compliance with data privacy regulations ensures that AI systems operate within ethical and legal boundaries. By adhering to these regulations, organizations can develop and deploy AI systems that respect individuals' privacy rights and operate transparently. This ethical approach to AI is crucial for gaining public acceptance and trust in AI technologies.

Summary

Data privacy regulations such as the GDPR and CCPA are essential for ensuring that personal information is collected, stored, and processed responsibly. These regulations mandate transparency in data practices, empowering individuals and building trust with users. Compliance with these regulations is crucial for organizations to avoid legal repercussions, enhance data security, and promote ethical AI.

As AI continues to evolve, the importance of robust data privacy regulations will only grow, ensuring that personal information is protected in an increasingly digital world.[†]

[†] ***Data Privacy***

Understanding Data Privacy: Importance, Examples and Differences
This article explains the concept of data privacy, its importance, and the differences between data privacy and data protection. https://atlan.com/what-is-data-privacy/.

The Benefits of Data Privacy: Why It Matters
This blog post discusses the importance of data privacy for individuals and businesses, highlighting the benefits of prioritizing data privacy. www.enzuzo.com/blog/data-privacy-benefits.

What Is Data Privacy? A Comprehensive Guide
This article provides an overview of data privacy, its significance, and the laws that govern it. www.cloudflare.com/learning/privacy/what-is-data-privacy/.

Securing AI Systems: Protecting Against Cyber Threats and Unauthorized Access

As AI systems are becoming more prevalent and sophisticated, securing them against cyber threats and unauthorized access is increasingly critical. AI systems often handle sensitive data, making them attractive targets for cybercriminals. This section explores why securing AI systems is essential, effective security strategies, and the importance of integrating privacy by design principles to ensure robust data protection.

Why AI Systems Are Attractive Targets

AI systems are designed to process vast amounts of data, often including sensitive personal, financial, and proprietary information. This makes them highly valuable targets for cybercriminals who seek to exploit vulnerabilities for various malicious purposes, such as data theft, financial gain, or disrupting operations.

Sensitive Data Handling

AI systems are used in numerous applications, from health care and finance to autonomous vehicles and smart cities. In health care, AI systems analyze patient data to improve diagnostics and treatment plans. In finance, they detect fraud and manage investments. The sensitivity and volume of data handled by these systems make them prime targets for cyberattacks.

High-Value Targets

The potential rewards for successfully breaching an AI system are significant. Cybercriminals can steal personal information, intellectual property, or financial data, leading to identity theft, financial loss, and reputational damage for organizations. The high value of the data processed by AI systems makes them particularly appealing to attackers.

Effective Security Strategies

To protect AI systems from cyber threats and unauthorized access, organizations must implement robust security measures. These strategies include encryption, access controls, and regular security audits.

Encryption

- Encryption is a fundamental security measure that protects data by converting it into a coded format that can only be read by authorized parties. There are two main types of encryption:
- **Data at Rest Encryption:** This type of encryption protects data stored on devices or servers. By encrypting data at rest, organizations can ensure that even if a cybercriminal gains access to the storage medium, the data remains unreadable without the decryption key.
- **Data in Transit Encryption:** This type of encryption protects data as it moves across networks. By encrypting data in transit, organizations can prevent interception and unauthorized access during transmission.

Access Controls

Access controls are mechanisms that regulate who can view or use resources in a computing environment. Effective access control measures include the following:

- **Authentication:** Verifying the identity of users before granting access to the system. This can be achieved through passwords, biometrics, or multifactor authentication (MFA).
- **Authorization:** Determining what an authenticated user is allowed to do. This involves assigning permissions and roles to users based on their responsibilities.

- **Audit Logs:** Keeping detailed records of who accessed the system, what actions they performed, and when. Audit logs help detect and investigate unauthorized access and suspicious activities.

Regular Security Audits

Regular security audits are essential for identifying and mitigating vulnerabilities in AI systems. Security audits involve:

- **Vulnerability Assessments:** Scanning the system for known vulnerabilities and weaknesses that could be exploited by attackers.
- **Penetration Testing:** Simulating cyberattacks to test the system's defenses and identify potential entry points for attackers.
- **Compliance Checks**: Ensuring that the system complies with relevant data protection regulations and industry standards.

Privacy by Design Principles

Incorporating privacy by design principles ensures that data protection is integrated into the development process of AI systems, rather than an afterthought. Privacy by design involves embedding privacy considerations into every stage of the system's life cycle, from initial design to deployment and maintenance.

Key Privacy by Design Principles

- **Proactive Not Reactive**: Anticipating and preventing privacy issues before they occur, rather than reacting to them after the fact.
- **Privacy as the Default Setting:** Ensuring that personal data is automatically protected without requiring user intervention.
- **Privacy Embedded Into Design:** Integrating privacy features directly into the design and architecture of the system.
- **Full Functionality:** Achieving privacy without compromising the system's functionality or user experience.

- **End-to-End Security:** Ensuring that data protection measures cover the entire data life cycle, from collection to disposal.
- **Visibility and Transparency**: Providing clear and transparent information about data practices to users and stakeholders.
- **Respect for User Privacy:** Prioritizing user privacy and providing options for users to control their data.

Prioritizing Security to Safeguard AI Systems

By prioritizing security, organizations can safeguard their AI systems against potential breaches and maintain the integrity of the data they handle. This involves:

- **Implementing Robust Security Measures:** Using encryption, access controls, and regular security audits to protect AI systems from cyber threats and unauthorized access.
- **Integrating Privacy by Design:** Embedding privacy considerations into the development process to ensure that data protection is a core component of the system.
- **Continuous Monitoring and Improvement:** Regularly reviewing and updating security measures to address emerging threats and vulnerabilities.
- **Training and Awareness:** Educating employees and stakeholders about the importance of data privacy and security and providing training on best practices.

Summary

Securing AI systems is essential for protecting sensitive data from cyber threats and unauthorized access. AI systems are attractive targets for cybercriminals due to the valuable data they handle. Implementing robust security measures, such as encryption, access controls, and regular security audits, is crucial for safeguarding these systems. Incorporating privacy by design principles ensures that data protection is integrated into the development process, rather than an afterthought.

By prioritizing security, organizations can maintain the integrity of their AI systems and the data they handle, building trust with users and stakeholders.[‡]

---

‡ ***Securing AI Systems Against Cyber Threats***

AI Cyber Security
Securing AI Systems Against Cyber Threats, www.exabeam.com/explainers/ai-cyber-security/ai-cyber-security-securing-ai-systems-against-cyber-threats/.

How Artificial Intelligence Can Help With Cybersecurity Threats
www.fortinet.com/resources/cyberglossary/artificial-intelligence-in-cybersecurity.

Securing AI Systems
Protecting Against Cyber Threats and Unauthorized Access www.exabeam.com/explainers/ai-cyber-security/ai-cyber-security-securing-ai-systems-against-cyber-threats/.

The Importance of Federated Learning in Addressing AI Data Privacy Concerns

As AI continues to evolve, the need to address data privacy concerns becomes increasingly critical. Traditional ML methods often require centralized data collection, which can expose sensitive personal information to potential breaches and misuse. FL offers an innovative solution to these privacy challenges by enabling AI models to be trained across multiple decentralized devices without sharing raw data.

This chapter explains why FL is essential for ensuring data privacy, how it works, and its benefits, particularly in sensitive industries such as health care and finance.

How Federated Learning Works

FL is a method where AI models are trained on decentralized data located on user devices, such as smartphones, tablets, or computers, rather than collecting data into a central server. The key idea is that the data never leaves the local devices. Instead, the AI model is sent to the devices, trained locally, and only the model updates (such as changes in parameters) are sent back to a central server. These updates are then aggregated to improve the global model without exposing individual data points.

Ensuring Data Privacy

By keeping data on local devices, FL significantly reduces the risk of data breaches. Since raw data is not transmitted to a central server, there is less opportunity for unauthorized access or misuse. This approach aligns well with data privacy regulations such as the GDPR in the European Union and the CCPA in the United States, which mandate strict control over the collection and processing of personal data.

Benefits of Federated Learning

Privacy Protection

FL ensures that personal data remains on local devices, which is crucial for maintaining privacy. Since only model updates are shared and not the raw data, the risk of exposing sensitive information is minimized. This is particularly important in industries that handle highly sensitive data, such as health care and finance.

Compliance With Data Privacy Regulations

FL helps organizations comply with stringent data privacy regulations such as GDPR and CCPA. These regulations require organizations to obtain explicit consent for data usage and give individuals greater control over their personal information. By avoiding the centralization of data, FL adheres to these regulatory requirements, reducing the risk of legal repercussions and building trust with users.

Enhanced Security

By decentralizing the data, FL reduces the liability associated with handling large volumes of sensitive information. Centralized data repositories are attractive targets for cybercriminals, but with FL, the data remains distributed across many devices, making it harder for attackers to access a significant amount of data.

Applications in Health Care and Finance

FL is especially beneficial in industries where data privacy is of utmost importance, such as health care and finance.

Health Care

In health care, patient data is highly sensitive and subject to strict privacy regulations. FL allows hospitals and medical research institutions to collaborate on AI models without sharing patient data. For example, hospitals can use FL to develop predictive models for disease outbreaks or treatment outcomes by training on local patient data and sharing only the model updates. This ensures that patient privacy is maintained while still benefiting from the collective insights of multiple institutions.

Finance

The finance industry deals with vast amounts of sensitive data, including personal financial information and transaction records. FL enables financial institutions to develop fraud detection models by training on local transaction data from multiple banks without sharing the raw data. This collaborative approach enhances the accuracy of fraud detection systems while ensuring compliance with data privacy regulations.

Challenges and Future Directions

While FL offers significant advantages for data privacy, it is not without challenges. One of the main issues is ensuring the quality and consistency of data across different devices. Variations in data quality can affect the performance of the global model. Additionally, there are potential security risks, such as model poisoning attacks, where malicious updates can be sent to corrupt the model.

To address these challenges, ongoing research is focused on improving the robustness and security of FL. Techniques such as differential privacy and secure multiparty computation are explored to enhance the privacy and security of model updates. Furthermore, efforts are made to develop methods for handling low-quality data and ensuring the integrity of the training process.

Summary

FL represents a significant advancement in addressing data privacy concerns in AI. By allowing AI models to be trained on decentralized data without sharing raw information, FL enhances privacy, reduces the risk of data breaches, and helps organizations comply with data privacy regulations. Its applications in sensitive industries such as health care and finance demonstrate its potential to revolutionize how one leverages AI while protecting personal information.

As research and development (R&D) in this field continue, FL is poised to become a cornerstone of privacy-preserving AI technologies.[§]

[§] ***The Importance of Federated Learning in Addressing AI Data Privacy Concerns***

The Promise of Federated Learning in Privacy-Preserving AI
This article discusses the potential of federated learning to enhance privacy in AI applications by training models without sharing raw data. www.linkedin.com/pulse/promise-federated-learning-privacy-preserving-ai-rajat-singhal.

How Federated Learning Protects Privacy
This interactive guide from Google explains how federated learning works and its benefits in protecting user privacy while training machine learning models. https://pair.withgoogle.com/explorables/federated-learning/.

Federated Learning: Bridging AI and Data Privacy
This article highlights how federated learning can bridge the gap between AI advancements and data privacy concerns, ensuring secure and efficient model training. www.linkedin.com/pulse/federated-learning-bridging-ai-data-privacy-naomi-kaduwela-iakuf.

AI-Driven Cybersecurity: A Proactive Defense Against Cyber Attacks

In today's digital age, cybersecurity is more critical than ever. Traditional methods of protecting data and systems, such as firewalls and antivirus programs, are often reactive and struggle to keep up with the rapidly evolving landscape of cyber threats. This is where AI-driven cybersecurity applications come into play, offering a proactive and dynamic defense mechanism. These applications use ML algorithms to detect and respond to threats in real time, providing a robust shield against potential cyberattacks.

How AI-Driven Cybersecurity Works

AI-driven cybersecurity applications leverage ML algorithms to analyze vast amounts of data and identify patterns and anomalies in network traffic. These algorithms are trained on large datasets that include both normal and malicious activities. By learning from this data, AI systems can recognize deviations from the norm that may indicate a cyber threat.

Detecting Patterns and Anomalies

One of the key strengths of AI in cybersecurity is its ability to detect patterns and anomalies. Traditional cybersecurity methods often rely on predefined rules and signatures to identify threats. However, these methods can miss new or evolving threats that do not match known patterns. In contrast, AI algorithms can identify subtle and complex patterns that may indicate a potential threat. For example, an AI system can detect unusual login attempts, abnormal data transfers, or unexpected changes in network behavior that could signify a cyberattack.

Real-Time Threat Detection

AI-driven cybersecurity applications operate in real time, monitoring network traffic and system activities. This real-time capability allows them to detect and respond to threats as they occur, rather than after the fact. For instance, if an AI system detects a sudden spike in data transfers that deviates from normal behavior, it can immediately flag this as a potential data breach and initiate a response to mitigate the threat.

Continuous Learning and Adaptation

A significant advantage of AI in cybersecurity is its ability to continuously learn and adapt to new threats. As cyber threats evolve, so too must the defenses against them. AI systems are designed to learn from new data, improving their ability to detect and respond to emerging threats.

Adaptive Defense Mechanisms

By continuously learning from new data, AI-driven cybersecurity systems can adapt to the ever-changing threat landscape. This adaptive capability ensures that the system remains effective even as cybercriminals develop new tactics and techniques. For example, if a new type of malware is detected, the AI system can learn from this instance and update its algorithms to recognize and defend against similar threats in the future.

Proactive Threat Prediction

In addition to detecting and responding to current threats, AI-driven cybersecurity applications can also predict potential future threats. By analyzing historical data and identifying trends, AI systems can forecast where and how future attacks might occur. This predictive capability allows organizations to strengthen their defenses proactively, reducing the likelihood of successful cyberattacks.

Ensuring Security and Transparency in AI Systems

While AI-driven cybersecurity applications offer numerous benefits, it is crucial to ensure that these systems are secure and transparent. AI systems can become targets for cyberattacks, and their effectiveness depends on the quality and integrity of the data they are trained on.

Securing AI Systems

AI systems must be protected from various types of attacks, such as data poisoning, adversarial examples, and model inversion attacks. Data poisoning occurs when attackers inject false data into the training dataset, leading the AI system to make incorrect decisions. Adversarial examples involve subtly altering inputs to fool the AI system into misclassifying them. Model inversion attacks aim to extract sensitive information from the AI model itself.

To mitigate these risks, organizations should implement strong security measures, including:

- **Data Integrity Checks:** Ensuring the accuracy and integrity of the training data to prevent data poisoning.
- **Robust Algorithms:** Developing algorithms that are resistant to adversarial examples.
- **Access Controls:** Restricting access to AI models and training data to prevent unauthorized manipulation.

Transparency and Accountability

Transparency in AI systems is essential for building trust and ensuring accountability. Users and stakeholders need to understand how AI-driven cybersecurity applications make decisions and respond to threats. This transparency can be achieved through XAI techniques, which provide clear and understandable explanations of the AI system's actions.

Ethical Considerations

Ethical considerations are also crucial in the deployment of AI-driven cybersecurity applications. Organizations must ensure that their AI systems do not inadvertently violate privacy rights or discriminate against certain groups. Adopting ethical AI practices and adhering to data privacy regulations, such as the GDPR and CCPA, can help address these concerns.

Summary

AI-driven cybersecurity applications represent a significant advancement in the fight against cyber threats. By using ML algorithms to detect patterns and anomalies in real time, these applications provide a proactive and dynamic defense mechanism. Continuous learning and adaptation ensure that AI systems remain effective against evolving threats. However, it is essential to secure these AI systems and maintain transparency to prevent them from becoming targets themselves.

As organizations increasingly rely on AI for cybersecurity, balancing security, transparency, and ethical considerations will be key to safeguarding the digital world.[5]

---

[5] ***AI-Driven Cybersecurity: A Proactive Defense Against Cyber Attacks***

AI in Cybersecurity: Revolutionizing Safety
This *Forbes* article examines how AI is changing the landscape of cybersecurity, making it more proactive and adaptive. www.forbes.com/sites/forbestechcouncil/2024/02/15/ai-in-cybersecurity-revolutionizing-safety/.

The Dark Side of AI Data Privacy
This blog post from Coalfire delves into the risks associated with AI, such as data leakage, bias, and over collection and offers recommendations for mitigation. https://coalfire.com/the-coalfire-blog/the-dark-side-of-ai-data-privacy.

How AI Could Help Cyber Security and Data Protection
This LinkedIn article discusses the dual role of AI in both causing and preventing cyber attacks and provides tips for using AI safely. www.linkedin.com/pulse/how-ai-could-help-cyber-security-data-protection-vision-raval-py1of.

CHAPTER 12

Becoming an AI-Driven Organization

A Holistic Transformation

This chapter explores what it means to be a truly AI-driven organization.

In the rapidly evolving business landscape, becoming an AI-driven organization is no longer just an option but a necessity for companies aiming to stay competitive. This transformation goes beyond simply implementing AI technologies; it requires a comprehensive overhaul of strategy, culture, processes, and skills. To fully leverage AI's potential, organizations must transform to become AI-driven. This involves adopting a culture that embraces innovation, investing in AI capabilities, and ensuring ethical AI use.

This chapter delves into the multifaceted journey of becoming an AI-driven organization, exploring the key elements that contribute to a successful transformation.

AI-driven organizations foster a culture of innovation where employees are encouraged to experiment with AI technologies and explore new applications. This requires leadership commitment and a willingness to invest in R&D. By embracing innovation, organizations can stay ahead of the competition and continuously adapt to changing market dynamics.

To support AI initiatives, organizations must invest in the necessary infrastructure, tools, and talent. This includes acquiring advanced computing resources, implementing robust data management systems, and hiring skilled professionals. Investing in AI capabilities ensures that an organization has the foundation needed to leverage AI effectively and achieve its strategic goals.

As AI becomes more integrated into business operations, ethical considerations are increasingly important. Organizations must ensure that their AI systems are fair, transparent, and accountable. This involves implementing ethical guidelines, conducting regular audits, and addressing potential biases. Ethical AI use not only builds trust with stakeholders but also mitigates risks associated with AI deployment.

An AI-driven organization leverages AI technologies to enhance decision making, improve operational efficiency, and create new value propositions. These organizations do not just use AI as a tool; they integrate it into the very fabric of their business, using it to drive innovation, strategy, and growth. Key characteristics of AI-driven organizations include data-centric decision making, automated and intelligent processes, continuous learning and adaptation, an AI-augmented workforce, and customer-centric personalized experiences.

Becoming an AI-driven organization requires a holistic transformation that touches every aspect of the business. This chapter explores the key elements of this transformation, including strategy, culture, processes, and skills. The chapter's sections delve deeper into each of these elements, providing insights and practical examples to guide organizations on their AI transformation journey. From aligning AI initiatives with business goals to fostering a culture of innovation and collaboration, this chapter offers a roadmap for organizations looking to harness the power of AI and thrive in the digital age.

By addressing these areas comprehensively, organizations can unlock the full potential of AI and achieve sustainable growth.

Embracing Innovation

This section delves into the critical aspects of fostering such a culture, highlighting the importance of leadership commitment and investment in R&D.

In the quest to become AI-driven, organizations must cultivate a culture of innovation that encourages employees to experiment with AI technologies and explore new applications.

The Role of Leadership in Fostering Innovation

Leadership plays a pivotal role in creating an environment where innovation can thrive. Leaders must not only endorse the use of AI but also actively promote a mindset that values experimentation and continuous learning. This involves:

- **Setting a Vision:** Leaders should articulate a clear vision for how AI can transform the organization. This vision should inspire employees and provide a sense of direction for AI initiatives.
- **Encouraging Risk-Taking:** Innovation often involves taking risks and venturing into uncharted territory. Leaders must create a safe space where employees feel comfortable experimenting with new ideas without fear of failure. Celebrating successes and learning from failures are essential components of this approach.
- **Providing Resources:** To foster innovation, leaders must allocate sufficient resources, including time, budget, and access to cutting-edge AI tools and technologies. This demonstrates a commitment to innovation and empowers employees to pursue their ideas.
- **Promoting Collaboration:** Innovation thrives in collaborative environments. Leaders should encourage cross-functional teams to work together, combining diverse perspectives and expertise to drive AI initiatives forward.

Investing in Research and Development

Investment in R&D is crucial for organizations aiming to stay at the forefront of AI innovation. This involves:

- **Building R&D Capabilities:** Organizations should establish dedicated R&D teams focused on exploring new AI technologies and applications. These teams should be equipped with the latest tools and resources to conduct cutting-edge research.

- **Collaborating With External Partners:** Partnering with academic institutions, research organizations, and AI start-ups can provide access to new ideas, technologies, and talent. These collaborations can accelerate innovation and help organizations stay ahead of industry trends.
- **Fostering a Learning Culture:** Continuous learning is essential for innovation. Organizations should invest in training and development programs to upskill employees in AI and related fields. Encouraging employees to attend conferences, workshops, and online courses can keep them updated on the latest advancements.
- **Supporting Pilot Projects:** Pilot projects are an effective way to test new AI applications and demonstrate their potential value. Organizations should support small-scale experiments that can provide quick wins and build momentum for larger AI initiatives.

Creating an Innovative Environment

To truly embrace innovation, organizations must create an environment that nurtures creativity and experimentation. This involves:

- **Encouraging Curiosity:** Employees should be encouraged to ask questions, explore new ideas, and challenge the status quo. A curious mindset can lead to breakthrough innovations and novel AI applications.
- **Providing Autonomy:** Giving employees the freedom to pursue their ideas and experiment with AI technologies can lead to unexpected discoveries. Autonomy fosters a sense of ownership and accountability, driving employees to innovate.
- **Recognizing and Rewarding Innovation:** Recognizing and rewarding employees for their innovative contributions can motivate them to continue pushing the boundaries.

This can be done through awards, promotions, or other forms of recognition.

- **Creating a Supportive Infrastructure:** Organizations should provide the necessary infrastructure to support innovation, including access to data, computing resources, and AI tools. A robust infrastructure can enable employees to experiment and iterate quickly.

Case Study: Embracing Innovation at Google

Google is a prime example of an organization that has successfully embraced innovation. The company's leadership has consistently promoted a culture of experimentation and risk-taking. Google's "20% time" policy, which allows employees to spend 20 percent of their time on projects of their choosing, has led to the development of groundbreaking products such as Gmail and Google News.

Additionally, Google invests heavily in R&D, with dedicated teams working on cutting-edge AI research. The company collaborates with academic institutions and research organizations to stay at the forefront of AI innovation. Google's commitment to continuous learning is evident in its extensive training programs and support for employees attending conferences and workshops.

By fostering a culture of innovation and investing in R&D, Google has been able to leverage AI to drive significant advancements and maintain its position as a leader in the tech industry.

Conclusion

Embracing innovation is a critical component of becoming an AI-driven organization. By fostering a culture that encourages experimentation, investing in R&D, and creating an environment that nurtures creativity, organizations can unlock the full potential of AI. Leadership commitment and a willingness to invest in innovation are essential for driving AI initiatives forward and achieving sustainable growth in the digital age.

Investing in AI Capabilities

In the journey to becoming an AI-driven organization, investing in the necessary infrastructure, tools, and talent is paramount. This section explores the critical components of such investments, highlighting the importance of acquiring advanced computing resources, implementing robust data management systems, and hiring skilled professionals.

Advanced Computing Resources

The foundation of any successful AI initiative lies in the availability of advanced computing resources. These resources enable organizations to process vast amounts of data, run complex algorithms, and develop sophisticated AI models. Key considerations:

- **High-Performance Computing (HPC):** HPC systems are essential for handling the computational demands of AI workloads. These systems provide the processing power needed to train large-scale ML models and perform real-time data analysis.
- **Cloud Computing:** Cloud platforms offer scalable and flexible computing resources that can be tailored to the needs of AI projects. Organizations can leverage cloud services to access cutting-edge AI tools, reduce infrastructure costs, and accelerate development cycles.
- **Edge Computing:** For applications requiring low latency and real-time processing, edge computing is a valuable investment. By processing data closer to the source, edge computing reduces the need for data transfer to centralized servers, enhancing efficiency and responsiveness.

Robust Data Management Systems

Data is the lifeblood of AI, and effective data management is crucial for the success of AI initiatives. Organizations must implement robust data management systems to ensure the availability, quality, and security of data. Key aspects:

- **Data Storage and Retrieval:** Efficient data storage solutions, such as data lakes and data warehouses, enable organizations to store and retrieve large volumes of structured and unstructured data. These solutions should be scalable and capable of handling diverse data types.
- **Data Integration:** Integrating data from various sources is essential for creating comprehensive datasets that drive AI models. Organizations should invest in data integration tools that facilitate seamless data aggregation, transformation, and synchronization.
- **Data Quality and Governance:** Ensuring data quality is critical for the accuracy and reliability of AI models. Organizations must implement data governance frameworks that establish standards for data quality, consistency, and integrity. Regular data audits and validation processes can help maintain high data quality.
- **Data Security and Privacy:** Protecting sensitive data is a top priority for AI-driven organizations. Implementing robust security measures, such as encryption, access controls, and anonymization techniques, can safeguard data from unauthorized access and breaches. Compliance with data privacy regulations, such as GDPR and CCPA, is also essential.

Hiring Skilled Professionals

The success of AI initiatives hinges on the expertise and skills of the professionals driving them. Organizations must invest in hiring and developing talent with the necessary knowledge and experience in AI and related fields. Key roles:

- **Data Scientists:** Data scientists are responsible for developing and deploying AI models. They possess expertise in ML, statistical analysis, and data visualization. Hiring skilled data scientists is crucial for creating accurate and effective AI solutions.

- **AI Engineers:** AI engineers focus on the implementation and optimization of AI systems. They work on integrating AI models into existing infrastructure, ensuring scalability, and improving performance. Their technical skills are essential for the successful deployment of AI applications.
- **Data Engineers:** Data engineers design and maintain the data pipelines that feed AI models. They are responsible for data collection, processing, and storage. Their expertise in data architecture and extract, transform, load (ETL) processes is vital for ensuring the availability of high-quality data.
- **AI Ethicists:** As AI becomes more integrated into business operations, ethical considerations become increasingly important. AI ethicists help organizations navigate the ethical challenges associated with AI use, ensuring that AI systems are fair, transparent, and accountable.
- **Cross-Functional Teams:** Creating cross-functional teams that combine domain expertise with AI skills can drive innovation and ensure the successful implementation of AI initiatives. Collaboration between data scientists, engineers, business analysts, and domain experts can lead to more effective and impactful AI solutions.

Case Study: Investing in AI Capabilities at Microsoft

Microsoft's commitment to AI is evident in its substantial investments in computing resources, data management, and talent development. The company leverages its Azure cloud platform to provide scalable and flexible AI services to businesses worldwide. Microsoft's investment in AI R&D has led to breakthroughs in NLP, computer vision, and ML.

Additionally, Microsoft has implemented robust data management systems to ensure the quality and security of its data. The company's focus on hiring skilled professionals, including data scientists, AI engineers, and ethicists, has been instrumental in driving its AI initiatives forward.

Conclusion

Investing in AI capabilities is a critical step for organizations aiming to become AI-driven. By acquiring advanced computing resources, implementing robust data management systems, and hiring skilled professionals, organizations can build a strong foundation for their AI initiatives. These investments enable organizations to harness the power of AI, drive innovation, and achieve sustainable growth in the digital age.

Ensuring Ethical AI Use

As AI becomes increasingly integrated into business operations, ethical considerations are paramount. Organizations must ensure that their AI systems are fair, transparent, and accountable.

This section explores the critical aspects of ethical AI use, highlighting the importance of implementing ethical guidelines, conducting regular audits, and addressing potential biases.

The Importance of Ethical AI

Ethical AI use is essential for building trust with stakeholders, including customers, employees, and regulators. It ensures that AI systems are used responsibly and do not cause harm or perpetuate inequalities. Key reasons for prioritizing ethical AI:

- **Fairness:** AI systems must be designed and deployed in a way that ensures fairness. This means avoiding biases that could lead to discriminatory outcomes. Fair AI systems treat all individuals and groups equitably, regardless of their background or characteristics.
- **Transparency:** Transparency in AI involves making the decision-making processes of AI systems understandable to stakeholders. This includes providing clear explanations of how AI models work and the factors influencing their decisions. Transparency fosters trust and allows stakeholders to hold organizations accountable.

- **Accountability:** Organizations must take responsibility for the actions and decisions of their AI systems. This involves establishing mechanisms for monitoring AI performance, addressing issues, and ensuring that AI systems operate within ethical boundaries.

Implementing Ethical Guidelines

To ensure ethical AI use, organizations must establish and adhere to ethical guidelines. These guidelines provide a framework for responsible AI development and deployment. Key components:

- **Ethical Principles:** Organizations should define a set of ethical principles that guide their AI initiatives. These principles may include fairness, transparency, accountability, privacy, and security. Articulated principles set the foundation for ethical AI practices.
- **Ethical Review Boards:** Establishing ethical review boards can help organizations evaluate AI projects from an ethical perspective. These boards, composed of diverse stakeholders, review AI initiatives to ensure that they align with ethical guidelines and address potential ethical concerns.
- **Ethical Training:** Providing ethical training for employees involved in AI development and deployment is crucial. Training programs should cover ethical principles, potential biases, and best practices for responsible AI use. Educating employees on ethical considerations helps create a culture of ethical awareness.

Conducting Regular Audits

Regular audits are essential for ensuring that AI systems operate ethically and comply with established guidelines. Audits involve evaluating AI models, data, and processes to identify and address ethical issues. Key aspects of AI audits:

- **Bias Detection:** Audits should include methods for detecting biases in AI models and data. This involves analyzing model outputs to identify patterns of discrimination or unfair treatment. Addressing biases is critical for ensuring fairness in AI systems.
- **Performance Monitoring:** Continuous monitoring of AI performance helps organizations identify and address issues promptly. Performance metrics should be tracked to ensure that AI systems operate as intended and do not deviate from ethical standards.
- **Compliance Checks:** Audits should assess compliance with ethical guidelines, legal regulations, and industry standards. Ensuring compliance helps organizations avoid legal and reputational risks associated with unethical AI use.
- **Stakeholder Feedback:** Gathering feedback from stakeholders, including customers and employees, provides valuable insights into the ethical implications of AI systems. Incorporating stakeholder perspectives helps organizations address ethical concerns and improve AI practices.

Addressing Potential Biases

Bias in AI systems can lead to unfair and discriminatory outcomes. Addressing potential biases is crucial for ensuring ethical AI use. Key strategies for mitigating biases:

- **Diverse Data:** Using diverse and representative data for training AI models helps reduce biases. Organizations should ensure that their datasets include a wide range of perspectives and do not disproportionately represent any particular group.
- **Bias Mitigation Techniques:** Implementing bias mitigation techniques, such as resampling, reweighting, and adversarial training, can help reduce biases in AI models. These techniques adjust the training process to minimize discriminatory patterns.

- **Human Oversight:** Human oversight is essential for identifying and addressing biases that AI systems may overlook. Involving human reviewers in the decision-making process ensures that AI outputs are scrutinized for fairness and ethical considerations.
- **Continuous Improvement:** Ethical AI use requires continuous improvement and adaptation. Organizations should regularly update their AI models, data, and processes to address emerging ethical challenges and incorporate new best practices.

Case Study: Ensuring Ethical AI at IBM

IBM is a leading example of an organization committed to ethical AI use. The company has established a comprehensive set of ethical guidelines, known as the *IBM Principles for Trust and Transparency*. These principles emphasize fairness, transparency, and accountability in AI development and deployment. IBM conducts regular audits of its AI systems to detect and address biases. The company also invests in ethical training for its employees and collaborates with external partners to advance ethical AI research.

Conclusion

Ensuring ethical AI use is a critical component of becoming an AI-driven organization. By implementing ethical guidelines, conducting regular audits, and addressing potential biases, organizations can build trust, mitigate risks, and promote responsible AI practices. Ethical AI use not only benefits organizations but also contributes to a fairer and more equitable society.

Understanding AI-Driven Organizations

AI-driven organizations are characterized by their ability to harness the power of data and ML to make informed decisions, automate processes, and continuously adapt to changing environments. By embedding AI into their core operations, these organizations can unlock new opportunities and stay ahead of the competition.

An AI-driven organization leverages AI technologies to enhance decision making, improve operational efficiency, and create new value propositions. These organizations don't just use AI as a tool; they integrate it into the very fabric of their business, using it to drive innovation, strategy, and growth.

Key Characteristics of AI-Driven Organizations

- **Data-Centric Decision Making:** AI-driven organizations prioritize data as a critical asset. They collect, analyze, and leverage vast amounts of data to make informed decisions. This data-centric approach enables them to identify patterns, predict trends, and make strategic choices that drive business growth. By utilizing advanced analytics and ML algorithms, these organizations can gain deeper insights into customer behavior, market dynamics, and operational performance.
- **Automated and Intelligent Processes:** Automation is a cornerstone of AI-driven organizations. They implement intelligent processes that streamline operations, reduce manual effort, and enhance efficiency. From RPA to AI-powered chatbots, these organizations leverage automation to handle repetitive tasks, improve accuracy, and free up human resources for more strategic activities. By automating routine processes, they can achieve higher productivity and cost savings.
- **Continuous Learning and Adaptation:** AI-driven organizations embrace a culture of continuous learning and adaptation. They recognize that AI technologies are constantly evolving, and they invest in ongoing training and development to stay ahead of the curve. These organizations foster a learning mindset, encouraging employees to acquire new skills and stay updated with the latest advancements in AI. By continuously learning and adapting, they can quickly respond to market changes, innovate, and maintain a competitive edge.

- **AI-Augmented Workforce:** In AI-driven organizations, the workforce is augmented by AI technologies. Rather than replacing human workers, AI complements their capabilities, enabling them to work more efficiently and effectively. AI-powered tools and systems assist employees in decision making, problem-solving, and task execution. This collaboration between humans and AI enhances productivity, creativity, and overall performance. By leveraging AI to augment the workforce, organizations can achieve higher levels of innovation and deliver superior customer experiences.

Conclusion

Becoming an AI-driven organization requires a holistic transformation that goes beyond simply adopting AI technologies. It involves integrating AI into the core of the business, fostering a data-centric culture, automating processes, embracing continuous learning, and augmenting the workforce with AI capabilities. By doing so, organizations can unlock new opportunities, drive innovation, and achieve sustainable growth in an increasingly competitive landscape.

Strategy Transformation

In the journey to becoming an AI-driven organization, strategy transformation is a critical step. AI should be at the core of the organization's strategy, not just an afterthought or a separate initiative. This holistic approach ensures that AI is fully integrated into the business, driving innovation, growth, and competitive advantage.

Becoming an AI-driven organization requires a holistic transformation that touches every aspect of the business. Let us explore the key elements of this transformation:

- **Aligning AI Initiatives With Business Goals:** To effectively leverage AI, organizations must align their AI initiatives with their overarching business goals. This alignment ensures that AI projects are not pursued in isolation but are directly contributing to the organization's strategic objectives. By integrating AI into the business strategy, organizations can enhance decision making, optimize operations, and create new value propositions. For example, a retail company might use AI to improve supply chain efficiency, enhance customer experiences, and drive sales growth.

- **Identifying AI-Driven Opportunities for Growth and Innovation:** AI presents numerous opportunities for growth and innovation. Organizations need to proactively identify areas where AI can create a significant impact. This involves analyzing market trends, customer needs, and internal processes to uncover AI-driven opportunities. For instance, a health care provider might use AI to develop predictive models for patient outcomes, enabling personalized treatment plans and improved patient care. By identifying and capitalizing on these opportunities, organizations can stay ahead of the competition and drive sustainable growth.
- **Developing a Clear AI Roadmap and Investment Plan:** A well-defined AI roadmap and investment plan are essential for successful strategy transformation. The roadmap should outline the organization's AI vision, goals, and key milestones. It should also include a detailed plan for AI implementation, covering aspects such as technology infrastructure, data management, and talent acquisition. Additionally, organizations need to allocate sufficient resources and budget for AI initiatives. By having a clear roadmap and investment plan, organizations can ensure that their AI projects are well-coordinated, adequately funded, and aligned with their strategic priorities.
- **Rethinking Business Models to Leverage AI Capabilities:** To fully harness the potential of AI, organizations may need to rethink their existing business models. This involves exploring new ways to deliver value to customers, optimize operations, and generate revenue. AI can enable organizations to create innovative products and services, enhance customer experiences, and streamline processes. For example, Netflix

transformed its strategy by using AI to personalize content recommendations, which became a key differentiator in the streaming market. By leveraging AI capabilities, organizations can create new business models that drive growth and competitive advantage.

Conclusion

Strategy transformation is a crucial component of becoming an AI-driven organization. By aligning AI initiatives with business goals, identifying AI-driven opportunities for growth and innovation, developing a clear AI roadmap and investment plan, and rethinking business models to leverage AI capabilities, organizations can fully integrate AI into their core strategy. This holistic approach ensures that AI is not just a tool but a driving force behind the organization's success.

Cultural Transformation

Creating an AI-driven culture is crucial for the successful transformation of any organization. This cultural shift involves fostering a data-driven mindset, encouraging experimentation, promoting collaboration between humans and AI systems, and addressing fears and misconceptions about AI.

By embedding these principles into the organizational culture, companies can fully leverage the potential of AI and drive sustainable growth.

- **Fostering a Data-Driven Mindset Across the Organization:** To become an AI-driven organization, it is essential to cultivate a data-driven mindset among employees at all levels. This involves emphasizing the importance of data in decision making and encouraging employees to rely on data insights rather than intuition or experience alone. Organizations can achieve this by providing training on data literacy, investing in data analytics tools, and promoting a culture where data is accessible and valued. By fostering a data-driven mindset, organizations can make more informed decisions, identify new opportunities, and drive innovation.

- **Encouraging Experimentation and Learning From Failures:** An AI-driven culture thrives on experimentation and learning from failures. Organizations should create an environment where employees feel empowered to experiment with AI technologies and explore new ideas without fear of failure. This can be achieved by promoting a growth mindset, providing resources for experimentation, and recognizing and rewarding innovative efforts. By encouraging experimentation, organizations can discover new AI applications, improve existing processes, and stay ahead of the competition. Learning from failures is equally important, as it allows organizations to refine their approaches and continuously improve.
- **Promoting Collaboration Between Humans and AI Systems:** Collaboration between humans and AI systems is a key aspect of an AI-driven culture. Rather than viewing AI as a replacement for human workers, organizations should emphasize the complementary nature of AI and human capabilities. This involves designing AI systems that augment human skills, enhance productivity, and enable employees to focus on higher value tasks. Organizations can promote collaboration by providing training on AI tools, encouraging cross-functional teams, and fostering a culture of trust and transparency. By promoting collaboration, organizations can harness the full potential of AI and achieve better outcomes.
- **Addressing Fears and Misconceptions About AI:** Addressing fears and misconceptions about AI is crucial for creating an AI-driven culture. Employees may have concerns about job displacement, privacy, and the ethical implications of AI. Organizations should proactively address these concerns by providing clear communication, offering reassurances, and involving employees in the AI transformation process. This can be achieved through workshops, open forums, and transparent discussions about the benefits and limitations of AI. By addressing fears and misconceptions, organizations can build trust, reduce resistance, and foster a positive attitude toward AI adoption.

Conclusion

Cultural transformation is a vital component of becoming an AI-driven organization. By fostering a data-driven mindset, encouraging experimentation, promoting collaboration between humans and AI systems, and addressing fears and misconceptions about AI, organizations can create a culture that fully embraces AI technologies. Amazon's culture of innovation and experimentation serves as a prime example of how an organization can successfully integrate AI across its business, from product recommendations to warehouse robotics.

Process Transformation

AI has the potential to revolutionize business processes, making them more efficient and effective. This transformation involves automating routine tasks, implementing AI-powered predictive maintenance, using AI for real-time decision making, and redesigning processes to fully leverage AI capabilities.

By embracing these changes, organizations can achieve significant improvements in productivity, cost savings, and overall performance.

- **Automating Routine Tasks and Workflows:** One of the most immediate benefits of AI is its ability to automate routine tasks and workflows. By leveraging AI technologies such as RPA, organizations can streamline repetitive and time-consuming tasks, freeing up human resources for more strategic activities. Automation can be applied to various functions, such as data entry, invoice processing, and customer service. This not only enhances efficiency but also reduces the risk of human error, leading to more accurate and reliable outcomes.
- **Implementing AI-Powered Predictive Maintenance:** Predictive maintenance is another area where AI can drive significant improvements. By using AI algorithms to analyze data from sensors and equipment, organizations can predict when maintenance is needed, preventing costly breakdowns and minimizing downtime. AI-powered predictive maintenance enables organizations to move from

reactive to proactive maintenance strategies, optimizing asset performance and extending the lifespan of equipment. For example, manufacturing companies can use AI to monitor machinery and identify potential issues before they escalate, ensuring smooth and uninterrupted operations.

- **Using AI for Real-Time Decision Making and Optimization:** AI can also enhance real-time decision making and optimization. By processing vast amounts of data in real time, AI systems can provide valuable insights and recommendations to support decision making. This is particularly useful in dynamic environments where quick and accurate decisions are crucial. For instance, in supply chain management, AI can analyze data from various sources to optimize inventory levels, predict demand fluctuations, and improve delivery schedules. By leveraging AI for real-time decision making, organizations can respond swiftly to changing conditions, reduce costs, and improve customer satisfaction.
- **Redesigning Processes to Fully Leverage AI Capabilities:** To fully harness the potential of AI, organizations may need to redesign their existing processes. This involves rethinking traditional workflows and identifying areas where AI can add the most value. By integrating AI into the core processes, organizations can achieve higher levels of efficiency, innovation, and competitiveness. For example, UPS has transformed its logistics processes using AI for route optimization, significantly reducing fuel consumption and delivery times. By redesigning processes to leverage AI capabilities, organizations can unlock new opportunities and drive sustainable growth.

Conclusion

Process transformation is a key component of becoming an AI-driven organization. By automating routine tasks, implementing AI-powered predictive maintenance, using AI for real-time decision making, and redesigning processes to fully leverage AI capabilities, organizations can achieve significant improvements in efficiency, cost savings, and overall performance.

Skills Transformation

To become an AI-driven organization, developing new skills and capabilities is essential. This transformation involves upskilling existing employees, hiring AI specialists, developing AI literacy across all levels, and creating cross-functional teams that combine domain expertise with AI skills.

By investing in skills transformation, organizations can build a workforce that is capable of leveraging AI technologies to drive innovation and growth.

- **Upskilling Existing Employees in AI and Data Science:** Upskilling existing employees is a critical step in the skills transformation journey. Organizations should provide training and development programs to help employees acquire the necessary skills in AI and data science. This can include online courses, workshops, certifications, and hands-on projects. By upskilling their workforce, organizations can ensure that employees are equipped with the knowledge and expertise to work with AI technologies and contribute to AI-driven initiatives. This not only enhances the organization's capabilities but also boosts employee morale and engagement.
- **Hiring AI Specialists and Data Scientists:** In addition to upskilling existing employees, organizations need to hire AI specialists and data scientists to bring in specialized expertise. These professionals possess the technical skills and experience required to develop and implement AI solutions. By building a team of AI experts, organizations can accelerate their AI transformation and drive innovation. Recruitment efforts should focus on attracting top talent in AI and data science, and organizations should offer competitive compensation packages and career development opportunities to retain these valuable professionals.

- **Developing AI Literacy Across All Levels of the Organization:** Developing AI literacy across all levels of the organization is crucial for fostering a culture that embraces AI. This involves educating employees about the basics of AI, its potential applications, and its impact on the business. AI literacy programs can include seminars, webinars, and interactive learning sessions. By promoting AI literacy, organizations can ensure that employees at all levels understand the value of AI and are comfortable working with AI technologies. This widespread understanding and acceptance of AI are essential for successful AI integration.
- **Creating Cross-Functional Teams That Combine Domain Expertise With AI Skills:** Creating cross-functional teams that combine domain expertise with AI skills is key to unlocking the full potential of AI. These teams bring together employees from different departments, such as marketing, finance, operations, and IT, to collaborate on AI projects. By combining domain knowledge with AI expertise, these teams can develop innovative solutions that address specific business challenges. Cross-functional teams foster collaboration, creativity, and a holistic approach to problem-solving, enabling organizations to leverage AI effectively.

Conclusion

Skills transformation is a vital component of becoming an AI-driven organization. By upskilling existing employees, hiring AI specialists, developing AI literacy, and creating cross-functional teams, organizations can build a workforce that is capable of leveraging AI technologies to drive innovation and growth. Google's investment in AI education for its employees serves as a prime example of how skills transformation can contribute to maintaining a leadership position in AI. Embracing skills transformation requires a commitment to continuous learning, investment in training and development, and a willingness to adapt to new technologies.

Roadmap for AI Transformation

In today's rapidly evolving technological landscape, becoming an AI-driven organization is not just a competitive advantage but a necessity. The journey to AI transformation is multifaceted, requiring a strategic approach that encompasses technology, culture, and governance.

Here is a comprehensive roadmap for organizations looking to embark on this transformative journey:

1. ***Assess Current State***
   The first step in the AI transformation journey is to evaluate the organization's current state of AI readiness. This involves a thorough assessment of existing technologies, data infrastructure, and skills. Understanding the starting point is crucial for identifying gaps and opportunities. Organizations should conduct an AI maturity assessment to gauge their readiness and identify areas that need improvement.
2. ***Define AI Vision and Strategy***
   Developing a clear AI vision and strategy is essential for guiding the transformation process. This vision should articulate how AI will drive the business forward and align with the overall organizational strategy. It should include specific goals, objectives, and key performance indicators (KPIs) to measure success. A well-defined AI strategy provides a roadmap for decision making and resource allocation.
3. ***Build Data Infrastructure***
   Data is the lifeblood of AI. Ensuring that the organization has the necessary data infrastructure to support AI initiatives is critical. This includes robust data collection, storage, and management systems. Organizations should invest in a scalable and secure data infrastructure that can handle large volumes of data and support real-time analytics. Data quality and governance are also essential to ensure the reliability and integrity of AI models.
4. ***Start With Pilot Projects***
   To build momentum and demonstrate the value of AI, organizations should start with small-scale pilot projects. These projects should be carefully selected to address specific business challenges and deliver

quick wins. Pilot projects provide an opportunity to experiment with AI technologies, learn from successes and failures, and build confidence in AI capabilities. Successful pilots can serve as a foundation for scaling AI initiatives across the organization.

5. ***Develop AI Capabilities***

   Building AI capabilities within the organization is a critical step in the transformation journey. This involves investing in training and development programs to upskill existing employees and hiring new talent with specialized AI skills. Organizations should also consider forming partnerships with academic institutions, research organizations, and technology vendors to access cutting-edge AI expertise. Developing a strong AI talent pool is essential for driving innovation and sustaining AI initiatives.

6. ***Scale AI Initiatives***

   Once pilot projects have demonstrated success, organizations should gradually expand AI initiatives across the organization. This involves scaling successful AI models and solutions to different business units and functions. Scaling AI requires a coordinated effort to ensure consistency, interoperability, and integration with existing systems. Organizations should also establish a centralized AI center of excellence to provide guidance, support, and best practices for scaling AI initiatives.

7. ***Transform Processes***

   AI transformation is not just about technology; it also requires rethinking and redesigning business processes. Organizations should identify processes that can be enhanced or automated using AI and redesign them to fully leverage AI capabilities. This may involve reengineering workflows, redefining roles and responsibilities, and implementing new tools and technologies. Transforming processes to be AI-driven can lead to significant improvements in efficiency, productivity, and customer experience.

8. ***Foster an AI Culture***

   Creating a culture of innovation, experimentation, and continuous learning is essential for sustaining AI transformation. Organizations should promote a mindset that embraces change and encourages employees to explore new ideas and technologies. This can be achieved through initiatives such as hackathons, innovation labs, and cross-functional collaboration. Leadership plays a crucial role in fostering an AI culture by setting the tone, providing support, and recognizing and rewarding innovation.

9. ***Establish Governance***
   Implementing AI governance frameworks is critical to ensure the ethical and responsible use of AI. Organizations should establish policies and guidelines for AI development, deployment, and monitoring. This includes addressing issues such as data privacy, security, bias, and transparency. AI governance frameworks should also include mechanisms for accountability and oversight to ensure compliance with regulatory requirements and industry standards.
10. ***Continuously Evolve***
   The AI landscape is constantly evolving, and organizations must be agile and adaptable to stay ahead. Regularly reassessing and adapting the AI strategy is essential to keep pace with technological advancements and changing business needs. Organizations should establish a continuous improvement process to monitor AI performance, gather feedback, and make necessary adjustments. Staying informed about emerging AI trends and innovations can help organizations remain competitive and drive ongoing transformation.

Conclusion

In conclusion, becoming an AI-driven organization requires a holistic approach that encompasses technology, culture, and governance. By following this roadmap, organizations can navigate the complexities of AI transformation and unlock the full potential of AI to drive business success.

Challenges and Considerations

While the benefits of becoming an AI-driven organization are significant, the journey is not without its challenges. Organizations must navigate a complex landscape of technical, ethical, and human factors to successfully implement AI.

Here are some key challenges and considerations:

1. ***Data Quality and Privacy***
   Data is the foundation of AI, and ensuring its quality is paramount. Poor data quality can lead to inaccurate models and unreliable outcomes. Organizations must invest in robust data governance practices to ensure data accuracy, consistency, and completeness. Additionally, protecting data privacy is crucial. With increasing regulatory scrutiny and public concern over data privacy, organizations must implement stringent data protection measures to safeguard sensitive information and comply with regulations such as the GDPR and the CCPA.
2. ***Ethical Considerations***
   The use of AI raises several ethical questions that organizations must address proactively. Issues such as bias in AI algorithms, transparency, and accountability are critical. AI systems can inadvertently perpetuate existing biases present in the training data, leading to unfair and discriminatory outcomes. Organizations must implement fairness and bias mitigation strategies to ensure ethical AI use. Transparency in AI decision-making processes and accountability mechanisms are also essential to build trust with stakeholders and ensure responsible AI deployment.
3. ***Change Management***
   AI adoption often requires significant changes to existing business processes and workflows. Overcoming resistance to change and managing the human impact of AI adoption is critical for success. Employees may fear job displacement or feel uncertain about their roles in an AI-driven organization. Effective change management strategies, including clear communication, training, and support, are essential to address these concerns. Engaging employees in the AI transformation journey and highlighting the benefits of AI can help build a positive and collaborative culture.
4. ***Technical Complexity***
   Integrating AI systems with existing infrastructure can be technically challenging. Legacy systems may not be compatible with modern AI technologies, requiring significant upgrades or replacements.

Additionally, AI implementation often involves complex data integration, model training, and deployment processes. Organizations must invest in the right tools, technologies, and expertise to navigate these technical challenges. Collaborating with technology vendors and leveraging cloud-based AI solutions can also help streamline the integration process.

5. ***Talent Shortage***

   There is a global shortage of AI talent, making it difficult for organizations to find and retain skilled professionals. The demand for AI experts far exceeds the supply, leading to intense competition for top talent. Organizations must adopt a multifaceted approach to address this challenge. This includes investing in training and development programs to upskill existing employees, partnering with academic institutions to nurture future talent, and creating an attractive work environment to retain skilled professionals. Additionally, leveraging external expertise through partnerships and collaborations can help bridge the talent gap.

Summary

Becoming a truly AI-driven organization is a complex but necessary journey for businesses looking to thrive in the future. It requires a holistic transformation that goes beyond technology implementation, touching every aspect of the organization from strategy to culture. The integration of AI into the workforce is redefining the division of labor between humans and machines. By automating routine tasks and augmenting human capabilities, AI is transforming how businesses operate. Organizations are creating new roles centered on AI development and oversight, rethinking their business models, and striving to become AI-driven. By following a structured roadmap and addressing key challenges, organizations can successfully leverage AI as a core driver of their business, unlocking new opportunities for innovation, efficiency, and growth.

As AI continues to evolve, its impact on the workforce will only grow. Businesses that embrace AI and adapt to these changing dynamics will be better positioned to thrive in the future. However, it is crucial to ensure that AI is used ethically and transparently to build trust and maintain a positive relationship between humans and machines.

Organizations that embrace this transformation will be well-positioned to lead in their industries, while those that lag may find themselves struggling to compete in an increasingly AI-driven business landscape.*

* ***Becoming an AI-Driven Organization: A Holistic Transformation***

The Impact of AI on Future Business Models
This article explores how AI is transforming business operating models and the potential benefits for stakeholders. https://taskflowsolutions.com/the-impact-of-ai-on-future-business-models/.

Five New Business Models Empowered by AI
This blog outlines five innovative business models that are being revolutionized by AI technologies. https://trybusinessagility.com/blogs/5-new-business-models-empowered-by-ai/.

How Artificial Intelligence Will Transform Businesses
This article examines the vast capabilities of AI and its impact on various business sectors, emphasizing the importance of adopting AI technologies. www.businessnewsdaily.com/9402-artificial-intelligence-business-trends.html.

CHAPTER 13

The Dangers and Weaknesses of Using AI in Business

Introduction

The Importance of Understanding AI's Limitations and Risks

AI has become a transformative force in the business world, offering unprecedented opportunities for innovation, efficiency, and growth. However, as businesses increasingly integrate AI into their operations, it is crucial to recognize and understand the limitations and risks associated with this powerful technology. Acknowledging these aspects is essential for making informed decisions, ensuring ethical practices, and safeguarding against potential pitfalls.

The Dual Nature of AI

AI's potential to revolutionize industries is matched by its capacity to introduce new challenges and vulnerabilities. While AI can automate tasks, provide insights, and enhance decision making, it is not infallible. AI systems are only as good as the data they are trained on and the algorithms that power them. This dual nature necessitates a balanced approach, where the benefits of AI are harnessed while its limitations and risks are carefully managed.

Ethical and Social Implications

One of the most pressing concerns surrounding AI is its ethical and social impact. AI algorithms can inadvertently perpetuate biases present in the training data, leading to discriminatory outcomes. For instance, biased hiring algorithms can unfairly disadvantage certain groups, while predictive policing tools may disproportionately target minority communities. Understanding these risks is vital for developing AI systems that promote fairness and inclusivity. Moreover, AI's ability to process vast amounts of personal data raises significant privacy concerns. Businesses must navigate the delicate balance between leveraging data for insights and respecting individuals' privacy rights. Failure to do so can result in legal repercussions and damage to a company's reputation.

Technical Limitations

Despite the remarkable advancements in AI, there are inherent technical limitations that businesses must be aware of. Current AI models excel in narrow, specific tasks but struggle with generalization and context understanding. This limitation can lead to errors when AI systems encounter scenarios that deviate from their training data. For example, an AI-powered customer service chatbot may provide incorrect responses to complex or nuanced queries, frustrating customers and undermining trust. Additionally, AI's reliance on large datasets means that the quality and representativeness of the data are critical. Poor-quality data can lead to inaccurate predictions and flawed decision making. Businesses must invest in robust data collection and curation practices to mitigate these risks.

Security Risks

AI systems are not immune to security threats. They can be vulnerable to hacking, adversarial attacks, and manipulation. Malicious actors can exploit these vulnerabilities to compromise AI systems, leading to data breaches, financial losses, and reputational damage. For instance, adversarial attacks can deceive AI image recognition systems into misclassifying objects, posing risks in applications such as autonomous vehicles and security surveillance. Understanding these security risks is essential for implementing robust safeguards and ensuring the integrity of AI systems.

Businesses must adopt a proactive approach to cybersecurity, continuously monitoring and updating their AI infrastructure to defend against emerging threats.

Economic and Operational Considerations

The integration of AI into business operations also presents economic and operational challenges. While AI can enhance productivity and efficiency, it can also lead to job displacement and workforce disruption. Businesses must consider the social impact of AI adoption and invest in reskilling and upskilling initiatives to support employees affected by automation. Furthermore, the deployment of AI systems requires significant investment in infrastructure, talent, and ongoing maintenance. Businesses must carefully evaluate the cost–benefit ratio and ensure that AI initiatives align with their strategic goals.

Conclusion

In conclusion, understanding the limitations and risks of AI is paramount for businesses seeking to harness its potential responsibly. By acknowledging the ethical, technical, security, and economic challenges associated with AI, businesses can make informed decisions, implement best practices, and navigate the complex landscape of AI adoption. A balanced approach that prioritizes transparency, fairness, and continuous monitoring will enable businesses to leverage AI for success while mitigating its inherent risks.

The Balance Between AI's Potential and Its Pitfalls

AI has emerged as a transformative force in the business world, offering unprecedented opportunities for innovation, efficiency, and growth. However, alongside its potential, AI also presents significant challenges and risks that businesses must navigate carefully. Striking the right balance between leveraging AI's capabilities and mitigating its pitfalls is crucial for sustainable success.

The Potential of AI in Business

AI's potential in business is vast and multifaceted. Here are some key areas where AI can make a significant impact:

- **Automation and Efficiency:** AI can automate repetitive and mundane tasks, freeing up HR for more strategic and creative endeavors. This can lead to significant cost savings and productivity gains.
- **Data-Driven Decision Making:** AI algorithms can analyze vast amounts of data quickly and accurately, providing valuable insights that can inform business strategies and decisions. This can enhance the precision and effectiveness of decision-making processes.
- **Customer Experience:** AI-powered tools, such as chatbots and personalized recommendation systems, can enhance customer interactions and satisfaction. By understanding and anticipating customer needs, businesses can deliver more personalized and timely services.
- **Innovation and Competitive Advantage:** AI can drive innovation by enabling the development of new products, services, and business models. Companies that effectively harness AI can gain a competitive edge in their respective markets.

The Pitfalls of AI in Business

Despite its potential, AI also comes with several pitfalls that businesses must be aware of:

- **Bias and Fairness:** AI systems can inadvertently perpetuate and amplify existing biases present in the data they are trained on. This can lead to unfair and discriminatory outcomes, which can harm a company's reputation and legal standing.
- **Privacy and Security:** The use of AI often involves the collection and processing of large amounts of personal data.

Ensuring the privacy and security of this data is paramount, as breaches can result in significant financial and reputational damage.

- **Job Displacement:** The automation of tasks through AI can lead to job displacement and workforce disruption. Businesses must consider the social and ethical implications of AI adoption and invest in reskilling and upskilling programs for their employees.
- **Dependence and Reliability:** Overreliance on AI systems can be risky, especially if these systems fail or produce inaccurate results. Businesses must ensure that they have robust contingency plans and maintain a level of human oversight.

Striking the Balance

To harness the benefits of AI while mitigating its risks, businesses should adopt a balanced approach.

- **Ethical AI Practices:** Implementing ethical AI practices is essential. This includes ensuring transparency, accountability, and fairness in AI systems. Businesses should establish clear guidelines and frameworks for ethical AI use.
- **Continuous Monitoring and Evaluation:** AI systems should be continuously monitored and evaluated to ensure that they are functioning as intended and not producing harmful outcomes. Regular audits and assessments can help identify and address potential issues.
- **Stakeholder Engagement:** Engaging with stakeholders, including employees, customers, and regulators, is crucial for understanding the broader implications of AI adoption. Open communication and collaboration can help build trust and address concerns.
- **Investment in Human Capital:** Investing in the development and training of employees is vital. Businesses should focus on reskilling and upskilling their workforce to adapt to the changing landscape and complement AI technologies.

Conclusion

In conclusion, while AI offers immense potential for businesses, it also presents significant challenges that must be carefully managed. By adopting a balanced approach that prioritizes ethical practices, continuous monitoring, stakeholder engagement, and investment in human capital, businesses can navigate the complexities of AI and achieve sustainable success.

AI Ethical Concerns

Bias and Discrimination in AI Algorithms

AI has the potential to revolutionize business operations, offering unprecedented efficiencies and insights. However, one of the most pressing ethical concerns surrounding AI is the issue of bias and discrimination in AI algorithms. This problem arises when AI systems, which are designed to make decisions or predictions, inadvertently perpetuate or even exacerbate existing biases present in the data they are trained on.

Understanding Bias in AI

Bias in AI can manifest in various forms, including but not limited to racial, gender, age, and socioeconomic biases. These biases often stem from the data used to train AI models. If the training data reflects historical inequalities or prejudices, the AI system is likely to replicate these patterns. For instance, an AI hiring tool trained on resumes from a predominantly male workforce might favor male candidates, thereby perpetuating gender bias.

Sources of Bias

- **Data Collection:** The data used to train AI models can be inherently biased if it is not representative of the entire population. For example, facial recognition systems have been found to have higher error rates for people with darker skin tones because the training data predominantly consisted of lighter-skinned individuals.

- **Algorithm Design:** The design of the algorithm itself can introduce bias. If the algorithm is not carefully crafted to account for potential biases, it may inadvertently favor certain groups over others.
- **Human Intervention:** Bias can also be introduced through human intervention. The individuals who label data or set parameters for the AI system may unconsciously inject their own biases into the process.

Consequences of Bias

The consequences of biased AI algorithms can be far-reaching and severe. In the business context, biased AI systems can lead to discriminatory practices, such as unfair hiring processes, biased loan approvals, and unequal access to services. These practices not only harm individuals but can also damage a company's reputation and lead to legal repercussions.

Mitigating Bias

Addressing bias in AI requires a multifaceted approach.

- **Diverse Data:** Ensuring that the training data is diverse and representative of the entire population is crucial. This can help mitigate the risk of the AI system learning and perpetuating biased patterns.
- **Algorithmic Fairness:** Developing algorithms with fairness constraints can help reduce bias. Techniques such as reweighting data, adjusting decision thresholds, and using fairness-aware ML models can be employed.
- **Transparency and Accountability:** Companies should strive for transparency in their AI systems. This includes documenting the data sources, algorithm design, and decision-making processes. Additionally, establishing accountability mechanisms can help ensure that biases are identified and addressed promptly.

- **Regular Audits:** Conducting regular audits of AI systems can help detect and rectify biases. These audits should be performed by independent third parties to ensure objectivity.

Ethical Considerations

Beyond technical solutions, addressing bias in AI also involves ethical considerations. Businesses must recognize the societal impact of their AI systems and strive to use AI responsibly. This includes fostering an inclusive culture that values diversity and actively works to eliminate discrimination.

Conclusion

While AI holds immense potential for transforming business operations, it is imperative to address the ethical concerns associated with bias and discrimination in AI algorithms. By understanding the sources of bias, implementing mitigation strategies, and fostering an ethical approach to AI development, businesses can harness the power of AI while promoting fairness and equality.

AI Privacy Issues and Data Security

In the rapidly evolving landscape of AI, privacy issues and data security have emerged as critical ethical concerns. As businesses increasingly rely on AI to drive decision making, optimize operations, and enhance customer experiences, the collection, storage, and analysis of vast amounts of data have become commonplace. However, this data-centric approach raises significant privacy and security challenges that must be addressed to ensure ethical AI deployment.

Data Collection and Consent

One of the primary privacy concerns associated with AI is the collection of personal data. AI systems often require large datasets to function effectively, and these datasets frequently contain sensitive information about individuals. The collection of such data without explicit consent can lead to privacy violations. Businesses must prioritize obtaining informed consent from individuals before collecting their data. This involves transparently communicating the purpose of data collection, how the data will be used, and the potential risks involved.

Data Anonymization and Deidentification

To mitigate privacy risks, businesses can employ techniques such as data anonymization and deidentification. Anonymization involves removing personally identifiable information (PII) from datasets, making it difficult to trace the data back to specific individuals. Deidentification, on the other hand, involves altering data in a way that prevents the identification of individuals. While these techniques can enhance privacy, they are not foolproof. Advances in AI and data analytics can sometimes reidentify anonymized data, posing a significant challenge to maintaining privacy.

Data Security and Breaches

Data security is another critical concern in the context of AI. The vast amounts of data collected and processed by AI systems make them attractive targets for cyberattacks. Data breaches can result in the exposure of sensitive information, leading to financial losses, reputational damage, and legal consequences for businesses. To safeguard data, businesses must implement robust security measures, including encryption, access controls, and regular security audits. Additionally, businesses should develop incident response plans to address potential data breaches promptly and effectively.

Bias and Discrimination

AI systems can inadvertently perpetuate bias and discrimination, leading to ethical concerns related to privacy and data security. Biased algorithms can result in unfair treatment of individuals based on race, gender, age, or other protected characteristics. To address this issue, businesses must ensure that their AI systems are trained on diverse and representative datasets. Regular audits and evaluations of AI systems can help identify and mitigate biases, promoting fairness and equity in AI-driven decision making.

Regulatory Compliance

Businesses must also navigate a complex landscape of data protection regulations and standards. Laws such as the GDPR in Europe and the CCPA in the United States impose strict requirements on data collection, processing, and storage. Noncompliance with these regulations can result in severe penalties and legal repercussions. To ensure compliance, businesses should establish comprehensive data governance frameworks and stay informed about evolving regulatory requirements.

Ethical Considerations

Beyond legal compliance, businesses have an ethical responsibility to protect the privacy and security of individuals' data. This involves adopting a proactive approach to data ethics, which includes principles such as transparency, accountability, and fairness. By fostering a culture of ethical AI use, businesses can build trust with customers, employees, and stakeholders, leading to the responsible and sustainable development of AI.

The Ethical Implications of AI Decision Making

AI has become an integral part of modern business operations, offering unprecedented efficiencies and capabilities. However, the deployment of AI systems in decision-making processes raises significant ethical concerns that must be carefully considered.

Bias and Fairness

One of the most pressing ethical issues in AI decision making is the potential for bias. AI systems are trained on large datasets, and if these datasets contain biased information, the AI can perpetuate and even amplify these biases. For example, if an AI system used for hiring decisions is trained on historical data that reflects gender or racial biases, it may continue to favor certain groups over others, leading to unfair and discriminatory outcomes. Ensuring fairness in AI requires rigorous testing, diverse training data, and ongoing monitoring to detect and mitigate biases.

Transparency and Accountability

AI decision making often involves complex algorithms that are not easily understood by humans. This lack of transparency sometimes referred to as the "black box" problem, can make it difficult to understand how decisions are made and to hold AI systems accountable for their actions. In business contexts, this can lead to challenges in explaining decisions to stakeholders, customers, and regulators. To address this, businesses must prioritize transparency by developing XAI systems and establishing clear accountability frameworks.

Privacy and Data Security

AI systems rely on vast amounts of data to function effectively. This raises significant privacy and data security concerns, as sensitive information may be collected, stored, and analyzed without individuals' explicit consent. Businesses must navigate the ethical implications of data usage by implementing robust data protection measures, ensuring compliance with privacy regulations, and being transparent about data collection practices. Respecting individuals' privacy rights is crucial to maintaining trust and ethical integrity.

Autonomy and Human Oversight

The increasing autonomy of AI systems poses ethical questions about the role of human oversight in decision-making processes. While AI can enhance efficiency and accuracy, it is essential to maintain a balance between automation and human intervention. Critical decisions, especially those with significant ethical or social implications, should involve human judgment to ensure that moral and ethical considerations are adequately addressed. Businesses must establish guidelines for when and how human oversight should be integrated into AI decision making.

Social and Economic Impact

The widespread adoption of AI in business has broader social and economic implications. AI-driven automation can lead to job displacement, affecting workers and communities. Ethical considerations must include the potential impact on employment and the need for reskilling and upskilling programs to support affected workers. Additionally, businesses should consider the societal impact of their AI systems and strive to use AI in ways that promote social good and minimize harm.

Conclusion

The ethical implications of AI decision making are multifaceted and complex. As businesses increasingly rely on AI, it is imperative to address these ethical concerns proactively. By prioritizing fairness, transparency, privacy, human oversight, and social responsibility, businesses can harness the power of AI while upholding ethical standards and fostering trust among stakeholders.

Technical Limitations of AI

The Challenge of Achieving True General Intelligence

AI has made significant strides in recent years, with advancements in ML, NLP, and computer vision. However, despite these achievements, the quest for true general intelligence—an AI that can understand, learn, and apply knowledge across a wide range of tasks, much like a human—remains elusive. This section explores the technical limitations that make achieving true general intelligence a formidable challenge.

The Complexity of Human Cognition

Human intelligence is characterized by its ability to perform a vast array of tasks, from abstract reasoning and problem-solving to emotional understanding and creativity. Replicating this level of cognitive flexibility in AI systems is incredibly complex. Current AI models are typically designed for narrow tasks, excelling in specific domains but failing to generalize across different contexts. For instance, an AI that can master the game of chess may struggle with tasks that require common sense reasoning or emotional intelligence.

Data Dependency and Bias

AI systems rely heavily on large datasets for training. These datasets often contain biases that can be inadvertently learned and perpetuated by the AI. Achieving general intelligence would require an AI to not only learn from diverse and unbiased data but also understand and mitigate these biases. This is a significant technical challenge, as biases can be deeply ingrained and difficult to identify. Moreover, the sheer volume of data required to train a truly general AI is staggering, posing practical limitations on data collection and processing.

Transfer Learning and Adaptability

One of the hallmarks of human intelligence is the ability to transfer knowledge from one domain to another. While transfer learning techniques have shown promise in AI, they are still limited in scope and effectiveness. True general intelligence would require an AI to seamlessly adapt its knowledge and skills to new and unforeseen tasks. This level of adaptability is currently beyond the reach of existing AI technologies, which are often rigid and task-specific.

Understanding Context and Ambiguity

Human communication is rich with context and ambiguity. We effortlessly navigate nuances in language, tone, and situational context to derive meaning. AI systems, on the other hand, struggle with these subtleties. NLP models, despite their advancements, often fail to grasp the full context of a conversation or the underlying intent behind ambiguous statements. Achieving general intelligence would necessitate a profound understanding of context and the ability to handle ambiguity with humanlike proficiency.

Ethical and Safety Considerations

The pursuit of general intelligence also raises ethical and safety concerns. An AI with humanlike cognitive abilities could potentially make decisions that have far-reaching consequences. Ensuring that such an AI operates within ethical boundaries and prioritizes human well-being is a significant technical and philosophical challenge. Researchers must develop robust frameworks for AI ethics and safety to prevent unintended harm.

Conclusion

In summary, the challenge of achieving true general intelligence lies in the complexity of human cognition, the dependency on vast and unbiased data, the need for effective transfer learning, the understanding of context and ambiguity, and the ethical and safety considerations. While current AI technologies have made impressive strides, the journey toward true general intelligence is fraught with technical limitations that require innovative solutions and interdisciplinary collaboration.

AI Dependence on Large Datasets and the Quality of Data

AI has revolutionized various industries by enabling businesses to automate processes, gain insights from data, and enhance decision making. However, the effectiveness of AI systems is heavily reliant on the availability and quality of large datasets. This dependence on data presents several technical limitations that businesses must navigate to fully leverage AI's potential.

The Necessity of Large Datasets

AI models, particularly those based on ML and deep learning, require vast amounts of data to learn and make accurate predictions. The more data an AI system has, the better it can identify patterns, understand context, and generalize from the training data to new, unseen data. For instance, in NLP, models like GPT-4 are trained on diverse and extensive text corpora to understand and generate humanlike text.

However, acquiring large datasets can be challenging. Data collection is often time-consuming and expensive, requiring significant resources. Additionally, some industries may not have access to the volume of data needed to train robust AI models. This limitation can hinder the development and deployment of AI solutions, particularly for small- and medium-sized enterprises (SMEs) that may lack the resources of larger corporations.

Quality Over Quantity

While large datasets are essential, the quality of the data is equally, if not more, important. Poor-quality data can lead to inaccurate models, biased predictions, and unreliable outcomes. Data quality issues can arise from various sources, including:

- **Incomplete Data:** Missing values or incomplete records can skew the training process, leading to models that do not accurately represent the real world.
- **Inconsistent Data:** Data collected from different sources may have inconsistencies in format, units, or definitions, making it difficult to integrate and analyze.
- **Noisy Data:** Data that contains errors, outliers, or irrelevant information can confuse AI models and degrade their performance.
- **Bias in Data:** If the training data is biased, the AI model will likely perpetuate and even amplify these biases, leading to unfair or discriminatory outcomes.

Ensuring data quality requires rigorous data cleaning, preprocessing, and validation processes. Businesses must invest in data governance frameworks to maintain high standards of data integrity and reliability. This includes establishing protocols for data collection, storage, and management, as well as implementing tools and techniques for data cleaning and anomaly detection.

The Impact of Data Quality on AI Performance

The quality of data directly impacts the performance of AI models. High-quality data enables AI systems to make accurate predictions, generate valuable insights, and support informed decision making. Conversely, poor-quality data can lead to several issues:

- **Reduced Accuracy:** Models trained on low-quality data are less likely to make accurate predictions, reducing their effectiveness and reliability.
- **Increased Bias:** Biases in the training data can result in biased models, which can have serious ethical and legal implications for businesses.
- **Higher Costs:** Poor data quality can lead to increased costs associated with data cleaning, model retraining, and error correction.
- **Loss of Trust:** Inaccurate or biased AI systems can erode trust among customers, stakeholders, and regulators, potentially damaging a company's reputation.

Strategies for Mitigating Data Quality Issues

To address the challenges associated with data quality, businesses can adopt several strategies:

- **Data Augmentation:** Techniques such as data augmentation can help increase the diversity and volume of training data, improving model robustness.
- **Synthetic Data:** Generating synthetic data can supplement real-world data, particularly in cases where data is scarce or sensitive.
- **Regular Audits:** Conducting regular data audits can help identify and rectify data quality issues before they impact AI performance.
- **Bias Mitigation:** Implementing bias detection and mitigation techniques can help ensure that AI models are fair and unbiased.

Conclusion

In conclusion, while AI holds immense potential for transforming businesses, its dependence on large datasets and the quality of data presents significant technical limitations. By understanding and addressing these challenges, businesses can harness the power of AI more effectively and responsibly.

The Limitations of Current AI Models in Understanding Context and Nuance

AI has made significant strides in recent years, enabling machines to perform tasks that were once thought to be the exclusive domain of humans. From NLP to image recognition, AI models have demonstrated remarkable capabilities. However, despite these advancements, current AI models still face significant limitations in understanding context and nuance. These limitations can have profound implications for businesses that rely on AI for decision making and customer interactions.

The Challenge of Contextual Understanding

One of the primary limitations of current AI models is their inability to fully grasp context. Contextual understanding involves recognizing the circumstances or background information that surrounds a particular event, statement, or idea. For humans, context is essential for interpreting meaning accurately. However, AI models often struggle with this aspect due to several reasons:

- **Lack of World Knowledge:** AI models are trained on large datasets, but they do not possess the same breadth of world knowledge that humans do. This lack of knowledge can lead to misunderstandings or misinterpretations of context.
- **Static Training Data:** AI models are typically trained on static datasets that do not evolve. As a result, they may not be able to adapt to new contexts or changes in the environment.

- **Limited Understanding of Ambiguity:** Human language is inherently ambiguous, with words and phrases often having multiple meanings. AI models can struggle to disambiguate these meanings without sufficient contextual information.

For example, consider the sentence "I saw her duck." Without additional context, it is unclear whether "duck" refers to the action of lowering one's head or the bird. While humans can often infer the correct meaning based on context, AI models may not be able to do so accurately.

The Nuance Problem

Nuance refers to the subtle differences in meaning, expression, or tone that can significantly impact communication. Understanding nuance is crucial for tasks such as sentiment analysis, customer service interactions, and content generation. However, current AI models often fall short in this area due to several factors:

- **Literal Interpretation:** AI models tend to interpret text literally, missing the subtleties and nuances that humans naturally pick up on. This can lead to misunderstandings or inappropriate responses.
- **Cultural Sensitivity:** Nuance is often influenced by cultural factors, including idioms, humor, and social norms. AI models trained on diverse datasets may still struggle to accurately interpret these cultural nuances.
- **Emotional Intelligence:** Understanding and responding to emotions is a complex task that requires a deep understanding of human psychology. While AI models can perform basic sentiment analysis, they often lack the emotional intelligence needed to fully grasp nuanced emotional expressions.

For instance, consider a customer service chatbot that is tasked with handling customer complaints. If a customer expresses frustration using sarcasm, the chatbot may not recognize the sarcasm and respond inappropriately, further aggravating the customer.

Implications for Businesses

The limitations of current AI models in understanding context and nuance can have several implications for businesses:

- **Customer Experience:** AI-driven customer service solutions may fail to provide satisfactory responses if they cannot accurately interpret customer queries and emotions. This can lead to decreased customer satisfaction and loyalty.
- **Decision Making:** AI models used for decision making may produce suboptimal results if they cannot fully understand the context of the data they are analyzing. This can result in flawed business strategies and missed opportunities.
- **Content Generation:** AI-generated content, such as marketing copy or social media posts, may lack the subtlety and nuance needed to resonate with target audiences. This can impact the effectiveness of marketing campaigns and brand perception.

Addressing the Limitations

To mitigate the limitations of current AI models in understanding context and nuance, businesses can adopt several strategies:

- **Human–AI Collaboration:** Combining the strengths of AI with human expertise can help bridge the gap in contextual and nuanced understanding. Human oversight can ensure that AI-generated outputs are accurate and contextually appropriate.
- **Continuous Learning:** Implementing mechanisms for continuous learning and adaptation can help AI models stay

up-to-date with changing contexts and environments. This can involve retraining models on new data and incorporating feedback loops.

- **Enhanced Training Data:** Using more diverse and representative training datasets can improve AI models' ability to understand context and nuance. This includes incorporating data from different cultures, languages, and domains.
- **Advanced NLP Techniques:** Leveraging advanced NLP techniques, such as transfer learning and contextual embedding, can enhance AI models' ability to capture context and nuance. These techniques enable models to learn from broader contexts and apply that knowledge to specific tasks.

Conclusion

In conclusion, while AI has made remarkable progress, current models still face significant limitations in understanding context and nuance. By recognizing and addressing these limitations, businesses can harness the power of AI more effectively and responsibly, ensuring that AI-driven solutions deliver accurate, contextually appropriate, and nuanced outcomes.

AI Security Risks

Vulnerabilities to Hacking and Adversarial Attacks

AI systems have become integral to modern business operations, offering unprecedented capabilities in data analysis, decision making, and automation. However, the increasing reliance on AI also brings significant security risks, particularly vulnerabilities to hacking and adversarial attacks. Understanding these risks is crucial for businesses to protect their AI assets and maintain operational integrity.

Hacking Vulnerabilities

AI systems, like any other digital infrastructure, are susceptible to hacking. Hackers can exploit weaknesses in the AI's software, hardware, or network to gain unauthorized access, manipulate data, or disrupt operations. Common hacking techniques:

- **Phishing Attacks:** Cybercriminals use deceptive emails or messages to trick individuals into revealing sensitive information, such as login credentials. Once inside the system, hackers can manipulate AI algorithms or steal valuable data.
- **Malware Injections:** Hackers can introduce malicious software into AI systems to corrupt data, alter algorithmic outputs, or take control of the system. This can lead to significant operational disruptions and financial losses.
- **Man-in-the-Middle Attacks:** In these attacks, hackers intercept and alter communications between AI systems and their users or other systems. This can result in unauthorized data access, data manipulation, or system hijacking.

Adversarial Attacks

Adversarial attacks are a unique threat to AI systems, exploiting the very nature of ML algorithms. These attacks involve subtly manipulating input data to deceive AI models, causing them to make incorrect predictions or decisions. Key types of adversarial attacks:

- **Evasion Attacks:** Attackers modify input data in a way that is imperceptible to humans but causes the AI model to misclassify it. For example, slight alterations to an image can trick a facial recognition system into misidentifying a person.
- **Poisoning Attacks:** In these attacks, adversaries inject malicious data into the training dataset, corrupting the AI model during its learning phase. This can lead to biased or incorrect outputs, undermining the system's reliability.
- **Model Inversion Attacks:** Attackers use the outputs of an AI model to infer sensitive information about the training data. This can compromise privacy and expose confidential business information.

Mitigation Strategies

To safeguard AI systems against hacking and adversarial attacks, businesses must implement robust security measures:

- **Regular Security Audits:** Conducting frequent security assessments can help identify and address vulnerabilities in AI systems before they are exploited.
- **Data Encryption:** Encrypting data both at rest and in transit can protect sensitive information from unauthorized access and tampering.
- **Adversarial Training:** Training AI models with adversarial examples can improve their resilience against evasion and poisoning attacks.
- **Access Controls:** Implementing strict access controls and monitoring user activities can prevent unauthorized access and detect suspicious behavior.

Conclusion

While AI offers transformative potential for businesses, it also introduces new security challenges. By understanding and addressing vulnerabilities to hacking and adversarial attacks, businesses can protect their AI assets and ensure the integrity and reliability of their operations. Proactive security measures and continuous vigilance are essential to mitigating these risks and harnessing the full potential of AI securely and responsibly.

The Potential for AI to Be Used in Malicious Ways

AI has the potential to revolutionize industries and improve our daily lives. However, it also poses significant security risks, particularly when used maliciously. Two prominent examples of such misuse are deepfakes and autonomous weapons.

Deepfakes

Deepfakes are synthetic media in which a person in an existing image or video is replaced with someone else's likeness. This technology leverages advanced AI algorithms, particularly deep learning, to create highly realistic but fake content. The potential for harm is substantial:

- **Misinformation and Disinformation:** Deepfakes can be used to spread false information, manipulate public opinion, and undermine trust in the media. For instance, a deepfake video of a political leader making inflammatory statements could incite violence or sway election results.
- **Reputation Damage:** Individuals can be targeted with deepfake content to damage their reputation. Celebrities, politicians, and business leaders are particularly vulnerable. A fabricated video of a CEO engaging in unethical behavior could lead to significant financial losses for a company.
- **Fraud and Extortion:** Deepfakes can be used for fraudulent activities, such as impersonating someone to gain access to sensitive information or financial assets. Additionally, malicious actors could create compromising deepfake content to extort money from victims.

Autonomous Weapons

Autonomous weapons, also known as lethal autonomous weapon systems (LAWS), are military systems that can select and engage targets without human intervention. The deployment of such weapons raises several ethical and security concerns:

- **Lack of Accountability:** Autonomous weapons operate without direct human control, making it difficult to hold individuals accountable for their actions. This lack of accountability could lead to violations of international humanitarian law and human rights abuses.
- **Escalation of Conflicts:** The use of autonomous weapons could lower the threshold for entering conflicts, as they reduce the risk to human soldiers. This could lead to an increase in the frequency and intensity of armed conflicts.
- **Proliferation and Misuse:** There is a risk that autonomous weapons could fall into the hands of nonstate actors, such as

terrorist organizations. The proliferation of such technology could lead to its use in attacks against civilian populations, causing widespread harm.

- **Technical Failures:** Autonomous weapons rely on complex algorithms and sensors, which are not infallible. Technical failures or hacking could result in unintended casualties or the targeting of noncombatants.

Mitigating the Risks

To address the security risks associated with the malicious use of AI, several measures can be taken:

- **Regulation and Legislation:** Governments and international bodies should establish regulations and laws to govern the use of AI technologies, particularly in sensitive areas such as deepfakes and autonomous weapons.
- **Technological Safeguards:** Researchers and developers should implement robust security measures to prevent the misuse of AI. This includes developing detection tools for deepfakes and ensuring that autonomous weapons have fail-safes and human oversight.
- **Public Awareness and Education:** Raising awareness about the potential risks of AI misuse is crucial. Educating the public, policy makers, and industry leaders can help foster a more informed and cautious approach to AI adoption.
- **International Cooperation:** Addressing the global nature of AI security risks requires international cooperation. Countries should work together to establish norms and agreements that prevent the malicious use of AI technologies.

The Risk of AI Systems Being Manipulated or Corrupted

AI systems have become integral to modern business operations, offering unprecedented efficiencies and capabilities. However, as with any technology, AI is not without its vulnerabilities. One of the most significant risks is the potential for AI systems to be manipulated or corrupted. This risk can manifest in various ways, each with potentially severe consequences for businesses.

Data Poisoning

Data poisoning is a form of attack where malicious actors intentionally introduce false or misleading data into the training datasets used by AI systems. Since AI models learn from the data they are trained on, corrupted data can lead to incorrect or harmful outputs. For example, in a financial institution, data poisoning could cause an AI system to make poor investment decisions, leading to significant financial losses. The challenge lies in detecting and preventing such attacks, as they can be subtle and difficult to identify.

Model Inversion Attacks

Model inversion attacks involve extracting sensitive information from an AI model. By querying the model and analyzing its responses, attackers can infer details about the data used to train the model. This can lead to severe privacy breaches, especially if the training data includes personal or confidential information. For instance, an attacker could potentially reconstruct images of individuals from a facial recognition system, compromising their privacy and security.

Adversarial Attacks

Adversarial attacks exploit the weaknesses in AI models by introducing small, carefully crafted perturbations to the input data. These perturbations are often imperceptible to humans but can cause the AI system to make incorrect predictions or classifications. In the context of autonomous vehicles, an adversarial attack could involve altering road signs in a way that causes the vehicle to misinterpret them, potentially leading to accidents. The ability to defend against such attacks is crucial for the safe deployment of AI systems in critical applications.

Insider Threats

Insider threats pose a unique risk to AI systems, as they involve individuals within an organization who have access to the AI infrastructure. These insiders could intentionally manipulate the AI system for personal gain or to harm the organization. For example, an employee with access to an AI-powered recommendation system could alter the algorithms to favor certain products or services, undermining the system's integrity and fairness. Mitigating insider threats requires robust access controls, monitoring, and a culture of security awareness.

Algorithmic Bias

Algorithmic bias occurs when AI systems produce biased or unfair outcomes due to inherent biases in the training data or the design of the algorithms. While not always the result of malicious intent, algorithmic bias can still have detrimental effects on businesses and individuals. For instance, biased hiring algorithms could lead to discriminatory hiring practices, damaging a company's reputation and exposing it to legal liabilities. Addressing algorithmic bias requires careful consideration of data sources, algorithm design, and ongoing monitoring to ensure fairness and equity.

Mitigation Strategies

To mitigate the risks of AI manipulation and corruption, businesses must adopt a multifaceted approach:

- **Robust Data Management:** Ensuring the integrity and quality of training data is paramount. This includes implementing rigorous data validation processes and monitoring for anomalies.
- **Security Measures:** Employing advanced security measures such as encryption, access controls, and regular security audits can help protect AI systems from external and internal threats.
- **Adversarial Training:** Training AI models to recognize and defend against adversarial attacks can enhance their robustness and reliability.

- **Transparency and Accountability:** Maintaining transparency in AI decision-making processes and establishing accountability mechanisms can help identify and address biases and other issues.
- **Continuous Monitoring:** Regularly monitoring AI systems for signs of manipulation or corruption is essential for early detection and response.

Conclusion

In conclusion, while AI systems offer significant benefits to businesses, they also present unique security risks. Understanding and addressing these risks is crucial for the safe and effective deployment of AI technologies. By implementing robust security measures and fostering a culture of vigilance, businesses can mitigate the risks of AI manipulation and corruption, ensuring that their AI systems remain reliable and trustworthy.

AI's Economic and Social Impact

Job Displacement and the Future of Work

This section explores the economic and social impact of AI on employment, highlighting the potential risks and opportunities that lie ahead.

The rapid advancement of AI technologies has brought about significant changes in the business landscape. While AI offers numerous benefits, such as increased efficiency and productivity, it also poses substantial challenges, particularly in terms of job displacement and the future of work.

The Threat of Job Displacement

One of the most pressing concerns associated with the widespread adoption of AI in business is the potential for job displacement. As AI systems become more capable of performing tasks traditionally carried out by humans, there is a growing fear that many jobs will become obsolete. This phenomenon is not limited to low-skilled or repetitive tasks; AI is increasingly capable of handling complex and cognitive tasks, which puts a wide range of occupations at risk.

Industries such as manufacturing, retail, and transportation are particularly vulnerable to automation. For example, the introduction of AI-powered robots in manufacturing plants can lead to significant reductions in the need for human labor. Similarly, the rise of autonomous vehicles threatens the jobs of truck drivers, delivery personnel, and taxi drivers. Even white-collar jobs, such as data analysis, customer service, and administrative roles, are not immune to the impact of AI.

Economic Implications

The economic implications of job displacement due to AI are profound. On one hand, businesses that adopt AI technologies can achieve substantial cost savings and productivity gains. However, these benefits often come at the expense of the workforce. As jobs are automated, displaced workers may struggle to find new employment opportunities, leading to increased unemployment rates and economic inequality.

Moreover, the transition to an AI-driven economy may exacerbate existing disparities between different regions and demographic groups. For instance, areas heavily reliant on industries susceptible to automation may experience higher levels of economic disruption. Similarly, workers with lower levels of education and skills may find it more challenging to adapt to the changing job market, further widening the gap between the skilled and unskilled workforce.

Social Impact and the Future of Work

The social impact of AI-induced job displacement extends beyond economic considerations. The loss of employment can have far-reaching consequences for individuals and communities. Job loss can lead to financial instability, reduced access to health care and education, and increased stress and mental health issues. Additionally, the erosion of job security can undermine social cohesion and contribute to a sense of uncertainty and anxiety about the future.

However, it is important to recognize that AI also presents opportunities for the future of work. While certain jobs may be displaced, new roles and industries are likely to emerge. The key to mitigating the negative impact of AI on employment lies in proactive measures such as reskilling and upskilling the workforce. By investing in education and training programs, governments and businesses can help workers transition to new roles that leverage their unique human skills, such as creativity, critical thinking, and emotional intelligence.

Furthermore, the development of AI should be guided by ethical considerations and a commitment to social responsibility. Policy makers, business leaders, and technologists must collaborate to ensure that the benefits of AI are distributed equitably and that the potential harms are minimized. This includes implementing policies that support workers during periods of transition, such as unemployment benefits, job placement services, and lifelong learning initiatives.

Conclusion

In conclusion, the economic and social impact of AI on job displacement and the future of work is a complex and multifaceted issue. While AI has the potential to revolutionize industries and drive economic growth, it also poses significant challenges that must be addressed. By acknowledging the risks and taking proactive steps to support displaced workers, society can navigate the transition to an AI-driven economy in a way that promotes inclusivity, resilience, and shared prosperity.

The Digital Divide and Unequal Access to AI Technology

The advent of AI has brought about transformative changes across various sectors, promising unprecedented efficiency, innovation, and economic growth. However, the benefits of AI are not uniformly distributed, leading to a significant digital divide that exacerbates existing inequalities. This divide manifests in several ways, impacting both individuals and businesses and poses a critical challenge to the equitable development of AI technology.

Economic Disparities

One of the primary factors contributing to the digital divide is economic disparity. Access to AI technology often requires substantial financial investment in infrastructure, education, and research. Wealthier nations and large corporations have the resources to invest in cutting-edge AI technologies while developing countries and small businesses struggle to keep pace. This economic divide results in a concentration of AI advancements in the hands of a few, leaving others at a significant disadvantage.

For instance, multinational corporations can afford to develop and deploy sophisticated AI systems to optimize their operations, enhance customer experiences, and drive innovation. In contrast, SMEs may lack the financial resources to invest in AI, limiting their ability to compete in an increasingly AI-driven market. This disparity not only stifles competition but also perpetuates economic inequalities, as those with access to AI technology continue to advance while others fall further behind.

Educational Inequities

Access to quality education is another critical factor influencing the digital divide. AI technology requires a skilled workforce capable of developing, implementing, and managing AI systems. However, educational opportunities in AI and related fields are often concentrated in wealthier regions and institutions. This creates a knowledge gap, where individuals from underprivileged backgrounds have limited access to the education and training needed to participate in the AI economy.

Moreover, the lack of diversity in AI education and research can lead to biased AI systems that fail to address the needs and perspectives of diverse populations. This further marginalizes underrepresented groups and reinforces existing social inequalities. To bridge this gap, it is essential to invest in inclusive education and training programs that provide equal opportunities for all individuals to acquire AI-related skills.

Technological Infrastructure

The availability of technological infrastructure is another key determinant of access to AI technology. High-speed internet, advanced computing resources, and reliable power supply are essential for the development and deployment of AI systems. However, many regions, particularly in developing countries, lack the necessary infrastructure to support AI initiatives. This infrastructure gap hinders the ability of businesses and individuals in these regions to leverage AI technology, further widening the digital divide.

Efforts to address this issue must focus on improving technological infrastructure in underserved areas. This includes expanding internet access, investing in renewable energy sources, and providing affordable computing resources. By enhancing infrastructure, we can create a more level playing field for AI development and ensure that the benefits of AI are accessible to all.

Social and Ethical Implications

The digital divide in AI technology also has significant social and ethical implications. Unequal access to AI can exacerbate social inequalities, as marginalized communities are left out of the AI revolution. This can lead to a concentration of power and influence in the hands of a few, raising concerns about fairness, accountability, and transparency in AI decision making.

Furthermore, the lack of diverse perspectives in AI development can result in biased algorithms that perpetuate discrimination and exclusion. It is crucial to promote inclusive and ethical AI practices that consider the needs and rights of all individuals. This includes involving diverse stakeholders in AI development, implementing robust ethical guidelines, and ensuring transparency in AI systems.

Bridging the Divide

Addressing the digital divide and ensuring equitable access to AI technology requires a multifaceted approach. Governments, businesses, and educational institutions must collaborate to create policies and initiatives that promote inclusive AI development. This includes investing in education and training programs, improving technological infrastructure, and fostering a culture of diversity and inclusion in AI R&D.

Conclusion

By taking proactive steps to bridge the digital divide, we can harness the full potential of AI technology to drive economic and social progress for all. Ensuring that the benefits of AI are accessible to everyone is not only a matter of fairness but also a critical factor in achieving sustainable and inclusive growth in the AI era.

The Potential for AI to Exacerbate Social Inequalities

AI has the potential to revolutionize industries, drive economic growth, and improve the quality of life for many. However, it also poses significant risks, particularly in exacerbating social inequalities. As AI systems become more integrated into various aspects of society, it is crucial to understand how they can contribute to widening the gap between different social groups.

Bias in AI Algorithms

One of the primary concerns is the inherent bias in AI algorithms. These biases often stem from the data used to train AI systems. If the training data reflects existing social prejudices, the AI system is likely to perpetuate these biases. For example, AI-driven hiring tools have been found to favor candidates from certain demographic groups over others, leading to discriminatory hiring practices. This can result in marginalized communities facing even greater barriers to employment.

Access to AI Technology

Access to AI technology is another critical issue. Wealthier individuals and organizations are more likely to afford and benefit from advanced AI systems, while economically disadvantaged groups may be left behind. This digital divide can lead to unequal access to education, health care, and other essential services. For instance, AI-powered educational tools can provide personalized learning experiences, but only for those who can afford them, leaving low-income students at a disadvantage.

Job Displacement

AI's impact on the job market is a double-edged sword. While AI can create new job opportunities, it can also lead to significant job displacement, particularly for low-skilled workers. Automation of routine tasks can result in job losses in sectors such as manufacturing, retail, and transportation. This displacement disproportionately affects workers with lower educational attainment and fewer resources to retrain for new roles, exacerbating economic inequalities.

Surveillance and Privacy Concerns

AI-driven surveillance technologies can also contribute to social inequalities. These systems are often deployed in ways that disproportionately target marginalized communities. For example, predictive policing algorithms have been criticized for reinforcing racial biases, leading to overpolicing of minority neighborhoods. Additionally, the lack of privacy protections for vulnerable populations can result in increased surveillance and control, further entrenching social disparities.

Health Care Inequities

AI has the potential to transform health care by enabling early diagnosis and personalized treatment plans. However, these benefits are not equally distributed. Disparities in access to health care data and AI-driven medical tools can result in unequal health outcomes. For example, AI systems trained on data from predominantly white populations may not perform as well for patients from other racial or ethnic groups, leading to misdiagnoses and inadequate treatment.

Policy and Regulation

Addressing the potential for AI to exacerbate social inequalities requires robust policy and regulation. Governments and organizations must ensure that AI systems are designed and deployed in ways that promote fairness and inclusivity. This includes implementing measures to mitigate bias, ensuring equitable access to AI technology, and protecting the rights and privacy of all individuals. Additionally, there must be a focus on retraining and upskilling workers to adapt to the changing job market.

Conclusion

While AI holds immense promise, it is essential to recognize and address its potential to exacerbate social inequalities. By understanding the risks and implementing thoughtful policies, we can harness the power of AI to create a more equitable and just society. Ensuring that AI benefits all members of society, regardless of their socioeconomic status, is crucial for building a future where technology serves as a force for good.

AI Legal and Regulatory Challenges

The Need for Robust Legal Frameworks and Regulations

This section explores the critical need for comprehensive legal and regulatory measures to ensure the ethical and responsible deployment of AI in business.

As AI continues to permeate various sectors of business, the necessity for robust legal frameworks and regulations becomes increasingly evident. The rapid advancement of AI technologies presents unique challenges that traditional legal systems are often ill-equipped to handle.

Addressing Ethical Concerns

One of the primary reasons for establishing robust legal frameworks is to address the ethical concerns associated with AI. AI systems have the potential to make decisions that significantly impact individuals and society. Without proper regulations, there is a risk of AI being used in ways that violate privacy, perpetuate biases, or even cause harm. For instance, AI algorithms used in hiring processes may inadvertently discriminate against certain groups if not properly regulated. Legal frameworks can help ensure that AI systems are designed and implemented in a manner that respects human rights and promotes fairness.

Ensuring Accountability and Transparency

Another critical aspect of AI regulation is ensuring accountability and transparency. AI systems often operate as "black boxes," making decisions without clear explanations. This lack of transparency can lead to mistrust and hinder the adoption of AI technologies. Robust legal frameworks can mandate transparency requirements, compelling businesses to provide clear explanations of how their AI systems work and the rationale behind their decisions. Additionally, regulations can establish accountability mechanisms, ensuring that businesses are held responsible for the outcomes of their AI systems.

Mitigating Risks and Unintended Consequences

AI technologies, while powerful, are not infallible. They can produce unintended consequences that may have far-reaching implications. For example, an AI system used in financial trading could make erroneous decisions, leading to significant financial losses. Robust legal frameworks can help mitigate such risks by setting standards for the development, testing, and deployment of AI systems. Regulations can also require businesses to implement safeguards and contingency plans to address potential failures or malfunctions.

Promoting Innovation and Competition

While regulations are essential for addressing the risks associated with AI, they should also be designed to promote innovation and competition. Overly restrictive regulations can stifle innovation and hinder the growth of the AI industry. Therefore, it is crucial to strike a balance between regulation and innovation. Legal frameworks should provide clear guidelines that protect consumers and society while allowing businesses the flexibility to innovate and compete in the global market.

International Collaboration and Harmonization

AI is a global phenomenon, and its regulation requires international collaboration and harmonization. Different countries have varying approaches to AI regulation, which can create challenges for businesses operating across borders. International cooperation is essential to develop harmonized legal frameworks that facilitate the global deployment of AI technologies. Collaborative efforts can help establish common standards and best practices, ensuring that AI is used responsibly and ethically worldwide.

Conclusion

In conclusion, the need for robust legal frameworks and regulations in the context of AI in business cannot be overstated. As AI technologies continue to evolve, it is imperative to establish comprehensive legal measures that address ethical concerns, ensure accountability and transparency, mitigate risks, promote innovation, and facilitate international collaboration. By doing so, we can harness the full potential of AI while safeguarding the interests of individuals and society.

The Difficulty of Assigning Accountability and Responsibility in AI Systems

The rapid advancement of AI technologies has brought about significant transformations in various business sectors. However, alongside these advancements, there are complex legal and regulatory challenges that need to be addressed. One of the most pressing issues is the difficulty of assigning accountability and responsibility in AI systems. This challenge arises from several factors, including the autonomous nature of AI, the involvement of multiple stakeholders, and the lack of clear legal frameworks.

Autonomous Nature of AI

AI systems, particularly those that employ ML and deep learning techniques, can make decisions and perform actions without direct human intervention. This autonomy can lead to situations where it is unclear who should be held accountable for the outcomes produced by the AI. For instance, if an AI system used in financial trading makes a decision that results in significant financial losses, it becomes challenging to determine whether the responsibility lies with the developers who created the algorithm, the company that deployed the system, or the AI itself.

Involvement of Multiple Stakeholders

The development and deployment of AI systems often involve a multitude of stakeholders, including software developers, data scientists, business executives, and end-users. Each of these stakeholders plays a role in the functioning of the AI system, making it difficult to pinpoint a single entity responsible for any negative outcomes. For example, if an AI-powered health care diagnostic tool provides an incorrect diagnosis, responsibility could be attributed to the developers who designed the algorithm, the medical professionals who provided the training data, or the health care institution that implemented the system.

Lack of Clear Legal Frameworks

The legal and regulatory landscape for AI is still evolving, and many jurisdictions lack comprehensive frameworks to address the unique challenges posed by AI systems. This lack of clarity can lead to ambiguity in assigning accountability and responsibility. In some cases, existing laws may not be well-suited to address the complexities of AI, leading to gaps in regulation. For instance, traditional product liability laws may not adequately cover the nuances of AI systems, leaving questions about who should be held liable for harm caused by an AI-powered product.

Potential Solutions

To address the difficulty of assigning accountability and responsibility in AI systems, several potential solutions have been proposed. One approach is to establish clear guidelines and standards for AI development and deployment. These guidelines could outline the responsibilities of different stakeholders and provide a framework for assessing accountability. Additionally, regulatory bodies could develop specific regulations for AI systems, ensuring that they are subject to appropriate oversight and scrutiny. Another potential solution is to implement mechanisms for transparency and explainability in AI systems. By making AI decision-making processes more transparent, it becomes easier to trace the origins of decisions and identify the responsible parties. This could involve requiring AI developers to document their design choices and provide explanations for the behavior of their systems.

Conclusion

Fostering collaboration between industry, academia, and regulatory bodies can help create a more comprehensive understanding of the challenges and potential solutions related to AI accountability. By working together, these stakeholders can develop best practices and share knowledge to ensure that AI systems are developed and deployed responsibly.

Lessons Learned From Past Incidents and How They Can Inform Future AI Development

The deployment of AI in business has led to remarkable advancements, but it has also exposed significant vulnerabilities. By examining past AI failures, we can extract valuable lessons to guide future AI development, ensuring more robust, ethical, and reliable systems.

The Importance of Ethical AI Design

One of the most critical lessons from past AI failures is the necessity of incorporating ethical considerations into AI design. The case of Microsoft's Tay chatbot, which quickly devolved into posting offensive content, underscores the need for ethical guidelines and safeguards. AI systems must be designed with mechanisms to prevent misuse and ensure that they operate within ethical boundaries.

Key Takeaways

- **Implement Safeguards:** Develop AI systems with built-in safeguards to prevent unethical behavior.
- **Ethical Training Data:** Use ethically sourced and diverse training data to minimize biases and ensure fair outcomes.

Addressing Bias and Discrimination

AI systems can inadvertently perpetuate existing biases, as seen in Amazon's AI recruitment tool and Apple Card's gender bias issue. These incidents highlight the importance of addressing bias and discrimination in AI algorithms. Ensuring that AI systems are trained on diverse and representative datasets is crucial to avoid biased outcomes.

Key Takeaways

- **Diverse Datasets:** Train AI models on diverse datasets to reduce bias and improve fairness.
- **Regular Audits:** Conduct regular audits of AI systems to identify and mitigate biases.

Ensuring Transparency and Accountability

Transparency and accountability are essential for building trust in AI systems. The failures of Tesla's Autopilot and Google's image recognition algorithm demonstrate the need for clear communication about AI capabilities and limitations. Organizations must be transparent about how AI systems make decisions and be accountable for their outcomes.

Key Takeaways

- **Clear Communication:** Provide clear information about AI system capabilities, limitations, and decision-making processes.
- **Accountability Mechanisms:** Establish mechanisms for accountability to address any negative consequences of AI deployment.

Prioritizing Safety and Reliability

Safety and reliability are paramount, especially in high-stakes applications such as autonomous driving. The crashes involving Tesla's Autopilot highlight the need for rigorous testing and validation of AI systems before deployment. Ensuring that AI systems can handle a wide range of scenarios and conditions is essential for their safe operation.

Key Takeaways

- **Rigorous Testing:** Conduct extensive testing and validation of AI systems to ensure safety and reliability.
- **Continuous Monitoring:** Implement continuous monitoring and updates to address any emerging issues.

Fostering Collaboration and Regulation

Collaboration between industry, academia, and regulatory bodies is vital for the responsible development of AI. The regulatory challenges faced by autonomous vehicles and biased AI systems underscore the need for clear guidelines and standards. Collaborative efforts can help establish best practices and ensure that AI development aligns with societal values.

Key Takeaways

- **Industry Collaboration:** Foster collaboration between industry stakeholders to share knowledge and best practices.
- **Regulatory Frameworks:** Work with regulatory bodies to develop clear guidelines and standards for AI development.

Learning From Mistakes

Finally, learning from past mistakes is crucial for continuous improvement. Each AI failure provides an opportunity to identify weaknesses and implement corrective measures. By adopting a mindset of continuous learning and improvement, organizations can develop more resilient and trustworthy AI systems.

Key Takeaways

- **Continuous Improvement:** Embrace a culture of continuous learning and improvement to enhance AI systems.
- **Feedback Loops:** Establish feedback loops to gather insights from AI deployments and refine systems accordingly.

AI Case Studies: Real-World Examples of AI Failures and Their Consequences

AI has the potential to revolutionize industries and improve efficiencies, but it is not without its pitfalls. Several high-profile AI failures have highlighted the risks and weaknesses associated with its deployment in business. This section explores some notable examples and the consequences they had on the organizations involved.

Microsoft's Tay Chatbot

In 2016, Microsoft launched Tay, an AI chatbot designed to engage with users on Twitter and learn from those interactions. Unfortunately, within 24 hours, Tay began to post offensive and inappropriate tweets. This was a result of the bot learning from and mimicking the behavior of users who interacted with it. Microsoft had to shut down Tay shortly after its launch, leading to significant reputational damage and raising concerns about the ethical implications of AI learning from unfiltered human input.

Consequences

- **Reputational Damage:** Microsoft faced public backlash and criticism for not foreseeing the potential misuse of Tay.
- **Ethical Concerns:** The incident sparked a broader conversation about the ethical considerations of AI and the importance of implementing safeguards.

Amazon's AI Recruitment Tool

Amazon developed an AI recruitment tool to streamline the hiring process by evaluating resumes and identifying top candidates. However, it was discovered that the tool was biased against women. The AI had been trained on resumes submitted over a 10-year period, which were predominantly from men, leading the system to favor male candidates. Amazon eventually scrapped the tool due to its inability to provide unbiased recommendations.

Consequences

- **Bias and Discrimination:** The tool's bias highlighted the risk of AI perpetuating existing inequalities and discrimination in the workplace.
- **Loss of Trust:** The failure undermined trust in AI-driven recruitment processes and emphasized the need for transparency and fairness in AI systems.

Tesla's Autopilot Crashes

Tesla's Autopilot, an advanced driver-assistance system, has been involved in several high-profile crashes. In some cases, the AI system failed to recognize obstacles or misinterpreted road conditions, leading to accidents. These incidents have raised questions about the safety and reliability of autonomous driving technology.

Consequences

- **Safety Concerns:** The crashes have led to increased scrutiny of autonomous driving technology and its readiness for widespread use.
- **Regulatory Challenges:** The incidents have prompted regulatory bodies to consider stricter guidelines and standards for autonomous vehicles.

Google Photos' Image Recognition Error

In 2015, Google Photos' image recognition algorithm mistakenly labeled photos of African Americans as "gorillas." This error was a result of the AI's inability to accurately classify images and highlighted the limitations of ML algorithms in handling diverse datasets. Google quickly apologized and took steps to address the issue, but the incident underscored the potential for AI to cause harm through unintentional biases.

Consequences

- **Public Outcry:** The error led to widespread criticism and highlighted the need for more inclusive and representative training data.

- **Algorithmic Bias:** The incident emphasized the importance of addressing algorithmic bias and ensuring that AI systems are trained on diverse datasets.

Apple Card's Gender Bias

In 2019, Apple faced criticism when its AI-driven credit card, Apple Card, was found to offer significantly lower credit limits to women compared to men, even when they had similar financial profiles. The issue was attributed to the AI algorithm used to determine creditworthiness, which appeared to exhibit gender bias.

Consequences

- **Regulatory Investigation:** The incident prompted an investigation by the New York Department of Financial Services into potential gender discrimination.
- **Reputation Damage:** Apple faced backlash for the perceived unfairness and bias in its financial product, leading to calls for greater transparency in AI decision-making processes.

These examples illustrate the potential dangers and weaknesses of using AI in business. While AI can offer significant benefits, organizations must be aware of the risks and take proactive measures to mitigate them. Ensuring transparency, fairness, and ethical considerations in AI development and deployment is essential to avoid similar failures and their associated consequences.

Conclusion

By learning from past AI failures, businesses can develop more robust, ethical, and reliable AI systems. Incorporating ethical considerations, addressing bias, ensuring transparency, prioritizing safety, fostering collaboration, and learning from mistakes are essential steps in creating AI that serves society effectively and responsibly.

AI Mitigation Strategies

Best Practices for Developing and Deploying AI Responsibly

AI has the potential to revolutionize business operations, offering unprecedented efficiencies and insights. However, with great power comes great responsibility. To mitigate the risks associated with AI, businesses must adopt best practices for its development and deployment. Here are some key strategies:

Ethical AI Frameworks

Developing an ethical AI framework is crucial. This involves setting clear guidelines on the ethical use of AI, and ensuring that AI systems are designed and used in ways that are fair, transparent, and accountable. Companies should establish ethics committees to oversee AI projects and ensure compliance with ethical standards.

Data Privacy and Security

AI systems rely heavily on data, making data privacy and security paramount. Businesses must implement robust data protection measures to safeguard sensitive information. This includes anonymizing data, using encryption, and ensuring compliance with data protection regulations such as GDPR and CCPA.

Bias Mitigation

AI systems can inadvertently perpetuate biases present in training data. To mitigate this, businesses should use diverse and representative datasets, regularly audit AI systems for bias, and implement bias detection and correction mechanisms. It's also important to involve diverse teams in the development process to bring different perspectives and reduce bias.

Transparency and Explainability

AI systems should be transparent and explainable. This means that businesses should be able to explain how their AI systems make decisions.

Implementing XAI techniques can help in understanding and interpreting AI models, making it easier to identify and rectify issues.

Continuous Monitoring and Evaluation

AI systems should be continuously monitored and evaluated to ensure that they are functioning as intended. This involves setting up monitoring systems to track AI performance, conducting regular audits, and updating AI models as needed. Continuous evaluation helps in identifying and addressing any issues promptly.

Human-in-the-Loop

Incorporating a human-in-the-loop approach ensures that human judgment is involved in critical decision-making processes. This helps in maintaining control over AI systems and allows for human intervention when necessary. It also helps in building trust in AI systems among stakeholders.

Regulatory Compliance

Businesses must ensure that their AI systems comply with relevant regulations and standards. This includes staying updated with evolving AI regulations and industry standards, and ensuring that AI systems are designed and deployed in compliance with these requirements.

Ethical AI Training

Providing ethical AI training to employees is essential. This helps in building awareness about the ethical implications of AI and equips employees with the knowledge to develop and deploy AI responsibly. Training programs should cover topics such as data privacy, bias mitigation, and ethical decision making.

Stakeholder Engagement

Engaging with stakeholders, including customers, employees, and regulators, is crucial for responsible AI deployment. Businesses should seek feedback from stakeholders, address their concerns, and involve them in the AI development process. This helps in building trust and ensuring that AI systems meet the needs and expectations of all stakeholders.

Social Responsibility

Businesses should consider the broader social impact of their AI systems. This involves assessing the potential societal implications of AI and taking steps to mitigate any negative impacts. Companies should strive to use AI in ways that benefit society and contribute to social good.

Conclusion

By following these best practices, businesses can develop and deploy AI systems responsibly, mitigating risks and maximizing the benefits of AI. Responsible AI deployment not only helps build trust among stakeholders but also ensures that AI systems are used in ways that are ethical, transparent, and beneficial to society.

The Role of Transparency and Explainability in AI Systems

In the rapidly evolving landscape of AI, transparency and explainability have emerged as critical components for ensuring the ethical and effective deployment of AI systems in business. As organizations increasingly rely on AI to drive decision-making processes, the need for clear and understandable AI models becomes paramount. This segment delves into the significance of transparency and explainability in AI systems and explores strategies to enhance these attributes.

Importance of Transparency and Explainability

- **Building Trust and Accountability:** Transparency in AI systems fosters trust among stakeholders, including customers, employees, and regulatory bodies. When AI-driven decisions are transparent, stakeholders can understand the rationale behind these decisions, leading to increased confidence in the technology. Explainability, on the other hand, ensures that AI models can be interpreted and scrutinized, promoting accountability and reducing the risk of biased or unethical outcomes.

- **Enhancing Regulatory Compliance:** With the growing emphasis on data privacy and ethical AI, regulatory frameworks are becoming more stringent. Transparent and explainable AI systems are better equipped to comply with these regulations, as they can provide clear documentation and justifications for their decisions. This not only helps businesses avoid legal repercussions but also demonstrates a commitment to ethical AI practices.
- **Facilitating Informed Decision Making:** In business environments, decision makers need to understand the underlying mechanisms of AI models to make informed choices. Transparent and explainable AI systems provide insights into how data is processed and how conclusions are drawn, enabling decision makers to assess the reliability and relevance of AI-generated recommendations. This, in turn, leads to more effective and strategic business decisions.

Strategies to Enhance Transparency and Explainability

- **Model Documentation and Reporting:** Comprehensive documentation of AI models, including their design, training data, and decision making processes, is essential for transparency. Businesses should maintain detailed records of model development and updates, ensuring that stakeholders can access and review this information. Regular reporting on AI performance and outcomes further enhances transparency and accountability.
- **Implementing XAI Techniques:** XAI techniques, such as feature importance analysis, decision trees, and rule-based models, can help demystify complex AI systems. By breaking down AI decisions into understandable components, these

techniques enable stakeholders to grasp the factors influencing outcomes. Businesses should prioritize the use of XAI methods to ensure that AI models remain interpretable and accessible.

- **Stakeholder Engagement and Education:** Engaging stakeholders in the AI development process and educating them about AI technologies can significantly enhance transparency and explainability. Businesses should involve diverse teams in model development, including domain experts, ethicists, and end-users, to ensure that AI systems align with organizational values and ethical standards. Additionally, providing training and resources on AI literacy empowers stakeholders to critically evaluate AI-driven decisions.
- **Continuous Monitoring and Auditing:** Transparency and explainability are not one-time efforts but ongoing commitments. Businesses should establish mechanisms for continuous monitoring and auditing of AI systems to identify and address potential biases, errors, and ethical concerns. Regular audits and assessments ensure that AI models remain transparent, explainable, and aligned with evolving regulatory and ethical standards.

Conclusion

Transparency and explainability are indispensable for the responsible and effective use of AI in business. By prioritizing these attributes, organizations can build trust, ensure regulatory compliance, and facilitate informed decision making. Implementing strategies such as model documentation, XAI techniques, stakeholder engagement, and continuous monitoring can significantly enhance the transparency and explainability of AI systems. As AI continues to shape the future of business, embracing these principles will be crucial for harnessing the full potential of AI while mitigating its risks.

The Risk of Nontransparent AI

Lack of transparency can erode confidence in the technology, leading to skepticism and resistance from users, customers, and regulatory bodies.

- **Lack of Trust and Credibility:** When AI systems operate as "black boxes" with opaque decision-making processes, it becomes challenging for stakeholders to trust the outcomes.
- **Unintended Bias and Discrimination:** Nontransparent AI systems can inadvertently perpetuate biases present in the training data. Without clear visibility into how decisions are made, it becomes difficult to identify and mitigate these biases. This can result in discriminatory outcomes that disproportionately affect certain groups, leading to ethical and legal concerns.
- **Difficulty in Error Detection and Correction:** Opaque AI systems make it challenging to pinpoint the source of errors or inaccuracies in their outputs. This hampers the ability to diagnose and rectify issues, potentially leading to persistent mistakes that can have significant negative consequences for businesses and individuals.
- **Regulatory and Legal Risks:** As regulatory frameworks around AI and data privacy become more stringent, nontransparent AI systems may struggle to comply with these requirements. The inability to provide clear explanations for AI-driven decisions can result in legal challenges, fines, and reputational damage for businesses.
- **Reduced Accountability:** Without transparency, it is difficult to hold AI systems and their developers accountable for the outcomes they produce. This lack of accountability can lead to ethical lapses and irresponsible use of AI, undermining the overall integrity of the technology.
- **Impaired Decision Making:** Decision makers rely on understanding the rationale behind AI-generated recommendations to make informed choices. Nontransparent

AI systems obscure this rationale, making it harder for decision makers to assess the reliability and relevance of the AI's outputs. This can lead to suboptimal or misguided decisions.

- **Negative Impact on User Experience:** Users interacting with AI-driven products and services expect clarity and fairness in their interactions. Nontransparent AI systems can create frustration and dissatisfaction among users, as they may not understand why certain decisions or recommendations are made. This can negatively impact user experience and loyalty.

Conclusion

The risks associated with nontransparent AI systems highlight the importance of prioritizing transparency and explainability in AI development and deployment. By addressing these risks, businesses can build trust, ensure ethical and legal compliance, and enhance the overall effectiveness of AI-driven decision-making processes.

Nontransparent AI Examples

These examples illustrate the potential risks and challenges associated with nontransparent AI systems.

- **Credit Scoring Algorithms:** Many financial institutions use AI-driven credit scoring algorithms to assess the creditworthiness of loan applicants. These algorithms often operate as black boxes, making it difficult for applicants to understand why they were approved or denied. The lack of transparency can lead to concerns about fairness and potential biases in the decision-making process.
- **Predictive Policing Systems:** Some law enforcement agencies use predictive policing systems to forecast criminal activity and allocate resources. These systems analyze vast amounts of data to identify patterns and predict where crimes are likely to

occur. However, the algorithms behind these predictions are often opaque, raising concerns about potential biases and the reinforcement of existing prejudices in policing practices.

- **Hiring and Recruitment Tools:** AI-powered hiring tools are increasingly used to screen job applicants and make hiring decisions. These tools analyze resumes, social media profiles, and other data to rank candidates. When the decision-making process is not transparent, it can be challenging to ensure that the AI is not perpetuating biases based on gender, race, or other protected characteristics.
- **Social Media Algorithms:** Social media platforms use complex algorithms to curate content and recommend posts to users. These algorithms are often nontransparent, making it difficult for users to understand why certain content is prioritized or why they see specific advertisements. This lack of transparency can lead to concerns about manipulation, echo chambers, and the spread of misinformation.
- **Health Care Diagnosis Systems:** AI systems are increasingly used in health care to assist with diagnosing medical conditions. While these systems can provide valuable insights, their decision-making processes are often opaque. This lack of transparency can make it difficult for health care professionals to trust and validate the AI's recommendations, potentially impacting patient care.

Conclusion

By prioritizing transparency and explainability, businesses and organizations can mitigate these risks and ensure that AI technologies are used responsibly and ethically.

The Importance of Continuous Monitoring and Evaluation of AI

In the rapidly evolving landscape of AI, continuous monitoring and evaluation are paramount to ensuring the safe, ethical, and effective deployment of AI systems in business. As AI technologies become increasingly integrated into various business processes, the potential risks and weaknesses associated with their use also grow. Therefore, organizations must implement robust monitoring and evaluation strategies to mitigate these risks and harness the full potential of AI.

Ensuring Ethical Compliance

One of the primary reasons for continuous monitoring and evaluation of AI systems is to ensure ethical compliance. AI systems can inadvertently perpetuate biases present in the data they are trained on, leading to unfair or discriminatory outcomes. By continuously monitoring AI outputs and evaluating their impact, businesses can identify and address any ethical concerns that arise. This proactive approach helps maintain the integrity of the AI system and ensures that it aligns with the organization's ethical standards and values.

Enhancing Performance and Accuracy

AI systems are not static; they learn and evolve. Continuous monitoring allows businesses to track the performance and accuracy of AI models in real time. By regularly evaluating the outputs and comparing them against expected results, organizations can identify any deviations or anomalies that may indicate a decline in performance. This ongoing assessment enables timely interventions, such as retraining the model with updated data or fine-tuning its parameters, to maintain optimal performance and accuracy.

Mitigating Security Risks

AI systems are vulnerable to various security threats, including adversarial attacks and data breaches. Continuous monitoring and evaluation play a critical role in identifying and mitigating these risks. By implementing robust security measures and regularly assessing the system's vulnerability, businesses can detect and respond to potential threats before they cause significant harm. This proactive approach helps safeguard sensitive data and ensures the resilience of AI systems against evolving security challenges.

Facilitating Regulatory Compliance

The regulatory landscape for AI is continuously evolving, with new guidelines and standards being introduced to address emerging risks and challenges. Continuous monitoring and evaluation help businesses stay compliant with these regulations. By regularly assessing the AI system's adherence to regulatory requirements, organizations can identify any gaps or areas of noncompliance and take corrective actions promptly. This not only helps avoid legal repercussions but also demonstrates a commitment to responsible AI usage.

Building Trust and Transparency

Trust is a critical factor in the successful adoption of AI in business. Continuous monitoring and evaluation contribute to building trust and transparency by providing stakeholders with insights into the AI system's performance and decision-making processes. By maintaining an open and transparent approach, businesses can address any concerns or questions raised by stakeholders, fostering a sense of confidence and reliability in the AI system.

Adapting to Changing Business Needs

The business environment is dynamic, with changing market conditions, customer preferences, and technological advancements. Continuous monitoring and evaluation enable businesses to adapt their AI systems to these evolving needs. By regularly assessing the system's performance and relevance, organizations can make informed decisions about updating or modifying the AI models to align with current business objectives. This agility ensures that the AI system remains a valuable asset in achieving business goals.

Some Common Misconceptions About AI That Businesses Should Be Aware of

There are several common misconceptions about AI that businesses should be aware of to make informed decisions and avoid potential pitfalls:

- **AI Can Replace Human Jobs Completely:** One of the most prevalent misconceptions is that AI will entirely replace human jobs. While AI can automate certain tasks, it is more likely to augment human capabilities rather than replace them. Many roles will evolve, requiring humans to work alongside AI systems to achieve better outcomes.
- **AI Is Infallible:** Some believe that AI systems are always accurate and free from errors. In reality, AI models are only as good as the data they are trained on. They can make mistakes, especially if the data is biased or incomplete. Continuous monitoring and validation are essential to ensure that AI systems perform reliably.
- **AI Can Understand Context Like Humans:** AI systems can process and analyze large amounts of data, but they cannot often understand context and nuance in the same way humans do. This limitation can lead to misinterpretations and inappropriate responses in certain situations.
- **AI Implementation Is Quick and Easy:** Many businesses underestimate the complexity and time required to implement AI solutions. Successful AI integration involves significant planning, data preparation, model training, and ongoing maintenance. It is not a plug-and-play solution.
- **AI Is Only for Large Enterprises:** There is a misconception that AI is only accessible to large corporations with substantial resources. However, AI technologies are becoming more affordable and accessible to small- and medium-sized businesses. Cloud-based AI services and open-source tools have democratized AI adoption.
- **AI Can Solve All Problems:** AI is a powerful tool, but it is not a panacea for all business challenges. It is essential to

identify specific use cases where AI can add value and to set realistic expectations about its capabilities and limitations.

- **AI Systems Are Self-Sufficient:** Some believe that once an AI system is deployed, it can operate independently without human intervention. In reality, AI systems require continuous monitoring, updates, and adjustments to remain effective and relevant.
- **AI Is Always Ethical:** AI systems can inadvertently perpetuate biases present in the training data, leading to unethical outcomes. It is crucial to implement ethical guidelines and conduct regular audits to ensure that AI systems align with ethical standards.
- **AI Can Replace Human Creativity:** While AI can assist in creative processes, it cannot replicate human creativity and intuition. AI-generated content often lacks the originality and emotional depth that human creativity brings.
- **AI Is a One-Time Investment:** AI implementation is an ongoing process that requires continuous investment in terms of time, resources, and expertise. Regular updates, retraining of models, and adaptation to changing business needs are necessary to maintain the effectiveness of AI systems.

By understanding and addressing these misconceptions, businesses can make more informed decisions about AI adoption and implementation, ultimately leading to more successful and sustainable outcomes.

Summary

A balanced approach to harnessing AI for business success while mitigating its risks is essential when implementing AI.

AI has emerged as a transformative force in the business world, offering unprecedented opportunities for innovation, efficiency, and growth. However, the rapid adoption of AI also brings with it a host of risks and challenges that must be carefully managed. To fully leverage the potential of AI while safeguarding against its dangers, businesses must adopt a balanced approach that integrates both the benefits and the mitigation of associated risks.

Leveraging AI for Business Success

AI technologies have the potential to revolutionize various aspects of business operations. From automating routine tasks to providing deep insights through data analysis, AI can significantly enhance productivity and decision-making processes. For instance, AI-driven predictive analytics can help businesses anticipate market trends, optimize supply chains, and personalize customer experiences. By harnessing these capabilities, organizations can gain a competitive edge and drive sustainable growth.

Identifying and Assessing Risks

While the benefits of AI are substantial, it is crucial to recognize and address the inherent risks. AI systems can be prone to biases, errors, and security vulnerabilities. Additionally, the reliance on AI can lead to over-automation, where critical human judgment is overlooked. To mitigate these risks, businesses must conduct thorough risk assessments and identify potential pitfalls associated with AI implementation. This involves evaluating the quality of data used for training AI models, assessing the robustness of algorithms, and considering the ethical implications of AI decisions.

Implementing Robust Governance Frameworks

A balanced approach to AI requires the establishment of robust governance frameworks. These frameworks should encompass policies, procedures, and guidelines that govern the development, deployment, and monitoring of AI systems. By implementing clear governance structures, businesses can ensure accountability, transparency, and ethical compliance. This includes defining roles and responsibilities, setting standards for data privacy and security, and establishing mechanisms for continuous monitoring and evaluation.

Fostering a Culture of Collaboration

Successful AI integration necessitates collaboration between various stakeholders, including data scientists, business leaders, and regulatory bodies. By fostering a culture of collaboration, businesses can ensure that diverse perspectives are considered in AI decision-making processes. This collaborative approach helps in identifying potential risks, developing effective mitigation strategies, and ensuring that AI systems align with organizational goals and values. Additionally, engaging with external experts and industry peers can provide valuable insights and best practices for AI implementation.

Prioritizing Human-Centric AI

While AI can automate many tasks, it is essential to prioritize human-centric AI that augments human capabilities rather than replacing them. Human oversight and intervention are critical in ensuring that AI systems operate ethically and effectively. By maintaining a human-in-the-loop approach, businesses can leverage the strengths of both AI and human intelligence. This involves designing AI systems that are transparent, explainable, and accountable, allowing humans to understand and trust AI decisions.

Continuous Learning and Adaptation

The AI landscape is constantly evolving, with new advancements and challenges emerging regularly. To stay ahead, businesses must adopt a mindset of continuous learning and adaptation. This involves staying updated with the latest developments in AI technology, regulatory changes, and industry trends. By investing in ongoing training and development for employees, businesses can build a workforce that is well-equipped to navigate the complexities of AI. Additionally, regularly reviewing and updating AI strategies ensures that businesses remain agile and responsive to changing needs and risks.

Balancing Innovation With Responsibility

Ultimately, the key to harnessing AI for business success lies in balancing innovation with responsibility. Businesses must strive to innovate and explore new AI-driven opportunities while maintaining a strong commitment to ethical practices and risk mitigation. This requires a proactive approach to identifying and addressing potential risks, fostering a culture of collaboration and transparency, and prioritizing human-centric AI. By achieving this balance, businesses can unlock the full potential of AI while safeguarding against its dangers, ensuring long-term success and sustainability.

Last Word

Navigating the AI Landscape: A Strategic Roadmap for Business Transformation

Developing a comprehensive AI strategy for business is a complex but essential process in today's rapidly evolving technological landscape. The six-step approach outlined in this book provides a structured framework for organizations to navigate the challenges and opportunities presented by AI integration.

By systematically assessing business needs, reviewing data assets, addressing technology gaps, identifying suitable use cases, leveraging existing AI solutions, and carefully weighing the benefits and risks, businesses can create a robust and tailored AI strategy. This approach ensures that AI initiatives are aligned with strategic objectives, grounded in data-driven insights, and supported by the necessary technological infrastructure.

The journey of AI integration is not a one-time effort but an ongoing process of adaptation and refinement. As AI technologies continue to advance and new applications emerge, organizations must remain agile and open to evolving their strategies. The six-step framework provides a foundation for this continuous improvement, allowing businesses to regularly reassess their AI initiatives and adjust courses as needed.

Successful AI implementation goes beyond mere technological adoption; it requires a holistic transformation that encompasses organizational culture, skills development, and ethical considerations. By following this comprehensive approach, businesses can not only harness the power of AI to drive efficiency, innovation, and competitive advantage but also navigate the associated challenges and risks responsibly.

In the future, AI will play an increasingly central role in business operations and strategy. Organizations that proactively develop and implement thoughtful AI strategies will be well-positioned to thrive in this new era of intelligent automation and data-driven decision making. By embracing AI with a strategic, measured approach, businesses can unlock new opportunities, enhance their capabilities, and create sustainable value in an increasingly AI-driven world.

The six-step framework presented in this book serves as a roadmap for this transformative journey, guiding organizations from initial assessment to successful implementation and ongoing optimization of AI solutions. As you embark on or continue your AI journey, remember that the key to success lies not just in the technology itself, but in how well it is integrated into your unique business context and aligned with your strategic goals.

By following this roadmap, organizations can develop a comprehensive AI strategy that aligns with their business objectives and capabilities. Developing an AI strategy is an iterative process. As you implement AI initiatives, continuously learn from your experiences and adjust your strategy accordingly.

The journey to becoming an AI-powered organization may be challenging, but with a well-thought-out strategy, it can lead to significant competitive advantages and transformative business outcomes.

By carefully assessing readiness, identifying opportunities, and creating a detailed integration roadmap, organizations can navigate the AI ecosystem successfully and harness the full potential of this revolutionary technology.*

---

* ***A Strategic Roadmap for Business Transformation***

How to Build an AI Business Strategy
A guide on structuring an effective AI strategy to enhance business growth and efficiency. www.bdc.ca/en/articles-tools/technology/invest-technology/how-to-build-an-ai-business-strategy

AI Ecosystem Reports—Vector Institute
Annual reports providing insights and benchmarks for measuring the progress of Canada's AI ecosystem. https://vectorinstitute.ai/ai-ecosystem-reports/.

Navigating Generative AI Ecosystem: Transforming Disruptions
Analyzes the impact of generative AI on marketing and business strategies in 2024. www.linkedin.com/pulse/navigating-generative-ai-ecosystem-transforming-disruptions-roy-liu.

About the Author

Dr. Frankl, MBA, PhD, has managed large-scale systems development projects; conducted numerous Information Technology, Telecommunications, and Business Reengineering strategic plans; and played major roles in key systems development initiatives. He has considerable experience in strategic management planning, project management, system development, system metrics and evaluation techniques, system feasibility studies, system quality assurance, and human resource planning. Dr. Frankl is involved in promoting Information Technology at the University level (as an academic) as well as at the Industry level (as a research associate) in the areas of systems development techniques and knowledge transfer.

Dr. Frankl held technical, marketing, and management positions with IBM Canada. He later joined the Quebec-based Desjardins Credit Union Confederation as Director of Clearing Systems. While with Desjardins and through the Canadian International Development Agency (CIDA), he spent some time in Latin America, implementing a generalized financial infrastructure project for the Latino-American Cooperative Movement (COLAC) out of Panama City. Next, he joined CGI as Director of Consulting Services and partner where he participated in a large number of strategic technology-related projects in the private and public sectors. After moving to Victoria in the early 1990s, he became CFO, President, and CEO of several hi-tech Canadian businesses. He is presently a professor emeritus with the University Canada West (UCW), a member of the UK-based Global University Systems, an adjunct professor with the School of Health Information Science at the University of Victoria, and a program chair of the Master in Information Technology Management at Yorkville University (all in BC, Canada).

Index

www.ingramcontent.com/pod-product-compliance
Lightning Source LLC
Chambersburg PA
CBHW061129220326
41599CB00024B/4212

* 9 7 8 1 6 3 7 4 2 8 0 0 9 *